Core Resource

Education, Society, and Economic Opportunity

Education, Society, and Economic Opportunity

A Historical Perspective on Persistent Issues

Maris A. Vinovskis

Yale University Press / *New Haven and London*

Set in Ehrhardt and Futura type by Clarinda, Clarinda, Iowa.

Printed in the United States of America by BookCrafters, Inc., Chelsea, Michigan.

Library of Congress Cataloging-in-Publication Data

Vinovskis, Maris.
    Education, society, and economic opportunity : a historical
    perspective on persistent issues / Maris A. Vinovskis.
        p.   cm.
    Includes bibliographical references and index.
    ISBN 0-300-06269-9 (alk. paper)
    1. Public schools—United States—History.   2. Education—Social
aspects—United States—History.   3. Education—Economic aspects—
United States—History.   4. School attendance—United States—
History.   I. Title.
LA212.V56   1995
370'.973'09—dc20

                                                          95–5892
                                                          CIP

A catalogue record for this book is available from the British Library.

The paper in this book meets the guidelines for permanence and durability of the Committee on Production Guidelines for Book Longevity of the Council on Library Resources.

10 9 8 7 6 5 4 3 2 1

For Carl Kaestle

Contents

Acknowledgments

One of the great pleasures of studying and researching this volume on the history of American education has been the opportunity to work closely with colleagues. The stimulus of another's considered reflections on the issues at hand and the motivation provided by the close scrutiny of another's sincere interest in one's own ideas has provided for me an ideal way of working. Dean May coauthored the original essay on infant schools that appears here as Chapter 2; David Angus and Jeffrey Mirel were my coauthors for the study of age-stratification in schooling that is reproduced here as Chapter 10. Dean, Dave, and Jeff were ideal collaborators in terms of their enthusiasm, knowledge, and skills, as well as their friendship and support throughout all our mutual endeavors.

This book is dedicated to another long-time academic colleague and friend—Carl Kaestle. I first encountered Carl more than two decades ago, when I arrived at the University of Wisconsin to begin my first academic position. While I had already done some work in the area of educational history, my focus at that time was on demographic and family history. In the course of conversations with Carl about American educational developments, we found that we usually agreed on many things but often brought quite different perspectives and methodologies to our discussions. Our intellectual and social interactions blossomed into a long and productive collaboration exploring educational developments in nineteenth-century Massachusetts using both quantitative and qualitative evidence. Over time I have continued to learn from him, and my work and life have been greatly enriched by his collaboration with me. I certainly can think of no finer example of a researcher, teacher, and friend than Carl.

In the course of writing this book, many people read individual chapters and provided useful suggestions and criticism. Among those who provided such assistance are Andrew Achenbaum, David Angus, Vern Bengtson, Lawrence Cremin, Stephen Frank, Philip Gleason, Raymond Grew, Michael Grossberg, Tamara Hareven, Donald Horowitz, Carl Kaestle, Carol Karlsen, Jill Korbin, Kenneth Lockridge, Dean May, Jeffrey Mirel, Gerald Moran, Andrejs Plakans, William Reese, Peter Schuck, Carl Schneider, Stephan Thernstrom, James Turner, and David Tyack. As always, my family has played a major role in facilitating my research.

The publication of this book was made much easier by the help of several individuals. My editor at Yale University Press, Gladys Topkis, was supportive and helpful throughout the entire process, and Eliza Childs did an excellent job of editing the manuscript. At the University of Michigan, Jeanette Diuble helped assemble the final draft, while Stephen Frank and Jennifer Mittelstadt prepared the index and assisted me in proofreading the manuscript.

Social science research is often associated with large-scale funding. In this case, however, a project that did not need a single large grant was successfully accomplished because a number of institutions were willing to fund small-scale investigations. These types of grants are sadly often unavailable—with the result that valuable research is difficult to sustain. Evidence of the usefulness of this level of funding may encourage granting agencies to continue to provide research assistance.

This project was aided by four small grants. The former U.S. Office of Research (USOE) provided funding for the study of infant schools; the former National Institute of Education (NIE) supported my original reanalysis of the controversy over the Beverly Public High School. Two indispensable research grants from the Spencer Foundation supported the analysis of the crisis in moral education in Massachusetts as well as the investigation of high school attendance in Newburyport, Massachusetts. Without the financial assistance of these groups, the research for this book could not have been completed.

Introduction

The field· of American educational history is an exciting and challenging area of research today. Since the 1960s, scholars with a variety of perspectives and methodologies have made invaluable contributions to our understanding of American educational development. Particularly important are the contributions of social and economic historians, who have broadened the definition of educational history and significantly expanded our understanding of the nature and development of public schools in the past. Much of this work has been expertly summarized by the late Lawrence Cremin in his three-volume survey of American education (1970, 1980, 1988) and in more focused analytic studies by scholars such as Carl Kaestle (1983).

Nontraditional or "revisionist" interpretations have led the study of educational history in new directions. In the late 1960s and early 1970s such scholars as Michael Katz, Samuel Bowles, and Herbert Gintis, using the latest social science methodology, challenged the accepted interpretations of educational development and pointed to darker aspects of common school reform. They questioned the motives of nineteenth-century educational reformers and tended to minimize the benefits of schooling for children of working-class parents.

The work of these revisionists has not gone unchallenged. Other scholars have criticized their ideological assumptions, their empirical findings, and, especially, their overall interpretations of American educational development. At times these debates have been acrimonious and counterproductive, but the net result has been to advance the field of American educational history generally, by expanding the issues addressed and the research strategies employed. One very useful consequence has been to focus attention on the motivations of educational reformers and the nature of the public schools as institutions. Perhaps the greatest contribution has been to bring a new excitement and vigor to the study of our educational past.

Inadvertently, the controversies over revisionism may have diverted our attention from investigations of the role of education in other facets of society, such as the family. More than three decades ago, Bernard Bailyn, in his seminal overview of colonial education, called for the integration of educational and family history, and while some work has been done along this line, especially in the area of familial determinants of school attendance, his pleas have gone largely unheeded as revisionists and their critics have focused on school reformers and the workings of the public schools. Yet the field of family history has blossomed during these years—without, however, paying much attention to the education of children in the household. Perhaps this is an opportune time to bring these histories together by looking more closely at the changing role of the family in the education of its members and by examining such topics as early childhood education—topics that involve both parents and schools.

Other areas of educational history also need further study. For example, while considerable work has been done on the nature and extent of common school attendance in nineteenth-century America, less attention has been paid to high school attendance—especially in small and moderate-sized communities. Similarly, despite the growing contemporary concern about the economic rewards of education, historians of American education have paid little attention to this topic—even though it has been a cornerstone of the rationale for public school support since the mid-nineteenth century. Indeed, educators and policy makers alike might benefit considerably if historians could provide them with a more detailed and nuanced historical perspective on contemporary educational problems. Current policy discussions on such issues as early childhood training, schooling to alleviate poverty, and educational programs to help immigrants would surely benefit from a more historical perspective.

Much useful work has already been done on American educational development, but syntheses of the accumulated research are needed, in part to point the directions of future investigations. Social historians and policy makers who are not familiar with the recent rich literature on American education in the past will benefit from a critical review and synthesis of the relevant studies. Yet at the same time considerable empirical work remains to be done on crucial aspects of educational history, such as patterns of early childhood education and high school attendance. As scholars are becoming more adept in theorizing and using linguistic analysis, there seems to be an unfortunate and unnecessary retreat from undertaking time-consuming, in-depth quantitative investigations of the past, like those that have proved so important in advancing the field of American educational history over the past few decades. The issue is not quantitative versus qualitative studies or theoretical versus empirical investigations, but how to do both in a more coordinated and thoughtful way. The agenda for scholars of American educational history should be to review the existing work in our field critically and integrate it thoughtfully, continue to improve our theoretical perspectives, and simultaneously conduct more sophisticated empirical analyses of crucial unexplored and unanswered questions. One of the major purposes of this volume is to encourage further research on topics that have not yet been thoroughly analyzed.

Most of the essays in this book were written during the past five years and build on the pioneering works of the previous generation of educational historians. While nine of the twelve chapters have been published as articles or essays in other collections, it is only by bringing them together in a single volume that one can fully appreciate the wide variety of important topics and issues in American educational development that remain to be explored in much more depth. All the essays have been updated, and some have been considerably expanded for this book.

The first part of the book examines families, schools, and the challenges of economic opportunity. Chapter 1 explores the relation between family and schooling in colonial and nineteenth-century America. It investigates the shift from a primary reliance on the family for the education of the young in seventeenth-century America to a dependence on the public schools by the mid-nineteenth century. Although this is sometimes seen as a competition between parents and schools for the right to educate children, the transfer of educational responsibility to the state in the late eighteenth and early nineteenth centuries was actually rather harmonious and complementary. Moreover, the interactions between parents and the schools in the training of the young continued to play an important role in defining the nature of the educational experiences of children throughout the nineteenth century.

Early childhood education in the 1820s and 1830s is explored in chapter 2. While some individuals today might think that early childhood education was invented and developed by the Headstart Program in the 1960s, formal programs for the education of very young children were tried much earlier. This chapter examines the infant schools that became widespread in the United States in the second quarter of the nineteenth century and shows how children and their educational needs were viewed very differently in the past from the way they are today. In 1840 approximately 40 percent of Massachusetts three-year-olds were enrolled in school, but by 1860 there were almost no three-year-olds attending school. The rise and fall of infant schools in American education is analyzed with particular attention to the important role women and physicians played in bringing about changes in the enrollment of very young children in the schools as well as in facilitating changes in how children were perceived by adults.

Chapter 3 investigates the crisis in moral education in Massachusetts in the mid-nineteenth century. Public schools had always prided themselves on teaching children morality and proper behavior. Therefore it was a shock when in 1856 six girls from the Boston Hancock Grammar School, ranging in age from eleven to thirteen, either were seduced by three prominent businessmen or were their willing accomplices. The public outrage over this incident and the accusations against the Massachusetts public education system reveal the difficulties of teaching morality while trying to avoid sectarianism in the schools. The incident led to renewed efforts by the public schools of the Commonwealth to pay more attention to morality and proper behavior in the classroom. At the same time it reduced the excessive confidence nineteenth-century people had in the ability of public education to eradicate all forms of immoral and criminal behavior.

Like early childhood education, special education programs for the poor have proliferated since the 1960s, but there were significant efforts during the nineteenth century to help economically disadvantaged Americans. Chapter 4 examines how monitorial charity schools, Sunday schools, and infant schools were designed in the early 1800s to help impoverished children. Moreover, contrary to the claims of revisionist historians, schooling does appear to have promoted individual economic and social mobility in the nineteenth century. Yet prejudice against certain segments of the population, African-Americans, for example, minimized the economic value of that training and reduced the prospects for individual or group social mobility.

At a time when the economic productivity of education is being stressed by policy makers, most American educational historians continue to neglect this topic. Chapter 5 examines the ideas of Horace Mann. While such British economists as Adam Smith minimized the importance of education for economic productivity, Mann almost single-handedly introduced the notion in America. His attempts to calculate the economic productivity of education were biased and methodologically flawed, but they paved the way for more rigorous scholars and solidified support for public schooling by American taxpayers in the nineteenth century.

Recent concerns about the assimilation of immigrants and the role of education in providing them with economic opportunities were the impetus for a historical reexamination of these issues. Chapter 6 analyzes the relation of schooling and immigrants in the past. While some contemporaries then and many historians today are pessimistic about the ability of education to help immigrants, it appears that many nineteenth- and twentieth-century immigrants and their children received the skills and credentials necessary to advance in our society in American public schools. While current immigrants differ considerably from earlier ones demographically and in terms of their country of origin, there is reason for some hope that many of them may also benefit from additional schooling. Again, however, social and occupational discrimination against these new minorities threatens to minimize or undo many of the benefits of the education they are currently receiving.

In the second half of the book I look at school attendance, institutional arrangements, and social support for education. One of the central debates among historians has been about the intent and motivation of antebellum educational reformers. The classic work of Michael Katz (1968) on the origins of the Beverly High School in Massachusetts in the 1850s has been cited frequently by the so-called revisionists as evidence that public schooling was imposed upon a hostile or indifferent working class by self-interested capitalists and manufacturers. My own reexamination of this controversy reveals a quite different picture, one that seriously challenges the revisionist interpretation (Vinovskis, 1985). Chapter 7 reprints unedited the thoughtful and provocative essay reviews of my book, *The Origins of Public High Schools: A Reexamination of the Beverly High School Controversy*, by Michael Katz and Edward Stevens, Jr., as well as my response to their critiques. This exchange provides a useful glimpse into the continuing differences among historians on the origins and development of American high schools in the antebellum period and the problems involved in using social science techniques to analyze the history of education.

Chapter 8 continues the reexamination of the role of public high schools in Massachusetts on the eve of the Civil War. Scholars argue that only a very small proportion of children ever attended one of these institutions before 1900—even in states like Massachusetts, which pioneered the development of public secondary education. However, on the basis of a detailed, individual-level study of public high school attendance in Newburyport, Massachusetts, as well as an analysis of aggregate school-enrollment data for all other Essex County towns in 1860, it appears that nearly one out of five children in those cities and towns did attend a public or private high school. Moreover, the results also suggest that in some communities, such as Newburyport, a surprisingly large percentage of children of lower-class parents attended those institutions.

The issue of public high school attendance is examined further in chapter 9. Using aggregate-level information on public high schools for all 341 Massachusetts townships in 1875, a new statewide estimate of secondary school attendance was calculated. Approximately 18 percent of Massachusetts children attended a public high school at some point in their lives—again a much higher figure than other scholars have suggested. In addition, a detailed regression analysis of the determinants of the levels of public high school attendance in 1875 reveals that children in medium-sized cities and towns were the most likely to enroll in one of these institutions, while those living in communities with a high percentage of foreign-born children were least likely to attend.

Many educators today complain about the automatic promotion of unprepared students and the strict age-grading of pupils within classrooms. Most analysts have assumed that age-grading developed in the mid-nineteenth century and was widely in place by the turn of the century. However, there have been few detailed attempts to examine age-grading historically. Chapter 10 looks at the development of age-grading in the nineteenth century and finds, surprisingly, that it was not until the 1920s and 1930s that most urban school systems succeeded in assigning children to grades by age. Perhaps even more startling was the discovery that the age-grade homogeneity so common in classrooms today and so widely accepted as normal was not achieved in most schools before the 1940s and not evident in many schools until the late 1950s.

The volume concludes with an examination of the variations in support for schooling by different age cohorts. While differences in school support by age do not appear to have played a major role in the past, there are hints that the growing proportion of elderly in our population will not be as willing to vote for higher taxes to finance public education as were elders in the past. Although many gerontologists today try to minimize or deny age differences in school support, a detailed regression analysis of survey data from 1988 suggests otherwise. Some proponents of more funding for children today argue that the elderly receive a disproportionate amount of government assistance. Nevertheless, an understanding of how Horace Mann and others mobilized public opinion on behalf of education in the past suggests that it may be counterproductive to promote any hostility against the elderly in appealing for future funding of public schools.

This book is not intended as a comprehensive analysis of American educational development. Rather it focuses attention on some important aspects of American education in the past that allow for a better understanding of the relation between schooling and other broad changes in society. It also provides a historical perspective for contemporary efforts at school reform and debates about educational developments today that may help us to provide quality education for all our children in the future.

Part One / *Family, Schools, and the Challenges of Economic Opportunity and Social Reform*

Chapter 1 / *Family and Schooling in Colonial and Nineteenth-Century America*

In 1960 Bernard Bailyn called for a new and broader interpretation of how American education developed during colonial times—one that recognized the important historical role of the family in the transmission of culture from one generation to the next. Many of the specific elements of his analysis need to be reconsidered and revised, but Bailyn's challenge to historians to study the interactions between the family and schooling in the socialization of the young continues to inspire and guide researchers.

In spite of the wide circulation and acceptance of Bailyn's views on education in early America, few scholars have written directly about the relation between family and schooling—especially during the nineteenth century. Most historians have analyzed facets of either colonial and nineteenth-century family life or educational developments without paying explicit attention to the interactions between the two.[1] In this chapter, I shall survey some of the findings in the fields of American family and educational history from the perspective of the changing relation between the family and schools in the seventeenth, eighteenth, and nineteenth centuries. Rather than providing a detailed review or a comprehensive synthesis of the large number of studies in each field, I hope to create a stimulus for further research by exploring some of the more salient points raised in those studies. Although some references will be made to educational developments throughout the United States, New England will be the primary focus because of the greater availability of secondary analyses relating to family and education in that region.

Family and Schooling in Colonial America

Bailyn's seminal book on early American educational development is based on several assumptions about the nature of English society on the eve of colonization and the transformation of the American family in the inhospitable environment of the New World. English families were seen as patriarchal and extended: "The family familiar to the early colonists was a patrilineal group of extended kinship gathered in a single household. By modern standards it was large. Besides children, who often remained in the home well into maturity, it included a wide range of their dependents: nieces and nephews, cousins, and, except for families of the lowest rung of society, servants in filial discipline. In the Elizabethan family the conjugal was only the nucleus of a broad kinship community whose outer edges merged almost imperceptibly into the society at large" (Bailyn, 1960: 15–16).

These patriarchal families and the larger communities they formed were the central agencies for the socialization and education of children. Formal schools were not readily available or particularly important, but the church played a key role in educating the young. "Family, community, and church together accounted for the greater part of the mechanism by which English culture transferred itself across the generations. The instruments of deliberate pedagogy, of explicit, literate education, accounted for a smaller, though indispensable, portion of the process" (Bailyn, 1960: 18–19).

Settlers coming to the New World did not anticipate any major changes in the way children were raised and educated. Yet within a few decades, the colonists, particularly in Puritan New England, had to reconceptualize and reorder their system of educating the young. The unexpected destruction of the stable, extended English family was central to this change:

> In many ways the most important changes, and certainly the most dramatic, were those that overtook the family in colonial America. In the course of these changes the family's traditional role as the primary agency of cultural transfer was jeopardized, reduced, and partly superseded.
>
> Disruption and transplantation in alien soil transformed the character of the traditional English family life. Severe pressures were felt from the first. Normal procedures were upset by the long and acute discomforts of travel; the ancient discipline slackened. But once reestablished in permanent settlements the colonists moved toward recreating the essential institution in its usual form. In this, despite heroic efforts, they failed. At first they laid their failure to moral disorder; but in time they came to recognize its true source in the intractable circumstances of material life. (Bailyn, 1960: 22)

In reasoning reminiscent of Handlin's (1951) analysis of nineteenth-century immigration, Bailyn argued that the role of children in the new environment was greatly enhanced at the expense of paternal authority.[2] As a result, the civil authorities intervened to prop up the weakened and endangered family and required communities in Massachusetts to maintain schools to educate children who were no longer being properly trained at home. Thus, for Bailyn the demise of the stable extended English family in the New World led to the establishment of elementary schools—an unexpected but crucial step in the long-term development of schooling in America.

In the three decades since the publication of Bailyn's interpretation of family life and education, much more has been learned about English society in the sixteenth and seventeenth centuries. Contrary to Bailyn's assumption that most English families were extended and geographically immobile, it appears that English families were much smaller and predominantly nuclear (Houlbrooke, 1984; Laslett, 1969, 1972, 1977). Although there is still controversy over the prevalence of extended families as seen from a more dynamic view of family life (Berkner, 1972; Vinovskis, 1988), there is general agreement that most English families in the sixteenth and seventeenth centuries were nuclear with fewer than five members present at any given time. In addition, although a few families remained in the same community over several generations, there was much more geographic mobility than Bailyn assumed (Prest, 1976).

The availability of formal schooling in England in the sixteenth and seventeenth centuries appears to have been greater than Bailyn portrayed. Lawrence Stone (1964) argued that the extent of schooling and literacy in the seventeenth century was considerably higher than scholars had previously acknowledged. More recent work on English education (O'Day, 1982) suggests that the improvements in education and literacy were more gradual than Stone proposed but accepts his notion of the relatively high rates of schooling and literacy in England on the eve of North American colonization.

If Bailyn exaggerated the stability, size, and complexity of English families and underestimated the extent of formal schooling, he also overestimated the disruption of family life in the New World—especially in New England, which was the pioneer in establishing local schools. Studies of the migration of settlers to Massachusetts (Allen, 1981; Powell, 1963), for example, emphasize either the continuation of many English customs and practices or a more orderly process of adjustment to the new environment than the cataclysmic picture portrayed by Bailyn. Indeed, Greven (1970), one of Bailyn's students, found that parental authority in seventeenth-century Andover, Massachusetts, was stronger and family life more stable than in England. "The remarkable success with which Andover's first generation rerooted themselves in the soil of New England and maintained their families for generations to come reflects the opportunities for the establishment of orderly and cohesive families and communities in the midst of the American wilderness. In no significant sense were the lives of the first and second generations in disorder, once their permanent roots had been firmly established in early Andover" (Greven, 1970: 271).[3] As a result, Bailyn's claim that the sudden and unexpected disintegration and transformation of the family in the New World led to the creation of schools no longer seems as convincing and compelling as when it was first proposed thirty years ago.

Yet if Bailyn's specific explanations for the development of colonial education no longer appear as satisfactory, his emphasis on the importance of the family and the church for the education of the young in England was well founded. Protestants in England generally promoted household religion, and the Puritans emphasized this more than other religious groups (Axtell, 1974; Morgan, 1966). The Puritans assumed that the family had the primary responsibility for educating its members and that the state would intervene only when the family failed to provide instruction in reading and religion. The late Renaissance in England was a time of expanding familial responsibility for education, as well as a period of school expansion. Rather than the establishment of schools being a substitute for household education (Aries, 1962), the two processes were complementary (Cremin, 1970).

In the New World, the role of the family in educating the young was even more important than in England—partly out of necessity because other institutions such as the school and the church were not readily available.

> The family, then, was the principal unit of social organization in the colonies and the most important agency of popular education; and it assumed an educational significance that went considerably beyond that of its English counterpart. Whereas England had by the 1640s and 1650s placed churches within reach of virtually every household, schools within the reach of most, and universities within the reach of at least the more ambitious and able, the colonies were only beginning in those directions. Hence, while metropolitan families could take for granted the ready availability of other institutions to assist in the educational task, colonial families could not. As a result, the colonial household simply took unto itself, by force of circumstance, educational responsibilities that the English family commonly shared with other agencies. (Cremin, 1970: 135)

Indeed, even when local churches were available nearby, the New England Puritans before the 1660s continued to emphasize the role of the family over that of the church in the catechizing of children and servants (Axtell, 1974).[4]

For the New England Puritans, the father, as the head of the household, was expected to catechize his own children and servants. Although the mother might assist him, it was primarily the father's responsibility (Moran and Vinovskis, 1985).[5] After the Anne Hutchinson turmoil in the 1630s, however, the Puritan leaders were reluctant to entrust religious instruction to females.[6] In addition, the appropriateness of the father as the principal educator was reinforced by the fact that husbands usually were more literate than wives. An estimated 60 percent of men among the early settlers could sign their wills, whereas only about 30 percent of women were able to do so (Lockridge, 1974). Indeed, Linda Auwers (1980) found that female literacy in seventeenth-century Windsor, Connecticut, was associated with the literacy of the father but not that of the mother.

Although parents were expected to teach their children how to read and to catechize them, Massachusetts passed legislation in 1647 requiring communities of one hundred or more households to maintain a grammar school and those of fifty or more households to establish schools to teach reading and writing. As in England, this legislation was intended to complement rather than replace parental efforts in the home (Sheldon S. Cohen, 1974; Cremin, 1970). Joanne Geraldine Murphy found that in the first decade after the enactment of this law, only a third of the eligible towns complied with the requirement to establish petty or dame schools to teach elementary reading and writing, whereas all eight of the towns required to maintain a grammar school did so (1960). Thus, by the mid-seventeenth century, many of the larger Massachusetts communities provided some formal schooling for their inhabitants even though the emphasis was still on having parents educate and catechize their household members.[7]

Bailyn was correct in pointing to a crisis in Puritan society in the seventeenth century. The exact nature of that crisis, however, may have been slightly different from what he had envisioned. As Bailyn observed, church membership declined in the seventeenth century, and this led many Puritans to conclude that there was a serious decline in religious commitment in their society. Although more recent scholarship (Hall, 1972; Moran, 1979, 1980; Moran and Vinovskis, 1992; Pope, 1969) on Puritan church membership portrays a more complex picture of declension than the one suggested by Miller (1953), there is little doubt that many Massachusetts residents in the seventeenth century were deeply concerned about this trend.

Rather than seeing the enactment of these early school laws as evidence of the disintegration of the stable family in New England, it is probably more accurate to see it as a reflection of the attempts to promulgate correct religious views and to overcome the growing indifference of many families to religion and home education. In the aftermath of the Antinomian crisis, Puritan ministers and magistrates were very anxious about threats to their religion and wanted to make sure that correct doctrine was being taught in schools and at home (Foster, 1984; Hall, 1968). They also were reacting to the apparent growing indifference or unwillingness among many parents to catechize their own children (Axtell, 1974). As a result, the Puritans not only required the establishment of schools in towns and the use of approved catechisms in the home, sometimes they were willing to remove children from households that failed to educate and catechize them properly (Morgan, 1966).

In addition to the overall decline in church membership in the mid-seventeenth century, church membership became increasingly feminized. Although control of the congregation still rested in the hands of male elders and deacons (Moran, 1979, 1980; Moran and Vinovskis, 1982, 1992), adult males were increasingly unwilling to join the church. As a result, many of the male heads of households were not church members and so could no longer be entrusted with the education and catechism of their children and servants. This led to a variety of experiments to provide alternative sources of education, including more emphasis on catechism within the churches and an increasing reliance on schoolteachers (Axtell, 1974; Hall, 1972). It also led in the long run to a greater reliance on mothers, who continued to join the church in larger proportions than their husbands, to educate and catechize their children—thus increasing the need for educating women beyond the simple ability to read the Bible. Not surprisingly, the literacy rate for women increased substantially during the colonial period, from about 30 percent in the early seventeenth century to at least 60 percent at the end of the eighteenth century (Lockridge, 1974).[8]

If there is general agreement that the rates of literacy for both males and females in colonial New England rose, there is considerable disagreement over how this was achieved. Lockridge (1974), Daniels (1979), Auwers (1980), and Soltow and Stevens (1981) argue that the expansion in the number of schools in New England as the population density increased led to the rise in literacy. Lockridge (1974: 58) specifically dismisses home education as a possible explanation for the rise in literacy.

Some scholars (Moran and Vinovskis, 1985, 1992) have questioned rejecting household education as a possible factor in increased literacy by pointing out that since the emphasis in Puritan religion was on being able to read the Bible, it is not surprising that many girls might be taught to read but not to write, whereas boys were more likely to be educated in both skills as part of their career preparation. In addition, Auwers's (1980) study of literacy suggests an increase in female literacy even in those sections of Windsor that were far removed from any schools. Furthermore, some educational historians (Cohen, 1974) have argued that opportunities for formal education may have declined for many children in the eighteenth century even though literacy was increasing during these years.[9] The relative role of the household and the schools in the education of Americans in the late seventeenth and eighteenth centuries still awaits further research.[10]

The manner of maintaining and running schools in colonial New England varied considerably. As Bailyn pointed out, the expectation that rents from lands granted for educational purposes would produce sufficient income for schooling did not materialize. Therefore several other sources of income were used, such as tuition, subscription, and, increasingly, annual grants from the town treasury (Cohen, 1974; Cremin, 1970; Murphy, 1960). The direct costs to parents of educating children also differed among Massachusetts communities. In some towns all pupils attended school without any additional expense while in others all students except the children of the poor paid tuition.

Taxpayers were reluctant to assume the costs of elementary education, and town meetings frequently reaffirmed the responsibility of parents for educating their children. Yet once schools were established—especially at the expense of all taxpayers—parents were quite willing to send their children to these schools rather than teaching them at home (May and Vinovskis, 1977). Thus, even though the general increase in literacy in colonial America made parents more capable of training their children at home, most parents preferred, whenever possible, to send their offspring to public or private schools.

The Puritans emphasized education more than most other colonists (Cohen, 1974; Cremin, 1970, 1976; Morgan, 1966). New England led the rest of the colonies in literacy and schooling (Cremin, 1970; Lockridge, 1974). Although efforts were made to establish schools in the South, they failed owing to the greater dispersion of population and the lack of sustained financial support locally (Cohen, 1974). Educating children was more difficult in the South because high rates of mortality in the early decades of settlement made family life very unstable (Beales, 1985; Earle, 1979; Rutman and Rutman, 1979). Nevertheless, southern parents frequently tried to provide for their children's education by setting aside funds for schooling in their wills (Carr and Walsh, 1977).

As southern society became more settled and family life more stable, it became easier to plan and provide for education. Yet southern parents did not seem to value education as much as their northern counterparts. Indeed, some planter sons were educated more as a sign of family respectability and achievement than as a reflection of a commitment to learning (Smith, 1980). Rather than trying to establish schools, most planters were content to hire tutors to educate their sons at home, then sending them abroad or to the North for a university education. Although planters also provided for the training of their daughters, they usually did not encourage education much beyond reading and writing (Smith, 1980). Since the South did not develop an extensive system of schools, most children of less wealthy parents received only a rudimentary education, and many did not even acquire literacy (Cohen, 1974; Cremin, 1970, 1976).

Nineteenth-Century Patterns and Practices

The relation between family and schooling has been a central concern for students of American colonial history but not for investigators of nineteenth-century educational or family development. One explanation for this is that in the nineteenth century children received most of their education in schools and not at home. New England colonists stressed the importance of educating and cat-echizing children in the home; nineteenth-century parents assumed that learn-ing to read and write would occur in a classroom. The role of parents, especially mothers, was not ignored in the socialization of the child in the nineteenth century, but it was not seen as an alternative to sending children to school. Therefore, it is not surprising that most analysts of antebellum education have devoted relatively little attention to the family.

Although some scholars infer an inevitable conflict between the family and the schools as the latter multiplied in number and scope during the nineteenth century and seemingly competed with parents for the attention of children, the process was actually more complementary. The role of women in the raising of children, for example, expanded considerably during the antebellum period (Kuhn, 1947; Ryan, 1981). Mothers were now seen as the natural and logical caretakers of young children as fathers continued to reduce their active involve-ment in the socialization of children (Demos, 1982; Vinovskis, 1986). The doc-trine of separate spheres rationalized and reinforced the growing expectations and obligations of the mother even though schools were playing a larger role in the formal instruction of the child (Cott, 1977; Norton, 1980). Furthermore, as women replaced men as school teachers for young children, any apparent separation between the home and the school was minimized; women continued their primary role of educating the young (Bernard and Vinovskis, 1977; Fitts, 1979; Boylan, 1985; Hoffman, 1981; Morain, 1980; Tyack and Hansot, 1990).

Parents did not oppose the expansion of schools in principle although in practice they often voted against any increases in taxes for public education.[11] According to a Massachusetts statute of 1789, children who enrolled in gram-mar schools were expected to be able to read and write. Some citizens of Boston complained that since the community did not provide public primary schools, children of poor parents, who could not afford to go to private schools to learn to read and write, were in effect excluded from the grammar schools (Schultz, 1973). The Boston School Committee appointed a subcommittee in 1817 to investigate the issue. The subcommittee reaffirmed the traditional colonial view that parents could and should educate their own children at home rather than in a public school (Wightman, 1860).

Although the Boston School Committee emphasized the role of parents in educating their children, it acknowledged that most parents who could afford to send their children to private schools were already doing so. After some heated discussions, the committee relented and in 1818 established a few free primary schools for children ages four to six. The demand for these schools was much greater than had been anticipated. Not only did the new public schools enroll children from poor families, but also many whose parents were more affluent and had been sending their children to private schools (Wightman, 1860). Thus, while parents as taxpayers sometimes opposed an expansion of public schools, as individuals they were quite willing to send their children to public schools to learn how to read and write.

If many early-nineteenth-century parents were eager to send their children to school, they were more reluctant to have them stay in school beyond the time necessary to obtain a basic common school education. Unfortunately, there is very little analysis of the relative role of students and their parents in the decision to leave school. Most scholars simply seem to assume that the parents exercised the most influence in deciding when their children would end their schooling; some recent work on high school attendance in the late nineteenth century, however, suggests that the experiences of the students themselves may have influenced that decision. Perlmann (1985b) has found that the grades students received in high school were a better predictor of whether or not they decided to stay in school than were the occupations of their fathers.[12]

Historians of colonial education have found it difficult to analyze the characteristics of students and their families because of the lack of readily available information. Scholars of nineteenth-century education, however, have been more successful because they can ascertain the characteristics of school attendance from the decennial federal manuscript censuses from 1850 to 1880 and 1900 to 1910, which asked each person under twenty if he or she had attended any school during the past year.[13]

The classic work by Stephan Thernstrom (1964) on school attendance in Newburyport, Massachusetts, found that Irish Catholics were much less likely to keep their children in school than native-born Protestants. Thernstrom argued that Irish parents, eager to purchase their own home, sacrificed the future social mobility of their children by sending them into the labor force. Thernstrom's emphasis on the ethnicity and religion of the Irish as the explanation for the differential school attendance rates has been challenged by revisionists such as Michael Katz (1975), who interpret variations in school attendance as class differences.[14] More recent studies (Kaestle and Vinovskis, 1980; Katz and Davey, 1978), using more sophisticated statistical techniques such as multiple classification analysis, have found that both ethnicity and occupation influence the likelihood of remaining in school. Furthermore, the argument that Irish families prematurely sent their children into the labor force in order to purchase a home has not been substantiated. In fact, several investigators (Katz, 1982; Perlmann, 1985a) have found a positive rather than negative relation between home ownership and school attendance.[15]

Most studies of the influence of family characteristics on school attendance focus on the ethnicity and occupation of the head of the household. Yet this provides only a limited sense of the needs and resources of the family as a whole. Some scholars (Kaestle and Vinovskis, 1980) have tried to develop a work-consumption index that takes into account the number of workers and consumers in each family according to information from the federal manuscript censuses. Yet the results from these investigations do not show a strong relation between school attendance and the economic well-being of the family as a whole—perhaps suggesting that the particular work-consumption indices may not be an accurate reflection of the overall economic circumstances of the family.[16]

Although studies of school attendance based on census data are useful, they do not have the type of financial information we would like to have in order to study the impact of a family's economic circumstances on the school attendance of its children. Historians are now turning to the more detailed industrial household budget data from the late nineteenth century. Using the household budgets of textile workers in 1890, David Angus and Jeffrey Mirel (1985) found that the economic situation of the family was an important predictor of whether or not a child stayed in school.[17]

The frustration of school reformers in getting some children, especially those of immigrant parents, to go to school led to the passage of compulsory school attendance laws in the nineteenth century. Massachusetts led the nation in enacting legislation that required children under fifteen years of age working in manufacturing establishments to attend school at least three months each year. In spite of repeated exhortations by reformers to the parents and manufacturers to comply with the laws as well as attempts to hire truant officers in several communities, there was such widespread evasion of the compulsory school attendance laws that most contemporaries doubted that they had much of an impact on school attendance (Kaestle and Vinovskis, 1980).

Many nineteenth-century Americans were convinced that cities were destroying the traditional family (Boyer, 1978). Conservatives also bemoaned the disestablishment of the state church and the rise of less orthodox religious groups such as the Unitarians (Howe, 1970; Turner, 1985). Many educational reformers saw urban public schools replacing the family and the church as the primary means of educating children. Thus, while nineteenth-century educational reformers continued to speak of the complementary roles of the family, the church, and the school in the proper upbringing of children, many of them openly or secretly feared that, in fact, the school was the last bastion for civilizing youths growing up in the cities (Schultz, 1973).[18]

Whereas considerable research has been done on trends in nineteenth-century schooling, as well as on the individual family characteristics of students, much less work is available on parent-school relations. Many of the studies that do look at parent-school interactions focus on the tension between school reformers, who wanted to professionalize teaching and advocated giving town school committees more control, and parents, who favored having local school district committees making decisions because they were more responsive to the particular needs of that area (Katz, 1971). Gradually the proponents of centralization in Massachusetts, for example, won control of the public schools in the second half of the nineteenth century.

In the rural Midwest, however, parents exercised control over the public schools longer since state governments gave local districts corporate powers with only minimal restrictions on how they were to be administered. The governance of these small school districts involved a high proportion of local families, providing them with an important sense of participation and power (Fuller, 1982).

Professional educators objected to the decentralization of education in the rural Midwest, but farmers welcomed it. While nineteenth-century educators pointed to the inefficiencies and ineffectiveness of the decentralized system, at least one researcher (Fuller, 1982) argues that the centralization of schooling at the township level in the Midwest hurt education overall by reducing local interest and support.

If town school committees and administrators clashed with parents over hiring teachers and running local schools, they were eager to involve the parents in the classroom. Nineteenth-century educators frequently complained about parental apathy or indifference that allowed or even encouraged children to be absent from school or tardy. In addition, teachers recognized the need for parental involvement in order to stimulate better performances by students and therefore encouraged parents to attend classes and special examinations. Most nineteenth-century teaching manuals advised teachers to encourage parents to visit classrooms regularly: "The teacher should encourage parents frequently to visit his school. There is almost everywhere too great backwardness on the part of parents to do this duty. The teacher should early invite them to come in. It is not enough that he do this in general terms. He may fix the time, and arrange the party, so that those who would assimilate, should be brought together. It will frequently be wise to begin with the mothers, where visitation has been unusual. They will soon bring in the fathers. As often as they come they will be benefited. When such visits are made, the teacher should not depart from his usual course of instruction on their account" (Page, 1859: 251–52).

If educators sought parental cooperation and participation in the classroom, they were also aware of the conflicts that arose. Immigrant parents, especially those who were Catholic, often complained bitterly that their children were being indoctrinated in Protestantism in the public schools (Angus, 1980a; Ravitch, 1974). This often led to the removal of foreign-born children from the public schools and the establishment of parochial schools at great additional expense to the parents. In some cities, such as St. Louis, school reformers allowed instruction in German in order to attract more support for the public schools (Troen, 1975).

Parents also objected to the type and extent of discipline used in the classroom, as well as to how and what was taught. During the course of the nineteenth century parents reluctantly and often unhappily relinquished much of their involvement and influence over activities within the classroom.

In general, parents in nineteenth-century America wanted schools to take custody of their children, and they wanted schools to train their children in basic skills and attitudes. The eventual price that they paid was the loss of authority and control over their children's education. The trade-off was made. The state successfully exerted its right to discipline all children in values that served, first and foremost, the operational necessities of the school, but that also served the social leaders' image of appropriate adult behavior and the parents' image of appropriate childhood behavior. Despite the apparent grounds for consensus, this differentiation of function and shift of authority to the school ultimately produced not just different, but substantially contrary goals.

Elements of antagonism between school and family did not end with a new nineteenth-century equilibrium; they persist today. Clearer boundaries did not necessarily eliminate conflict, but in some ways merely prevented its expression. Compulsory attendance laws, the professionalization of teaching and administration, the development of pedagogical expertise, and the construction of fortress-like urban schools—these helped to insure that parents would interfere less; they did not insure that parents would feel happier or be better served. (Kaestle, 1978: 15)[19]

During the nineteenth century parents increasingly turned their children over to the schools even though it sometimes meant that they had to accept educational and disciplinary practices they did not favor. Nevertheless, the interactions between parents and schooling continued to influence the nature of the nineteenth-century educational system because schoolteachers and administrators in most communities were not sufficiently powerful simply to ignore the demands of parents.

Throughout human history, the family has played an important role in the socialization of its young. As civilizations developed, there was an increasing tendency to supplement the efforts of the family through such institutions as churches and schools. The growth of these additional and alternative institutions of education reflect in large measure the recognition that the task of training the young is so vital to the interests of society that it cannot be entrusted exclusively to the family.

The family was an important source of education for children in colonial and nineteenth-century America. But from the very beginning churches and schools were directed to assist parents in the socialization of the young. Indeed, by the mid-nineteenth century, the role of the schools had expanded to such an extent that many of the educational tasks initially assigned to parents, such as teaching children the alphabet and how to read, became the responsibility of the schools.

Throughout the seventeenth, eighteenth, and nineteenth centuries, both parents and schools played an important part in the education of young Americans. While historians of the family and of education have frequently acknowledged the contributions of these complementary, if sometimes conflicting, institutions, very little effort has been made to examine the interactions between them. Few historians have responded directly to Bailyn's call for a more comprehensive approach to the study of education. Nevertheless, as this chapter suggests, many of the particular components of a broader interpretation of the role of parents and schools in the education of the young now have been completed and prepare the way for a more dynamic and family-oriented analysis of the education of children in early America.

Notes

This chapter appeared in an earlier form in *Journal of Family History* 12, nos. 1–3 (1987): 19–37. Reprinted by permission of *Journal of Family History*, JAI Press, Greenwich, Conn.

1. For an introduction to post-Bailyn work on family history, see Coontz (1988), Degler (1980), Gordon (1978), Mintz and Kellogg (1988), McCall and Vinovskis (1991), Ryan (1982), Vinovskis (1988a), and Wall (1990). For developments in educational history, see Angus (1983b), Cremin (1970, 1980, 1988), Graff (1977), and Vinovskis (1983a, 1983b, 1985a). Three useful essays on the relation between the family and education are Angus (1980b), Cremin (1978), and Hiner (1989).

2. Bailyn makes no specific references to Handlin's book, but he probably drew on some of the ideas espoused by Handlin—especially Handlin's chapters on the reactions of parents and children to the New World.

3. Although critics (Vinovskis, 1971) have quarreled with some of Greven's methodology and findings, no one has contested his assertion that family life in New England was relatively stable. Similar results have been reported (Demos, 1970; Lockridge, 1970) for other communities in seventeenth-century Massachusetts.

4. The most detailed and comprehensive treatment of the role of education and the family among the New England Puritans is still Morgan (1966). His account discusses the difficulties that Puritans experienced in trying to get families to fulfill their responsibilities, but it does not convey the sense of disintegration and instability that Bailyn's (1960) account does. For a recent review of this topic, see Moran and Vinovskis (1992).

5. Hiner (1973: 12) points out that "hardly any attention was devoted to mothers in seventeenth-century recitations of parental duties." Indeed, "if the Puritan father had a relatively equal teaching partner, it was not his wife, but his minister" (13). Many historians, however, continue to ignore or minimize the role of the father in teaching young children in early America. For example, see Hall (1989).

6. On the changing role of women and religion during the seventeenth century, see Dunn (1980), Koehler (1980), Moran (1979, 1980), Moran and Vinovskis (1982, 1985), and Ulrich (1980, 1982).

7. According to Hiner (1973), seventeenth-century Puritans did not emphasize the importance of the lower schools. Beginning in the 1690s, however, Cotton Mather and others began to stress the need for these schools as a way of cultivating civility among unregenerate children.

8. There is considerable disagreement on just how high female literacy rates were at the end of the eighteenth century. For example, Beales (1978), Gilmore (1982, 1989), Main (1991), and Perlmann and Shirley (1991) all argue that female literacy in New England was higher than Lockridge's (1974) estimate.

9. Whether or not educational facilities increased or decreased proportionate to the population in eighteenth-century New England is not clear. Part of the confusion stems from the fact that much of the evidence of school decline comes from data on grammar schools. Yet Teaford (1970) argues that although classical grammar schools did decline in the late seventeenth and eighteenth centuries, they were replaced by other secondary schools that taught English. According to Teaford, there was a transformation in the nature of secondary education in Massachusetts before the American Revolution rather than a decrease in interest in education. The question of the relative availability of elementary schools in the eighteenth century awaits further research.

10. The question of literacy and illiteracy needs to be considered further as the simple dichotomy presented in earlier studies is no longer seen as accurate. For useful recent works on historical literacy in America, see Brown (1989), Gilmore (1989), Hall (1989), and Kaestle et al. (1991).

11. For a fuller discussion of how concern about how tax dollars were being spent affected support for education in nineteenth-century America, see chap. 4.

12. In general, there is very little concern among historians with the experiences of students in the classroom. For a good introduction to this issue, see Boylan (1985) and Finkelstein (1979, 1989). For a discussion of how nineteenth-century children learned to draw at home and in school, see Korzenik (1985).

13. Nineteenth-century school attendance is treated in depth in chaps. 8 and 9.

14. For a reanalysis of the patterns of school attendance in Newburyport, see chap. 8.

15. Hogan (1985) maintains that home ownership and early school leaving are related in his study of Chicago, but he does not have any individual-level data that would either support or refute that proposition.

16. The work-consumption index seems to predict the likelihood of women going into the labor force (Mason, Vinovskis, and Hareven, 1978), but it does not explain school attendance. Since many nineteenth-century girls who dropped out of school stayed at home rather than entering the labor force, it may be that the process of school leaving and entry into the paid labor force are not identical for females.

17. For a thorough discussion of the household budget data, see Clubb, Austin and Kirk (1989).

18. Public elementary and secondary schools were not the only institutions devised by nineteenth-century Americans to cope with the perceived crisis of raising children in cities. Child-reform advocates also established orphan asylums (Hawes, 1971), Sunday schools (Boylan, 1979), and reform schools (Brenzel, 1983; Schlossman, 1977). For an introduction and interpretation of these and other institutions for children, see Finkelstein (1985) and Holloran (1989).

19. See also chap. 3 for a discussion of the parent-teacher relationship in mid-nineteenth-century Massachusetts.

Chapter 2 / *A Ray of Millennial Light: Early Education and Social Reform in the Infant School Movement in Massachusetts, 1826–40*

written with Dean May

But a ray of Millennial light has shone on us, and reveals a way in which poverty, with all its attendant evils—moral, physical, and intellectual, may be banished from the world.

—*Infant School Society of the City of Boston (1834)*

The editors of the *Boston Recorder and Religious Transcript* showed little restraint in their enthusiasm for a Boston infant school in 1829: "Infants, taken from the most unfavorable situations in which they are ever placed, from the abodes of poverty and vice, are capable of learning at least a hundred times as much, a hundred times as well, and of being a hundred times as happy, by the system adopted in infant schools, as by that which prevails in the common schools throughout the country. The conclusion most interesting to every friend of education is, that the infant school system can be extended through every department of *popular education*. And that in any school district where there is interest and liberality enough to raise Ten Dollars to procure apparatus, a *beginning* can be made the present session."

Infant schools were religious and educational institutions intended to provide instruction for children of the poor, beginning at the age of about eighteen months and continuing until the children were old enough to attend public schools. They were founded and underwritten by civic-minded persons in Europe and America during the third and fourth decades of the nineteenth century. The movement began in 1816 with Robert Owen, who opened an infant school at New Lanark, Scotland (Salmon and Hindshaw, 1904).[1] The schools rapidly spread throughout England, Scotland, and Ireland. Americans, always sensitive to reform movements in England, quickly picked up the idea. In February 1827, plans were made in Hartford, Connecticut, to establish the first infant school in America. In May of that year an infant school society was founded in New York City, and similar societies were soon organized in Philadelphia and other American cities.[2] The infant school movement spread to Massachusetts in 1828. In June, two different infant school societies established schools, one on Pleasant Street and one on Salem Street. Shortly thereafter, schools opened in a number of other towns, including Salem, Worcester, Concord, Haverhill, and Charlestown.[3]

The new institutions were very popular in the early 1830s, but by mid-decade there was a drastic decline in enthusiasm. By the end of 1835, almost all public comment on the infant schools in Massachusetts had ceased, and the activities of the once-flourishing infant school societies faded—not only from public memory, but even from the recollections of those who had actively participated in the movement. When kindergartens became popular in Massachusetts in the 1860s and 1870s, they were greeted as a unique European contribution with almost no association to the earlier infant school movement.[4]

The infant school movement provides an ideal opportunity to study the dynamics of an educational reform effort. The interaction of educational reformers, social reformers, civic-minded social elites, public school officials, and the general public buffeted the movement in directions that none of the groups alone would have planned. Attitudes toward infant schools and differing expectations of what the schools could accomplish also influenced the early successes and the abrupt decline of the movement.

The short duration of public enthusiasm for the infant education movement does not diminish its significance to the social historian. The discussion of infant schools focused public attention on the importance of infancy and stimulated a vigorous reexamination of the social institutions that related most directly to infants. The role of the family and the school in an infant's life received particular attention. These considerations gave rise to questions about the role of women as mothers, students, and teachers. The infant school movement provides an opportunity to explore these issues at the family level and in different social institutions.

Clearly it is impossible to discuss all the issues raised by the infant education movement here. In this chapter we will examine the major ideas and considerations that led to the founding of infant schools; trace the attitudes and interactions of the local groups that established these schools; and show how confusion as to objectives and lack of unanimity within and among the groups led to the decline of the schools at the very time when changing social conditions made the needs they were designed to meet more pressing than ever. This analysis will suggest tentatively that infant education may have been a major factor in encouraging parents to send their children at a very young age to public schools even after the movement itself had faded from the scene.

Educators in England developing the infant school system attempted to fuse two major European traditions of educational theory and practice. Much of the difficulty in making infant schools viable in America arose from the fact that these two traditions led the sponsoring groups to work at cross purposes.

The first of these traditions developed on the Continent from foundations laid by Jean-Jacques Rousseau with the publication of *Emile* in 1762 (Rousseau, 1979).[5] Rousseau proposed two major innovations in *Emile*. Viewing human society as essentially corrupt, he stressed that the role of education should be primarily that of encouraging the young mind to shake off the impositions of the old society and arrive at its own conclusions as to what was worthy of study and attention. According to Rousseau, education was not the transmission of a body of knowledge from master to pupil, but rather it was a process of freeing the pupil's mind to explore the world on its own.

The second major idea introduced by Rousseau was his division of youth into three periods and his contention that specific aspects of the child's total educational experience were appropriate to each period in the child's development. For example, before the age of five—a period when the senses are most important—education should consist of exposing the senses to as great a variety of concrete experiences as possible. Children are not young adults but rather developing individuals whose education must be appropriately attuned to their stages of development.

Aspects of these two ideas were further developed in a long series of educational experiments carried out by various proponents of reform during the next hundred years. Although each reformer had distinctive ideas that he sought to emphasize and develop in his own school, all members of this group agreed on some general principles. All shared an implicit rejection of the old society and had a desire to isolate children from the its harmful influences. This found expression in the fact that schools were physically isolated from centers of population and were run as boarding schools, where the master could hope for greater control (Pollard, 1957).

These continental reformers shared a revulsion against force of any kind and a belief that if children were sufficiently exposed to the natural world, they would begin to ask questions and explore the world in their own way. Overall, the need to balance physical, moral, and intellectual development was emphasized. The reformers also stressed that certain teaching methods were appropriate to certain stages of development and that it was unnatural and hence wrong to try to thwart nature by attempting teachings that were not properly keyed to the developmental stage of a child.

It should be emphasized that none of these educators advocated institutions specifically for children younger than four or five, as the proponents of infant education later did. This might seem odd, given their common effort to remove the children from environments that might contaminate them. But here their distrust of old society and their love of nature came into conflict. It seemed obvious that parents were the most important conveyors of values in early childhood and that their teachings would most likely be those of the old society. But to remove infants from their home, from the loving care of the mother and the family, would violate their rule of strict adherence to nature (Kuhn, 1947).

Johann Heinrich Pestalozzi, the great eighteenth-century Swiss educator, studied the perceptual and learning faculties of infants. He concluded that children could begin to learn at a very early age, but that all such learning should take place in the home. Pestalozzi's work suggested that girls and mothers should be taught the new and progressive educational techniques so that they might apply them to their children. And, in fact, the emphasis on female education, maternal education, and fireside education, so common in the first half of the nineteenth century in America as well as in Europe, derived in part from Pestalozzi's ideas (Gutek, 1968; Monroes, 1907; Silber 1960).

But what if some parents were not sufficiently enlightened to be fit teachers of their offspring, as advocates of the infant schools contended? The fact that the European educational reformers provided no answer to this question suggests one of two beliefs. Either they felt that the infant was not sufficiently impressionable to experience irreversible harm in an unenlightened home, or they believed that natural affection and love were the most significant part of the education process at this age and that even an unenlightened mother was preferable to the most enlightened schoolmaster.

In England quite a different tradition dominated educational reform. The English produced no educators of the renown of Pestalozzi until the effects of industrialization and urbanization began to be felt late in the eighteenth century—a striking fact. The only educational innovations in England in the eighteenth century and early decades of the nineteenth century were the Sunday school movement, which began in 1780, and the Lancastrian-Bell system of monitorial instruction, which began in the first decade of the nineteenth century. Both of these movements were practical reforms designed to extend a modicum of education to the lower classes at the least possible cost. They did not involve new concepts about the content of education (Kaestle, 1973b; Lacquer, 1976; Pollard, 1957); nor did the English reformers advocate special teaching methods based upon novel conceptions of the infant mind, as did the continental reformers.

The first major educational innovation in England in the early nineteenth century was Robert Owen's infant school at New Lanark in 1816. The principles underlying the school, which formed part of his New Institution, were expressed by Owen in his *New View of Society*, where he recommended that: "the governing powers of all countries should establish rational plans for the education and general formation of the characters of their subjects. . . . These plans must be devised to train children from their earliest infancy in good habits of every description (which will of course prevent them from acquiring those of falsehood and deception). They must afterwards be rationally educated, and their labour be usefully directed. Such habits and education will impress them with an active and ardent desire to promote the happiness of every individual, and that without the shadow of exception for sect, or party, or country, or climate" (quoted from Silber, 1960: 76).

Owen's infant school was followed by a school on Brewer's Green, Westminster, founded in 1818 by an eminent group of English reformers. Another infant school was organized in the Spitalfields section of London shortly thereafter, and in July 1824, these same reformers founded the Infant School Society and began to solicit public subscriptions to support the institutions. Within a year, at least fifty-five infant schools were in operation in various parts of England, Scotland, and Ireland.[6]

The discussions at Freemason's Hall in London, which led to the founding of the Infant School Society, underline the fact that the infant schools were perceived as a means of dealing with pressing social problems. Whatever the designs of Robert Owen at New Lanark, it is strikingly obvious that the schools seemed a perfect answer to problems created by the factory system of production. With children safely in school, mothers and older children were free to work in the factories. This consideration was not lost on those who spoke at Freemason's Hall, although they emphasized in this context the positive advantage to the family of the incremental income of working mothers rather than the value to factory owners of the increased labor supply. It is clear that the growth of an urban pauper class was what occupied the minds of the London reformers. Participants in the meeting told tales of Fagin-like criminals who kept large numbers of impoverished vagrant children in their employ as thieves and pickpockets (Wilderspin, 1825).

The instructors hired by the London Infant School Society soon found the management of several dozen infants no easy task. These teachers, in their search for ideas and techniques that might prove useful in an infant school, turned to the European tradition, especially the work of Pestalozzi. They were the first to apply Pestalozzian principles for the teaching of infants in an institutional setting—although Pestalozzi had never intended the establishment of such institutions. In the process of working out a practical combination of Owen's idea of infant schools and Pestalozzi's principles of teaching infants, they created what became the infant school system (McCann and Young, 1982).

Early advocacy of infant schools in the United States coincided with the emergence of a group of educators and public-minded citizens. This in turn led to an increase in the number of publications specializing in the theory and practice of public education. Before 1826 only three journals concerned exclusively with education had been published in the United States. During the next twenty-five years over sixty magazines and papers devoted to education were established (Mott, 1957).

William Russell's *American Journal of Education,* published in Boston from 1826 through 1830 under his editorship, was the first journal to contribute significantly to this flowering of interest in educational theories and reforms. Russell's position on infant education was made clear in his opening editorial: "There seems to us to be no danger of beginning instruction too soon, if it is begun in the right way, and with expectations sufficiently moderate. . . . Within a few years public sentiment has undergone a favorable change on the subject of early education. . . . The establishment of infant schools we look upon as one of the most important epochs in the history of education. We shall use every endeavor to render this subject familiar to the minds of our readers by communicating all the information we can procure regarding the details of the system and its progress abroad and at home" (*American Journal of Education,* 1826: 4–6). Russell made good on his promise: nearly every issue of the journal contained articles advocating or reporting the progress of infant schools.

Russell was the chief figure among the American theorists of educational reform. His popular journal was a major influence in building the sentiments that led to the founding of the first infant school societies in 1828. Born in Scotland and trained at Glasgow under George Jardine, Russell was one of the first to begin teaching in America the new European doctrines that had become influential in England.[7]

The sequence of events leading to the establishment of infant schools in Boston was almost precisely the reverse of the process in England, where concern about social problems had preceded a knowledge of how to establish and manage an infant school. William Russell's attentions were drawn to the infant school system by the writings of Samuel Wilderspin, William Wilson, and other teachers in British infant schools. The system thus came to America more or less intact, where theorists of educational reform, such as Russell, were quick to notice its novelty and its possible applications in the American setting. Boston already had over fifty primary schools in operation—schools that accepted children as young as four years old. As a result, Russell's enthusiasm for the infant school system was understandably placed more on the pedagogical theories than on the idea of creating new institutions. Certainly he advocated the establishment of infant schools, but he saw them primarily as pilot schools for proving the value to the public school system of exciting new principles. His major problem was to find a group with the interest, the expertise, and the financial resources to found the first infant schools and to sustain them long enough to prove the efficacy of their principles.[8]

Russell's efforts were successful in 1828. Such schools had been in operation in Philadelphia and New York for nearly a year, and favorable reports had appeared in Boston newspapers, as well as in the *American Journal of Education.* In 1828, two separate infant school societies were founded, one opening a school on Salem Street and the other a school on Pleasant Street.[9] As there is only sketchy information available on the Salem Street society we will concentrate on the much more solidly documented activities of the Infant School Society of the City of Boston, which favored the Pleasant Street School. Because of the lack of evidence, our analysis also excludes the private infant schools in Boston that catered to middle- and upper-class pupils. (See table 2.1 for a list of known infant schools in Boston.)

In the June 1828 issue of the *American Journal of Education*, Russell announced with obvious satisfaction a meeting of some ninety women at the home of Mrs. William Thurston. Following an opening prayer by the Reverend Thomas H. Skinner, they proceeded to organize the Infant School Society of the City of Boston. Mr. Thurston, a lawyer of considerable wealth, was a leading figure in the orthodox Trinitarian reaction to the Unitarian establishment. Similarly, the Reverend Mr. Skinner had been recently called from Philadelphia to serve in one of Boston's newly organized Trinitarian churches. The women who formed the new society were a part of a remarkable group of Bostonians who set out with evangelical fervor in the second decade of the nineteenth century to rescue the city from the moral and spiritual lassitude of Unitarian complacency. Although well-to-do middle-class citizens, the Trinitarian commitment of the group kept them apart from the Unitarian-dominated elites of Boston.[10]

In a certain sense, the membership of this group was ideally suited to carry out William Russell's hope for an infant school. Their husbands had pursued a large variety of reform efforts during the decade since they had organized the Society for the Religious and Moral Instruction of the Poor in 1816. The credo of that society was set forth clearly in its third annual report; it emphasized the relation between poverty, vice, and ignorance and proposed that moral and religious instruction were much more effective deterrents to crime than "the mere dread of legal punishment" (Boston Society for the Religious and Moral Instruction of the Poor, 1819: 22).

The society had been a major influence in establishing primary schools in Boston, had pursued a program of bringing religious instruction to the city's seafaring population, and had founded and maintained an ambitious Sabbath-school program for the children of the poor. The Sabbath schools accepted children as young as five and offered instruction them during most of the day

Table 2.1 / *Known Infant Schools in Boston, 1828–35*

	Founded	Closed	Instructor	Enroll-ment[a]	Notes
Schools of the Infant School Society of the City of Boston					
Pleasant Street	June 1828	August 1828	Miss Blood	—	Moved to Bedford Street.
Bedford Street	August 1828	1833	Miss Blood	129	Closed by competition of two neighboring schools.
Stillman Street	1829	1835	—	73.8	Reported moved to Charlestown Street.
Charlestown Street	1835	—	—	—	Planned, but no evidence that school was opened.
Garden Street	October 1833	—	Miss Mary Jones	65.3	In the Mission House.
Schools of the "Other Infant School Society" of Boston					
Salem Street	June 1828	before July 1829	B. Alcott Mrs. Brush	50	Alcott left in September 1828 to found his own school.
Atkinson Street	by July 1829	before April 1832	Mrs. Brush		
Theatre Alley	by April 1832	—	—	—	New building built for the school.
Broad Street	by October 1835	—	—	—	Assumed to be supported by this society, though this is uncertain.
Private Schools					
Common Street	October 1828	April 1829	B. Alcott	20	Name of Common Street changed to Tremont
Tremont Street	April 1829	May 1830	B. Alcott	30	Street in 1830, and school in a new location near St. Paul's.
Belknap Street (African)	Summer 1830	—	—	—	Established by Miss E. O. Lane.
Near Bed-ford Street	by 1833	—	—	—	

[a]Annual average of all known figures.

on Sunday. The curriculum was not entirely the learning of scriptures and catechisms; a serious effort was made to instruct the children in rudimentary reading, writing, and ciphering.

The infant schools in Boston were thus initially underwritten by social reformers who saw in them a means of combating the ills of urban society. The first infant schools in London had drawn their support from a similar group. But there is a significant difference in the role played by the groups that founded and sustained the two movements. Whereas in London the social reformers first established infant schools and then called upon the educational theorists for guidance in teaching young children, the process was exactly the reverse in Boston. In the United States, educational theorists advocated the establishment of infant schools because they were attracted to the progressive pedagogical theories applied to infant education in Europe. The Boston social reformers responded to Russell's pleas willingly, though with very different goals in mind.

Most of the discussion about infant schools concerned their usefulness in dealing with urban problems. This was of particular relevance in a state such as Massachusetts, which at that time was more urbanized than the rest of the nation. Nonetheless, although the Commonwealth, particularly the eastern counties, was relatively urban by the 1820s, the great increase in percentage of people living in urban areas of more than 8,000 persons did not occur until the late 1830s (see figure 2.1)—after the decline of the infant education movement (Knights, 1971; Williamson, 1965).

Boston was the largest urban area in Massachusetts, and although it had a smaller population than such cities as New York and Philadelphia, it experienced many of the social problems caused by urban crowding and rapid population growth.[11] But just as in the state as a whole, the period of the most rapid population growth in Boston occurred after the peak of enthusiasm for the infant schools. It is difficult to obtain accurate estimates of levels and trends in poverty and crime for nineteenth-century Boston. One crude approximation of the concern about these problems is indicated by the per capita expenditures of the city on these issues (see figure 2.2). It is interesting to note that the per capita expenditures for institutions for the poor and the mentally ill, as well as for the police, were considerably less than what was spent on public schools. Furthermore, these expenditures did not increase drastically during the late 1820s when infant schools were being advocated.[12]

The crucial changes in social reform during this period were not in the amount of public expenditure but rather in the attitudes of the reformers. Social reformers began to distinguish among different types of poor and attempted to reform them morally as well as to provide them with a means of livelihood. More attention was given to breaking the vicious cycle of poverty by reaching young children and providing them with the social norms and necessary skills

Figure 2.1 / *Population of Massachusetts Living in Urban Areas, 1790–1860*

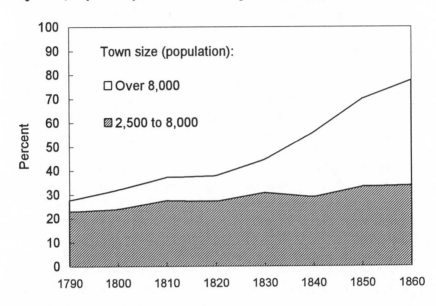

Source: Data from Vinovskis, 1981: 228–29

to escape from a life of continued dependence on society.[13] Poverty was the major factor motivating the founders of the first two infant schools in Boston. They saw the infant schools a means of permanently eliminating poverty by educating and properly socializing children from poor families.

Crime rather than poverty had been uppermost in the minds of the founders of the Infant School Society in London. But it appears that the incidence and severity of crime in Boston were much lower than in London. Although crime was often mentioned by the American advocates, they usually used the term *vice* rather than *crime* in describing the evils the schools were intended to prevent. In the arguments on behalf of infant schools in America there are few indications of concern for immediate public safety or references to gangs of young hoodlums such as the ones who terrorized whole districts of London.[14]

Since 1816, when Owen founded his infant school at New Lanark, the infant school movement in England had been viewed as an ideal means of dealing with the harmful effects of industrialization. It offered the advantage of providing moral and literary instruction for the urban poor at an early age and freed mothers to work. As Massachusetts was a leader in industrial development during the 1820s and 1830s, one might have expected American social reformers to reiterate the arguments of their English counterparts. Yet the nature of the manufacturing system in Massachusetts minimized the usefulness and need for relieving working mothers from caring for their children. Most

Figure 2.2 / *Per Capita Expenditures on Public Schools, Institutions, and Police in Boston, 1818–60*

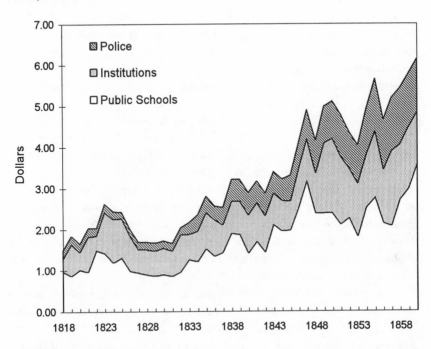

Source: Data from Huse, 1916: 348–51

Massachusetts manufacturing firms that used female labor tried to hire young, single women rather than married women with young children. In Boston, manufacturing was not of major economic importance during the 1820s and 1830s (Handlin, 1968; N. Ware, 1924; C. Ware, 1966). As a result, even when the advocates of infant education did use the argument that the schools freed the mothers to work, the nature of the employment opportunities for those women was not specified.

A sizable immigrant community existed in Boston by the 1830s, especially Catholic Irish. During the first three decades of the nineteenth century, native Bostonians and the immigrants lived in relative harmony. Tensions increased in the 1830s, but it seems unlikely that fear of immigrants was the major motivating factor in the establishment of infant schools. The Boston infant school societies had closed before the large waves of Catholic immigrants and the increasing hostility between the Catholics and Protestants of the 1840s (Handlin, 1968).

In Massachusetts in the 1820s population growth, poverty, crime rates, industrialization, and immigration were not yet causing problems sufficiently grave to account for the early support given the infant education movement. Rather, the importation of instruments of reform caused educational reformers to seek out ways to use these new techniques. The reformers emphasized the need to avoid the excesses of English urbanization and industrialization rather than stressing the need to combat social problems in Boston. Ironically, just as the infant education movement began its sudden decline, most of the social problems mentioned above became increasingly serious. This, however, did not save the faltering infant schools because the causes of their demise were not based on their relevance or lack of relevance to the social conditions of the city.

What, then, led to the decline of the infant schools? One circumstance arose from the hopes and expectations of the women who founded the Infant School Society of the City of Boston. They were less concerned about educational reform than they were about moral reform. They saw infant schools as an extension of their husbands' work with the Sabbath schools. Believing the infant mind to be especially susceptible to the influence of its environment— whether good or bad—and having used this argument to garner support for Sabbath schools, it was a natural step to extend the beneficent influence of such schools to still younger children.

The officers and managers of the society throughout its existence were a small, closely knit group. Nearly 20 percent of the entire membership were wives or relatives of men who were officers or patrons of the Society for the Religious and Moral Instruction of the Poor. The group was composed entirely of women. The only official relation men had to the society was through a group of five men, including an auditor of accounts and a physician, who were chosen each year to serve as a board of advisers. Management of the schools seems to have been entirely under the guidance of the women. This is in marked contrast to the Sabbath school movement, and a careful reading of the infant school movement's discussions reveals a modest degree of militancy in the insistence that the schools provided one educational cause that fell squarely and exclusively within women's province. Characteristic is the assertion in the *Ladies' Magazine* that "it is well observed that *'females* have many natural qualifications for instructors of infants,' which men have not—it is also true that females are competent, and might be advantageously employed in the business of education to a far greater extent than has ever yet been practiced" (April 1830: 189).

The relatively small group of women who were officers and managers of the Infant School Society are those we have designated the "social reform group." Their devotion to the cause sustained their activity and commitment whatever vicissitudes befell them. Their financial resources were not sufficient in themselves to be able to support the society. In their effort to raise funds they were able to mobilize the support of a much larger body of Boston women—mostly of the orthodox congregations. These women we call the "civic-minded social elites"—women who read their *Ladies' Magazine,* kept up on current fashions, and were quick to respond to causes that social reformers brought to their attention. These women formed the larger body of patrons of the society in its early years and supported the annual fund-raising fairs conducted by the society during its first three years of operation.

By 1829, the *Ladies' Magazine* was reporting that: "The interesting subject of Infant Schools is becoming more and more fashionable. . . . We have been told that it is now in contemplation, to open a school for the infants of others besides the poor. If such course be not soon adopted, at the age for entering primary schools those *poor* children will assuredly be the *richest* scholars. And why should a plan which promises so many advantages, independent of merely relieving the mother from her charge, be confined to children of the indigent?" (February 1829: 89). The editor of the magazine then added a long list of arguments for the founding of the infant schools for the well-to-do, including the evocation of the charming image of the father, after coming home from a hard day at "counting-room or shop," being pleased to hear his son "with his scarcely formed accents . . . singing our national air . . . to the words, 'Five times five are twenty-five, five times six are thirty, and five times seven are thirty-five, and five times eight are forty' " (89–90).

This enthusiasm mounted when the infant schools began to give public demonstrations early in 1829. The founding of infant schools for the children of the well-to-do had already begun, and extension to the outlying villages was under way. More public demonstrations followed in short order. Infant schools had clearly become a favorite charity of the Boston orthodox community.

Public demonstrations contributed to exaggerated public expectations and misunderstandings about the schools. As noted above, the leaders of the infant school societies were primarily interested in moral reform. And yet, how does one demonstrate the progress made in reforming the morals of infants? The very name chosen for the institutions, "infant *schools*"; the fact that those who taught were called "instructresses"; and the experience of the public with the concept "school" determined what the standard of success would be. A public trained over decades to think of schools as institutions where children were taught order and discipline so that they might master the fundamental skills of reading, writing, and ciphering found itself captivated by the idea that two- or three-year-olds were capable of learning what it had been previously thought only older children could learn.

The public assumption that infant schools were the same as primary schools, except that they taught younger children, was subversive to the intentions of William Russell, as well as to those of the women of the Infant School Society. The reformers were unsuccessful in convincing the public that infant schools embodied new principles, the efficacy of which could not be judged by the old standards and assumptions. The institutions had been tagged by their founders with the name "schools." The public demonstrations necessitated the display of their accomplishments as schools. Once the image had been firmly set, there was no other basis upon which the institutions could demonstrate their worthiness of public support and emulation. Initial tactical errors denied Russell his hope of seeing the pedagogical techniques of infant schools spread into the public school system.

In an 1829 address Russell stressed his desire that infant school methods be adopted by public schools: "An Important subject in immediate connection with the present subject, is the good effected by infant schools, through their influence on elementary instruction generally and the useful hints which they offer for the management of primary schools, and even of arrangements of the nursery" (13).

The Boston School Committee—and especially the Primary School Board—had a negative attitude toward introducing any teaching innovations in the schools, so there was little chance of the infant schools or their principles being adopted into the public schools in any major way. The persistent hints by Russell and others that infant schools offered great benefits to the public school system were specifically taken up by the Primary School Board in 1830. After gathering information from primary school teachers who had accepted children from infant schools, they cited the observation of John P. Bigelow as typical of the reports they had received: "With regard to children from 'Infant Schools,' it is the decided opinion of every instructress in the district, who has had any experience on the subject, that it is better to receive children into the Primary Schools who have had no instruction whatever, than those who have graduated with the highest honors of the Infant Seminaries. It is stated that these children are peculiarly restless in their habits, and are thereby the cause of restlessness and disorder among the other children; and it does not appear that their previous instruction renders them, in any respect, peculiarly proficient or forward in the studies of the Primary Schools" (Wightman, 1860: 123).

Other teachers reported infant school children as "intractable and troublesome, restless from want of constant excitement, and their attention fixed with difficulty upon their studies." The Primary School Board, in condemning occasional introductions of "Exercises in geometry, geography, and natural philosophy" into some primary schools, had already made it clear that it saw its mandate to be that of training the children in "correct reading and thorough spelling" only (Wightman, 1860: 125).[15]

It is no wonder that the Boston Primary School Board objected to the deportment of pupils from the infant schools. The issue was fundamentally between two different conceptions of the infant mind and its capabilities. Derived from these differing conceptions were opposite theories on the purposes and techniques of teaching children. The theory that lay behind the infant school movement was in essence an early challenge to the Enlightenment establishment by Romantic reformers. In the Boston of the 1830s, there could be little doubt as to the immediate victor.[16]

The Primary School Board had no objection to teaching children of tender years. The fact that the primary schools by law accepted children as young as four years was evidence of this. Moreover, very young children had been educated in dame schools for many years. But the board members could not imagine that the infant mind, blank and open as it was, should be approached in any manner other than through the strict discipline and the rote memorization that had always been their experience. Nor could they imagine that education could serve any purpose other than to prepare children to read and write—to make them more efficient recipients of the knowledge that society had to offer them. This, to them, was the meaning of schools and schooling.

Added to this conflict of opposing ideas was the simple problem of expense. As we have already seen in figure 2.2, the period of retrenchment in public expenditures that followed Mayor Josiah Quincy's expensive reforms continued until about 1831 (McCaughey, 1970). When the expenditures began to rise again, the proportion spent on schools did not grow as rapidly as those spent on other city services. Boston public officials simply were unwilling to allocate much money to primary school education. While there are dramatic increases in the amounts spent on higher-level schools beginning in 1831, the expenditures on primary schools show only a moderate increase. Since the cost of educating a child in the infant schools was quite high, it was unlikely that the political leadership would have been willing to incur the additional expense even if it had approved of the institutions in principle.

There were also major obstacles that prevented the infant schools from continuing as private philanthropies. Pestalozzian principles made their dramatic entry into this country as part of the infant school idea, but by the late 1820s Pestalozzi's ideas were flowing to America through other channels as well—channels that gave American educators an opportunity to see them in another context.

The early literature of the infant school movement reveals a belief that under normal circumstances the home was the most desirable place to begin instruction. Both the theorists and the sponsors of infant schools belied their uneasiness in perpetuating the unnatural act of taking children from their homes when they defended the infant schools as homes themselves—homes likely to promote the happiness of both children and society in ways that natural homes would never do.

The enthusiasm shared by those in the movement for the reform potential of the schools, however, overcame whatever qualms may have existed about taking children from their parents: "Such is the power of bad example—especially that of parents—that it will probably do much to counteract the good influence of the infant school. Indeed there would be every thing to fear, were not its good influences brought to bear on the mind so early. Making every allowance for this evil, will not these children, trained up under the same system, be better than they; and perhaps, in the third generation, the work of moral renovation will be complete. Then ignorance and vice will be gone and poverty must go too" (Infant School Society of the City of Boston, 1833: 5–6).

But the later stream of Pestalozzian teachings—a stream that came to America free of the association with infant schools—reinforced a growing attitude among Boston's elites that the infant is better off at home whenever possible. An interesting expression of this evolution was made by the editors of the *Ladies' Magazine*, who in their early enthusiasm had suggested as part of their 1829 argument favoring infant schools that "it is nearly, if not quite impossible to teach such little ones at home, with the facility they are taught at an infant school. And if a convenient room is prepared, and faithful and discreet agents employed, parents may feel secure that their darlings are not only safe but improving" (February 1829: 89–90). Still enthusiastic about the schools a year later, they nonetheless had changed their emphasis to the importance of the schools in their effects on the common schools and especially on the home: "In the nursery—that retired and scarce heeded place of instruction, but which nevertheless shapes more minds than all the public schools on earth—these experiments on the infant mind will operate with a power that must cause a great and rapid change" (May 1830: 224). By 1832, although still urging support for the schools, the editors displayed a revealing lapse of memory when they maintained, "We have never urged their adoption, by those who have the means to provide for their infants, and the time to take care of them. These poor mothers have neither" (April 1832: 180).

Such a change in views suggests that the civic-minded social elites of Boston were imbibing through their *Ladies' Magazine* and the *American Annals of Education* the aspect of Pestalozzi's teaching that the advocates of infant schools had obscured—that the home was the proper institutional setting for the education of infants and that the informed mother was the best instructress. Pestalozzian principles, as embodied in the infant school system, had captured the public imagination by offering the promise that children could be taught at a very early age. This novel conception of making use of "what has hitherto been considered the waste years of human life" gave infant schools their early impetus (Infant School Society of the City of Boston, 1831: 12). But shortly the fuller exposition of Pestalozzi's thought began to work against the institutions, as his stress on the home and family as the ideal infant school permeated the attitudes of Boston's elites.

Still another strand of European educational theory tended to diminish enthusiasm for the infant schools as it came to be better understood in Boston by the early 1830s. This was the concept of the need for *balance* in a child's early education—that it not only train the intellect but also develop the body and the spiritual faculties. The Boston infant schools, at least throughout most of their history, appear to have been exemplars of this balance principle. Every effort was made to provide a playground and recess period for the children, and there was much emphasis on marching and clapping exercises and moral lessons. It is also clear that in the short run, physical and moral development is much more difficult to demonstrate than intellectual (or academic) achievement; and the leaders of the movement felt impelled to show quick, dramatic results in order to garner public financial support. Thus, in their early years the infant school became associated with the type of demonstration of intellectual precocity so glowingly referred to in the news media, such as the comments in the *Boston Recorder and Religious Transcript* at the beginning of this chapter. While these displays of the children's intellectual advancement were very helpful in gaining financial support for the infant schools, they also created an image of the schools that made them vulnerable to the charge that they were promoting premature intellectual precocity at the expense of a more balanced development.

In 1829 William Russell gave up his editorship of the *American Journal of Education* in order to assist Bronson Alcott in founding an infant school for a wealthy patron in Pennsylvania. His successor, William C. Woodbridge, had just returned from a long stay at Hofwyl, the estate of European educational reformer Philipp de Fellenberg. Fellenberg maintained the mind could not properly be instructed unless adequate attention was given to the development of the body. Physical exercise occupied nearly half the daily routine of pupils in his school (Pollard, 1957). The "manual training schools" that became popular about this time were undoubtedly influenced by his theories. William Woodbridge immediately began to stress in his journal the importance of physical development and of timing intellectual training with the proper stage of physical growth. While continuing to encourage early education, Woodbridge was hedging the idea with qualifications that were certain to diminish the shallowly rooted public enthusiasm for infant schools.

Woodbridge pushed the point in the August 1830 issue when he compared the training of children with that of plants, animals, or athletes. He said that training should begin early, but with great attention to the changing capacities of the child at each stage: "It is too little considered . . . *when the infant begins to be a proper subject of training, and at what age he may become in one respect or another, insensible to its influence.* . . . All the efforts of misjudging teachers and parents who wish to see their children early prodigies, only sacrifice the fruit in order to produce an earlier expansion of the flower, and resemble the hot-bed in their influence in 'forcing' a plant to maturity, whose feebleness or early decay must be proportional to the unnatural rapidity of its growth, and a consequent want of symmetry in its parts" (*American Annals of Education*, 1830: 355–56). Such expressions became increasingly common in the

American Annals of Education under Woodbridge's editorship. The dire hints of "feebleness" and "early decay" can hardly have escaped the notice of the civic-minded social elites whose donations were the major source of support for the infant schools. The increasing emphasis on a balance between physical and intellectual cultivation, itself a part of Pestalozzi's principles of education, was eroding public support for the idea of infant schools.

The final blow may well have been the Boston publication in 1833 of Amariah Brigham's *Remarks on the Influence of Mental Cultivation and Mental Excitement upon Health*. The preface to the first edition, which had appeared the year before in Hartford, made the author's intentions clear: "The object of this work is to awaken public attention to the importance of making some modification in the method of educating children, which now prevails in this country. It is intended to show the necessity of giving more attention to the health and growth of the body, and less to the cultivation of the mind, especially in early life, than is now given" (vii).

The influence of Brigham's book was nothing short of sensational. There is every indication that his intentions, as expressed in the preface, were quickly and dramatically realized. Favorable reviews were published in the *American Annals of Education,* the *Christian Examiner and General Reviewer,* and in the *Ladies' Magazine.* Especially significant is the fact that the *Ladies' Magazine,* which had made the schools objects of special attention almost since their founding, made no mention whatsoever of them in its 1834 editions. But its February issue did include excerpts from Brigham on the causes of insanity, which listed "the predominance given to the nervous system, by too early cultivating the mind and exciting the feelings of children" as the second most important cause (1834: 79). A tabulation of the number of articles opposing infant schools published in Boston journals in 1834 indicates that there were seven such articles. All of them related early instruction to the danger of either mental or physical debilitation in children.

It is important to note that Brigham's book did not cause poor parents to withdraw their children from the schools. The enrollment in schools for which we have records was higher in 1834 than in any year since 1831. Attendance figures were closer to enrollment figures in both the Stillman Street School and the Garden Street School than ever before—with both the attendance and enrollment being between sixty and sixty-five pupils for each school. Even more impressive was the fact that the token weekly payment that the ladies of the society asked of the pupils' families rose from a low of $.75 per pupil per year to $1.35 per pupil per year in 1835 (see figure 2.3). Apparently the parents were sufficiently convinced of the value of the schools their children attended and were willing to pay more for the privilege in spite of the dire warnings of Amariah Brigham.

Figure 2.3 / *Annual Budgets for the Infant School Society of the City of Boston, 1828–35*

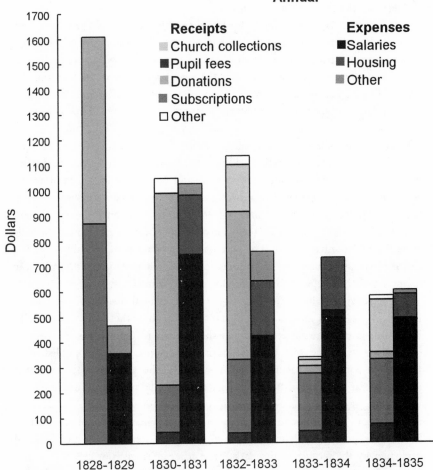

Note: Budget year runs from April to April.
Source: Data from Infant School Society of the City of Boston, Annual Reports, 1829, 1831, 1833, 1834, 1835

Nor did the women of the society lose faith in their reform movement. They did all within their power to correct the "hothouse" image they had been trapped into cultivating. They explained their position in their last annual report: "In commending Infant Schools to the attention of the Christian community, we wish their nature and design to be distinctly understood, and kept in mind. They are not *schools* in the common acceptation of the word. The use of this appellation has probably done much to excite a prejudice against them. They may with more propriety be termed neighborhood nurseries, or infant asylums" (Infant School Society of the City of Boston, 1835: 79). The report continued by urging financial contributions, not only for the existing schools, but also for funds to create several more.

If Amariah Brigham's book did not deter the parents of the infant poor from sending their children to the schools, nor the social reformers of the Infant School Society from continuing their support, how does one account for the collapse of the society? It appears that the key group involved in both the rise and decline of the movement was the large body of civic-minded women who were initially willing but later reluctant to support the society. Their donations and contributions at annual fund-raising fairs helped keep the society solvent when infant schools were a fashionable cause. Priding themselves on keeping in touch with the latest intellectual currents, literate and well informed, they were a most sensitive barometer of the rise and fall of intellectual fashions.

The women of the smaller reform group were more constant because they had invested much more in time and thought to sustaining the movement. Moreover, they were convinced that as instruments of reform the infant schools were as badly needed as ever. The parents of the infant poor probably were not aware of Amariah Brigham or the implications of his writings until after the infant schools had closed their doors for want of funds.

The surviving annual budgets of the Infant School Society of the City of Boston as portrayed in figure 2.3 substantiates this hypothesis. The most striking aspect is that the society's records show a decline from a positive balance of $380 in 1832, the year before Amariah Brigham's book was published in Boston, to a negative balance of $372 in 1833. The greatest volume of that decline by far was in donations—exactly the category where one would expect to find the large group of civic-minded social elites. A solid core of subscribers remained and even grew in the subsequent year. The church collections that brought the budget nearly into balance in fiscal 1834 were the result of a special campaign by the pastors of the Park Street, Essex Street, Bowdoin Street, and Federal Street Baptist churches, and they may represent an expression of loyalty to their pastors and their churches rather than any special enthusiasm to the cause of infant education.

The deficits occurred in spite of a continuing decrease in operating expenses gained through cutting back the costs of both housing and teachers' salaries from their peak in fiscal 1830. It is also worth noting that the contribution of pupils rose from 1832 in volume and even more dramatically in proportion to the total income of the society. There can be no doubt that the society continued to enjoy the solid support of those for whose benefit it was intended.

What, then, was the ultimate cause of the demise of the Infant School Society of the City of Boston? The trend in social conditions would seem to argue that the need for the schools was never greater than in the late 1830s.

One can only conclude that in this instance the underlying social conditions were not as important to those who might have sustained the society as were the tides of intellectual fashion. Convinced by ideas expounded in Amariah Brigham's book and in a number of current intellectual journals, the women recoiled from the thought that their benevolence—far from ensuring the eradication of poverty and vice—might be contributing to the insanity of future generations. The irony is that their reaction was against a misleading image of infant schools, one that was initially assumed to gain their support.

The demise of the Infant School Society of the City of Boston symbolized the end of efforts to create educational institutions designed specifically for infants in the Boston area until Elizabeth Palmer Peabody began the kindergarten movement in the 1860s.[17] An early hope of William Russell, among others, was that the principles and spirit of the infant schools would be adopted by the public schools and that if this were achieved, the survival of infant schools as separate institutions was not important. There is some evidence that in the 1830s and 1840s the Boston Primary School Board did institute some of the progressive techniques that had been advocated by theorists such as Russell, but it is impossible to say with confidence that these proposals came from the infant school movement because, as we have indicated, not all the innovations in educational techniques for children came directly from the infant schools themselves.

One distinctive feature of the infant school system was its advocacy sending children to school at much earlier ages than had hitherto been the practice. By studying at what age parents sent their children to school, one can perhaps find evidence of the possible influence of the infant school movement. In Boston such an influence is impossible to detect because children younger than four were specifically excluded from attending the public schools. In some other towns where infant schools existed, the public school systems did not specify an age for admission, and those areas provide a glimpse of public behavior on the issue of educating young children.

It this regard, it might be first useful to describe the process by which this investigation of the infant school movement in Boston was undertaken. Attention was called to the movement by an earlier analysis of the influence of Horace Mann upon public education in nineteenth-century Massachusetts. Data collected and analyzed independently by Albert Fishlow and Maris Vinovskis suggested that the enrollment rate in public and private schools was stable or even declining in Massachusetts during the period of Mann's tenure as secretary of the Board of Education. This appeared to be a startling reversal of traditional interpretations of Mann's impact on the school system in the state. Upon closer examination of the data, it appears that most of the decline in the rate of attendance came in the group of children under four and that the attendance record of children between four and sixteen, the category on which Mann had focused his efforts, actually increased. The reputation of Mann on this point seemed safe (Fishlow, 1966; Vinovskis, 1970b). But the observation had raised interesting questions about public attitudes toward the rearing and training of young children in the first half of the nineteenth century.

Vinovskis's data revealed that for the earliest period when relatively reliable school attendance data are available, a surprisingly large percentage of children under four still were attending schools. In 1840 at least 10 percent of children younger than four in the state were in school, and many localities showed a much higher percentage attending. Overall, perhaps about 40 percent of three-year-olds were enrolled in a public or private school that year.[18]

Not only were a high percentage of young children attending schools throughout the state in the 1840s and 1850s, but there was a steady decrease in the number of children under the age of five who attended school during those decades. The dramatic change in the ages at which parents chose to send children to school suggests that attitudinal changes toward young children, their place in society, and their aptitudes might lie behind the changes in school attendance.

The educational journals published in Massachusetts at that time made very little mention of the public education of very young children outside the context of infant schools, although there were some hints that attitudes on this subject may have shifted in the 1820s. William Russell mentioned that "within a few years public sentiment has undergone a favorable change on the subject of early education" (*American Journal of Education*, January 1826: 6), and there were occasional references to the fact that the Boston practice of accepting children in primary school as early as four years of age was quite unusual. The Sabbath school movement accepted no children younger than age five, and this was further evidence that the sending children younger than four to school was not a common practice.[19] In view of these findings, it seems possible that the flurry of intense devotion to the cause of educating young children generated by the infant school movement might bear a relation to the large numbers of children under four attending public schools in the 1840s and that some of the causes which led to the abrupt decline in enthusiasm for infant education among reformers in the mid-1830s might be related to the general decline in public practice of sending infants to school in the late 1840s and 1850s.[20]

Perhaps the reformers who pushed the cause of infant education in the 1820s and early 1830s might have been more effective than the abrupt and early end of the institutions they created would suggest. Unfortunately, there are very little data currently available to test this proposition. Statewide information on the numbers of children under age four attending school was not available until 1840. But data from one Concord primary school suggest very tentatively that the practice of sending infants to public schools may have been spurred by the infant school movement in areas where this practice was not banned outright by law.

Teachers in the East Centre District for the Concord school system kept a record of the names, dates of admission and withdrawal, parentage, ages, days attended, and days absent of all of their pupils from 1830 to 1842.[21] These data provide a glimpse of the public practices in sending children to school before reliable school reports on attendance are available for the state.

As figure 2.4 indicates, a sizable percentage of the children enrolled were under the age of four. One would like to examine changes over time in the percentage of children under four attending the East Centre District School, but the lack of information on the total number of children under four who lived in this school district precludes that possibility. One way of estimating changes over time would be to calculate the percentage of children under four in the school during this period. There is some danger, however, that the total population of the school might be a misleading base figure because there was no set age for entering the next higher school—the Concord grammar school. If there were a changing pattern in the ages of children entering the grammar school, it would distort the results. Consequently, it was decided to use the

Figure 2.4 / *Age Distribution of Students in Concord East Centre District School, 1830–42*

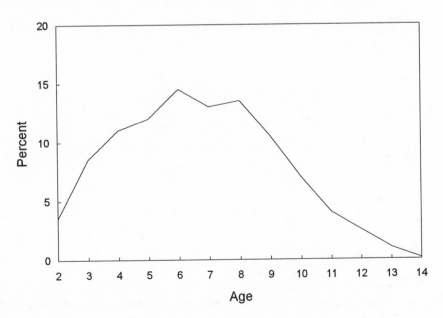

Source: Data from East Centre District School; Concord Public Library, Massachusetts

percentage of children attending the East Centre under age four compared to all students under nine since this age cutoff would minimize our chances of making a miscalculation because of any possible changes in the age when children left primary schools.

Figure 2.5 shows that the percentage of students under four of all students under nine in the Concord East Centre District School was following an upward trend in 1830 when the data are first available. The percentage of students under four continued a steady rise, to a peak of nearly 22 percent in 1833. It is interesting to note that this was the year when Amariah Brigham's book was published in Boston and that thereafter an erratic, though obvious, decline occurred until we lose the data in 1842. There are no satisfactory explanations for the changes in the percentage of students under four between 1838 and 1841, and one should be aware of the dangers of overgeneralizing from one case, especially when the total number of pupils in any given year was usually under one hundred. The data presented on Concord, however, are the only information currently available on enrollment practices of young children before 1840. On the basis of this limited statistical information and the few available literary references, a tentative hypothesis of the effect of infant schools on the school enrollment of the general public can be made.

Figure 2.5 / *Percentage of Students Younger Than Four of All Students Younger Than Nine in the Concord East Centre District School, 1830–42*

Source: Data from East Centre District School; Concord Public Library, Massachusetts

The infant school idea of sending children to school at younger ages did gradually influence the general public throughout the state. This was particularly true in towns like Concord that had infant schools, although one suspects that the general attitude penetrated other areas as well. The impact of the arguments against sending young children to school, which was felt so sharply in Boston, was less pronounced in outlying areas. The common people were not as responsive to new intellectual currents as were the well-to-do citizens of Boston. A decline in the practice of sending young children to school did occur, but as a secular trend it was very slow to return to the level of 1830. It lingered through the 1840s and gradually died out in response to the formalization of public school system regulations that eventually set lower limits on ages of admission. This probably resulted from a disinclination on the part of teachers to tolerate the extra attention and special techniques required to keep the youngest children from disrupting the work of older children. An analysis of the discussion in the Massachusetts state and local school reports of what the lowest ages of admission should be suggests that increasingly administrators and teachers did not want very young children in the classroom (Kaestle and Vinovskis, 1980).

The 1860s and 1870s saw a resurgence of interest in early education. The impetus for this came from the writings of Friedrich Froebel, a student of Pestalozzi, who had visited the famous school at Yverdun while the great master was still alive and who in 1840 began his own infant school, which he christened with the felicitous name *Kindergarten*. The kindergarten movement spread rapidly in America, achieving a degree of establishment that the infant school movement had never approached.

It cannot be said definitively, at this stage of our knowledge, why the kindergarten movement flourished whereas the infant school movement declined. There was little difference in the principles or techniques of the two systems. In fact, David Salmon treats the kindergarten as part of the movement that had begun at New Lanark.[22] In America the connection seems to have been almost completely forgotten. One immediately thinks of the great influx of immigration that had taken place since the 1830s and the possibility that educators felt a more pressing need to find a means of acculturating the children of immigrants into American society. One also suspects that the magnitude of the problems due to poverty, urbanization, and industrialization were much more severe than in the 1830s. Also, by 1870 the cause of public education had a wide following and a strong professional bureaucracy to support it. There was no ambiguity over responsibility for public education and objectives of educational innovation such as had characterized the Boston infant movement. In addition, the kindergartens took children no younger than three years of age, thus mitigating the threat to the home and the family implicit in the infant education movement. Significantly, proponents of kindergartens did not emphasize the intellectual aspects of early childhood training. Moreover, one suspects, the leaven of the continental tradition of educational reform had by 1870 time to do its work. The theories and techniques recommended by kindergarten advocates and the conceptions of infancy from which they came were not as alien to the American mind in 1870 as they were in 1830. And perhaps there was something to Froebel's fortunate choice of a name for his institution. A garden seemed an entirely appropriate place for even the youngest of children. A school did not.[23]

Notes

Reprinted from *Family and Kin in Urban Communities, 1700–1930,* ed. Tamara K. Hareven (New York: New Viewpoints, 1977), 62–99, by permission of Franklin Watts.

1. Salmon and Hindshaw (1904) and others refer to Frederic Oberlin (1767–1826), who founded several schools for the children of Alsatian peasants in the last quarter of the eighteenth century. Oberlin's work was not continued, however, and Owen's infant school was the model for later infant schools on the Continent as well as in England and America. For Owen's account of the founding of the infant school at New Lanark, see his autobiography (Owen, 1920).

2. An account of plans for an infant school in Hartford, Connecticut, was reprinted from the Hartford *Observer* in the *Boston Recorder and Religious Telegraph* (February 22, 1827). The *Recorder* enthusiastically reported the founding of infant schools in Philadelphia on February 1 and 8, 1828. The *American Journal of Education,* 3 (June 1828), 346–56, reported the founding of the Infant School Society of the City of New York.

3. The most complete account of the founding of the Infant School Society of the City of Boston is in the *Boston Recorder and Religious Telegraph,* April 18, 1828. The first annual report of that society (1829: 7–8) includes a report on the opening of its first infant school. The Salem Street school, which opened the same month under Amos Bronson Alcott, was sponsored by another infant school society. We have been able to find little concerning this latter society. Alcott left the Salem Street school to found his own infant school in October 1828, as described in Dorothy McCuskey (1940). There are references to the

opening of other infant schools in Boston and in Massachusetts in the third annual report (1831) of the Infant School Society of the City of Boston. Scattered references to infant schools in other Massachusetts towns have been found in several sources, especially the *American Journal of Education* and in occasional surviving annual reports of the societies that sponsored the schools. *Ladies' Magazine,* published in Boston under the editorship of Sarah J. Hale from January 1828 to December 1836 was unusually attentive to the progress of infant schools. This publication reported on the African infant school in vol. 3 (May 1830) and (October 1830).

4. The most striking example is Elizabeth Palmer Peabody. Through her association with Alcott she was actively involved in the infant school movement in the 1830s. Yet when she became a leader in the kindergarten movement in the 1860s, she made only a few explicit references to her earlier experiences and did not stress the obvious similarities and common antecedents of the two movements. For a study of her career, see Baylor (1965).

5. For an analysis of Rousseau's life and ideas, see Cranston (1983, 1991).

6. Samuel Wilderspin (1792–1866) gave an extensive account of the founding of the first infant schools in London in his *Infant Education; or Remarks on the Importance of Educating the Infant Poor, from the Age of Eighteen Months to Seven Years* (1825). A list of infant schools functioning in 1825 is found on page 284 of that publication. Wilderspin was instructor of the second infant school founded in London and became self-appointed apostle of the movement, traveling extensively throughout England, Scotland, and Ireland to promote the schools. His *Infant Education* was

probably the most widely read of all infant school manuals. For an excellent analysis of the work of Wilderspin, as well as a general introduction to British infant schools, see McCann and Young (1982).

7. Russell's close friend and colleague Amos Bronson Alcott contributed to the infant education movement as instructor and as author of an important tract, *Observations on the Principles and Methods of Infant Education* (1830). Alcott's primary activity was as instructor rather than publicist, however, and his opinions as to the objectives of instruction quickly became so idiosyncratic as to limit his influence on the broader movement. For Alcott, the purpose of educating young children was to elicit the spiritual nature of those who in point of time he thought to be closest to undefiled spirit. In encouraging the free expression of the infant mind, he was a practitioner and advocate of continental theory. But while he promoted the methods of the continental theorists his objectives were almost wholly theological—to better understand the nature of spiritual existence. His schools were founded not so much as institutions to better instruct children as to better instruct himself in eternal truths. Thus his contribution to the infant education movement was not as significant as that of William Russell, and I have not treated him as a major figure in this book. For a discussion of Alcott's relation to the infant education movement, see Shepherd (1937).

8. For a statement on his position on infant schools, see William Russell (1831).

9. See notes 2 and 3 above.

10. For a thoughtful comparative analysis of the types of women who founded these early reform groups in both Boston and New York, see Boylan (1986).

11. For a general introduction to the problems of Boston during this period, see Handlin (1968). Although Boston experienced many of the same social problems as New York and Philadelphia, before 1860 living conditions there were probably significantly better (Vinovskis, 1972a). Indeed, the impetus for establishing a special program for instructing the poor did not arise as a result of conditions in Boston itself, but rather as a conscious effort to copy similar institutions in New York (Bos-

ton Society for the Religious and Moral Instruction of the Poor, 1817: 1).

12. Most scholars agree that poverty was less prevalent in America than in England in the first half of the nineteenth century. There is considerable debate, however, on whether there was an increase or decrease in the amount of poverty in America during this period. For instance, Mohl (1971) argues that there was an intensification of poverty in northern cities at the beginning of the nineteenth century. Unfortunately, we do not have adequate quantitative studies of the level or the extent of poverty in nineteenth-century America to arrive at a definitive judgment at this time. It is unlikely that the increases in the levels or the extent of poverty in American cities before 1840 was of such a large magnitude that they by themselves account for the sudden increased interest in this subject by social reformers. Rather, I suspect that the growing belief that poverty was not inevitable in all societies led social reformers, as well as the general public, to become more aware of and interested in solving its problems.

13. Carroll Smith-Rosenberg (1971) dates this shift in attitudes toward the poor to the 1820s and 1830s in New York City. Barnett's (1973) analysis of the poor in Massachusetts places it between 1812 and 1820. For a useful analysis of the changing views toward charity and the growth of institutions to help the poor in New England, see Conrad Wright (1992).

14. Lane's (1971) investigation of the development of the Boston police found little evidence of a high level of crime in Boston during this period. In fact, before the 1830s Bostonians were content to rely on constables and watchmen for their safety, and it was only after the police were unable to handle the anti-Catholic mob violence that a new and more professional police force was recruited.

15. For a useful, comprehensive discussion of Boston public schools during this period, see Schultz (1973).

16. See Thomas (1965) for an insightful overview of prewar reform. Thomas's emphasis on the tendency of the Romantic reformers to place their hopes for reform in the moral regeneration of the individual rather than in established institutions is supported by this

book. Although the social reformers in this case created a new institution, they expected infants schools to be the institution to end all institutions. The infant schools, by giving proper moral instruction to the young children of unregenerate parents and by insulating the children as much as possible from the harmful influences of home and street life, were expected eventually to eliminate the need for all other reform institutions.

17. One school founded in 1833 in Charlestown did last into the 1870s, though in a significantly altered form. By 1870 its primary activities were the care of orphaned children, although it apparently continued, with little success in attracting a clientele, to serve as a day-care center. It is interesting that by 1870 its director was not called an instructress but a matron. This school survived by successfully achieving the change from school to home, a transition that was made official in 1870 when its name was changed to the Infant School and Children's Home Association. By then it had become a very modest enterprise with fewer than ten children in residence (Infant School and Children's Home Association, 1870).

18. In 1840 when Mann first inaugurated the procedure of requiring school committees to report the number of children under four in school, many were unable to respond because they had not kept sufficiently detailed records. In his annual report, Mann did not distinguish between towns that were able to provide information on this question and those that could not. As a result, calculating the percentage of children under four who were attending school from Mann's annual report underestimates that figure. An examination of local manuscript returns for 1840 indicates that the actual percentage of children under four in school would be about 13 percent, rather than the 10 percent figure derived from Mann's report. Most school committees were able to provide information on this question by 1841, so that the number of children under four reported by Mann is a very good estimate of the actual number of children in that age-group in school after 1840. For a further discussion of the problems of Massachusetts

school data, see Kaestle and Vinovskis (1980) and Vinovskis (1972b).

19. Interestingly, whereas the Sabbath schools initially accepted only children ages five and above, after the popularization of the infant schools, most of the Sabbath schools enrolled children as young as three or four (Boston Society for the Religious and Moral Instruction of the Poor, 1828: 24).

20. Of course the practice of educating young children in dame schools was quite common in colonial and early-nineteenth-century Massachusetts. Unfortunately, we do not have any data on the extent of dame schools or on the age distribution of the pupils who attended them during this period.

21. We would like to thank the Concord Free Public Library for permission to use the manuscript records of the East Centre District School, and we are indebted to Mrs. William Henry Moss, reference librarian, for her invaluable help and guidance.

22. Lazerson (1971) provides important insights into public education in Massachusetts between 1870 and 1915. In dealing with the kindergarten movement, however, he has apparently followed the lead of its nineteenth-century promoters and failed to notice that four decades earlier the founders of infant schools had sought to employ early education as an instrument of urban social reform. Especially puzzling, in view of the widespread attention to early education in the 1830s (of which infant schools were only one expression) is Lazerson's assertion that "not until the end of the nineteenth century did American educators generally acknowledge the importance of the early years in shaping adult behavior" (41).

23. For a more general discussion of early child care in nineteenth- and twentieth-century America, see Getis and Vinovskis (1992). For an analysis of the infant school movement outside Massachusetts, see John Jenkins (1978). A useful comparative investigation of kindergartens in Massachusetts and Michigan is provided by Robert Tank (1980). For an interesting study of the concerns about the dangers of instructing young children in kindergartens, see Caroline Winterer (1992).

Chapter 3 / *The Crisis in Moral Education in Antebellum Massachusetts*

The citizens of Massachusetts had always prided themselves on their commitment to schooling and the role education played in fostering public morality. Yet concern about public education became evident in the early 1850s as the growing numbers of Irish immigrants raised questions about the ability of public schools to facilitate the assimilation of the newcomers. At the same time, Catholic calls for a parochial school system sparked a spirited defense of the religious and moral training provided by the public schools.

It was quite a shock, therefore, when the Boston newspaper headlines in November 1856 suddenly revealed "Corruption and Crime in a Public School," "Recent Outrages upon School Girls," "Debauching Children," and "Horrible Depravity among School Children" (*Boston Daily Evening Transcript*, November 22, 1856; *Boston Pilot*, November 29, 1856; *Boston Post*, November 20, 1856; *Boston Daily Bee*, November 20, 1856). Six girls from the Boston Hancock Grammar School, ranging in age from eleven to sixteen, were accused of either being seduced by several prominent businessmen or acting as wanton prostitutes. As the Catholic *Boston Pilot* accurately and almost gleefully noted, "The boasted purity of our public schools has received a severe shock" (November 29, 1856).

This unusual but highly publicized event provides an opportunity to explore a variety of important and neglected topics such as attitudes toward public education, the role of law and the courts in protecting children, nineteenth-century gender relations, the nature of early adolescence, and attitudes toward early sexual activity.[1] Particularly interesting is the fact that this incident created a crisis in antebellum Massachusetts education that led to renewed efforts to improve moral training in the public schools. While historians of nineteenth-century education have devoted considerable attention to such issues as the use of schools for social control or social mobility, relatively little effort has been paid to the nature and role of moral training in the public schools.[2] Therefore, an investigation of this crisis will provide a useful perspective on the development of schooling.

Moral Education in Colonial and Nineteenth-Century Massachusetts

Religion and education were closely linked in colonial Massachusetts. The Puritans placed a high value on literacy; they felt everyone should be able to read the Bible. Although parents were responsible for the education of their children and servants, the local community often monitored the educational and religious progress of children and rebuked negligent parents. In the larger towns, schools were established to help parents, and schoolmasters were expected to assist in the catechizing of pupils (Axtell, 1974; Cremin, 1970; Murphy, 1960).

As Massachusetts moved from a colony to a state, the religious emphasis in public education was maintained (Dunn, 1958; Smith, 1926). Article 3 of the Massachusetts Constitution of 1780 stated that:

> As the happiness of a people, and the good order and preservation of civil government, essentially depend upon piety, religion, and morality; and as these cannot be generally diffused through a community, but by the institution of the public worship of GOD, and of public instructions in piety, religion and morality: Therefore, to promote their happiness, and to secure the good order and preservation of their government, the people of this Commonwealth have a right to invest their legislature with power to authorize and require, . . . the several towns, parishes, precincts, and other bodies-politic, or religious societies, to make suitable provision, at their own expense, for the institution of the public worship of GOD, and for the support and maintenance of public Protestant teachers of piety, religion, and morality, in all cases where such provision shall not be made voluntarily. (Handlin and Handlin, 1966: 442–43)

The Massachusetts legislature readily complied with the linkage of religion and education by passing in 1789 "An Act to Provide for the Instruction of Youth, and for the Promotion of Good Education," which required teachers at all public institutions "to take diligent care, and exert their best endeavors, to impress on the minds of children and youth, committed to their care and instruction, the principles of piety, justice, and a sacred regard to truth, love to their country, humanity, and universal benevolence, sobriety, industry, frugality, chastity, moderation and temperance, and those other virtues which are the ornament of human society, and the basis upon which the Republican Constitution is structured" (Sheldon S. Cohen, 1974: 2:795).

Throughout the early nineteenth century, the Massachusetts legislature and other elected officials frequently restated the close connection between religion and public education (Dunn, 1958; Smith, 1926). In a revision of earlier laws, the General Court in 1827 reiterated the Commonwealth's commitment to religious instruction but added a clause that local school committees "shall never direct any school books to be purchased or used, in any of the schools under their superintendence, which are calculated to favor any particular religious sect or tenet" (Sheldon S. Cohen: 1974, 2:1148). Although this clause attracted little attention at the time, Horace Mann later cited it to justify his efforts to keep both sectarian writings and teachings out of the public schools.[3]

Horace Mann, the first secretary of the Massachusetts Board of Education, was a deeply religious Unitarian who believed that education and religion could and should coexist in the classroom. In spite of attacks by his critics, Mann did not want to remove religion and moral training from the public schools. He was opposed only to the introduction of the specific doctrines of the orthodox Calvinists. He believed that broad religious principles acceptable to all Protestants should be taught and that all public school children should read the Bible in class. His critics pointed out that while Mann claimed he was against the introduction of any sectarian materials or teachings in the public schools, in fact he was really promulgating a particularly Unitarian version of religious instruction (Culver, 1929; Dunn, 1958).

Responding in part to these continued personal attacks, Mann frequently discussed the value of moral and religious education in his annual reports. He was enthusiastic about the ability of moral education to eliminate crime:

> Indeed, so decisive is the effect of early training upon adult habits and character, that numbers of the most able and experienced teachers,— those who have had the best opportunity to become acquainted with the errors and the excellence of children, their waywardness and their docility,—have unanimously declared it to be their belief, that, if all the children in the community, from the age of four years to that of sixteen, could be brought within the reformatory and elevating influences of good schools, the dark host of private vices and public crimes, which now embitter domestic peace and stain the civilization of the age, might in ninety-nine cases in every hundred, be banished from the world. (Massachusetts Board of Education, *Annual Report*, 1849: 95–96)

As I noted in chapter 1, nineteenth-century educational reformers placed growing emphasis on schools as the last bastions for civilizing youth. Mann was not alone in believing that moral and religious education could prevent juvenile delinquency and eventually eliminate adult crimes. This was a commonly held notion in mid-nineteenth-century America (Hawes, 1971; Mennel, 1973; Pickett, 1969). The only disagreements came over the particular type of moral and religious education that was needed and the role of the state in providing it (Kaestle, 1983).

Mann's two immediate successors as secretary of the Massachusetts Board of Education, Barnas Sears and George Boutwell, shared his belief in the efficacy of moral education (Dunn, 1958). But perhaps because they felt that the connection between moral education and the prevention of criminal or delinquent behavior had been so well established by Mann, neither of them devoted as much attention to this in their annual reports. Moreover, because Sears was an orthodox minister, he encountered less opposition from his religious compatriots than had Mann, who was suspected of trying to further his own Unitarian orientation (Hovey, 1902).[4] Instead, Sears and Boutwell focused on such administrative and management issues as the elimination of the local school districts and the grading of the schools by the ability of the pupils.[5]

In his seventh and final annual report, Sears did acknowledge the difficulties that public schools had in safeguarding youths from the corrupting influences of modern life: "Again, the crowds of young people rushing from the country into the cities, and the gregarious life of childhood and youth in our numerous manufacturing towns and villages, furnish peculiar facilities for the diffusion of corrupt principles and morals. The former find, in their new places of abode, pleasures set before them appealing to every sense, and in gradations adapted to every variety of the intellect. The current of sensuality, more or less refined, is so strong that it too often sweeps almost everything before it" (Massachusetts Board of Education, *Annual Report*, 1856: 43).

Because of these new and exaggerated temptations, especially in the cities, was it realistic to expect that the public schools by themselves could "turn back the tide of degeneracy?" Sears thought not. He continued: "The general tone of society, when at variance with the influence of the conscientious teacher, is a powerful check upon the success of his efforts. Indeed, as to manners and morals, it is society chiefly that educates. The school-room is limited in respect to time. . . . The adult portion of the community should remember that with them mainly rests the responsibility of forming the moral character of the young" (44).

Before this, Sears had not been particularly critical or anxious about the quality of moral training in the schools. But in his final report he questioned the attention paid to moral education, as well as the ways it was taught in the schools: "In respect to the moral training of the young, there are still greater deficiencies than in their intellectual training. The causes of this are various. Too frequently the subject receives but little direct attention. It is looked upon as a purely incidental part of education, and is either neglected or treated in a desultory manner" (58).

When the moral crisis generated by the so-called Hancock Grammar School girls erupted ten months later, Massachusetts public school officials discovered that Sears's belated acknowledgement of the deficiencies in moral training in the public schools seemed all too evident to both parents and policy makers. Boutwell was forced to admit that educators had inadvertently neglected the importance of moral and religious training in most of their recent annual reports (Massachusetts Board of Education, *Annual Report*, 1857).

Concerns about Crime and Juvenile Delinquency in Mid-Nineteenth-Century Massachusetts

Nineteenth-century Americans were deeply concerned about crime. Most contemporary observers associated the rising crime rate with increasing urbanization. Michael Hindus's (1980) analysis of criminal prosecutions and commitments to penal institutions in antebellum Massachusetts found that although the rates fluctuated, a peak was reached in the mid-1850s. Although some scholars (Monkkonen, 1975) now question the relation between urban development and increases in crime, Hindus found that commitment rates in Boston were significantly higher than in the rest of the state. Moreover, he found that in Massachusetts there was a shift in recorded crimes from the colonial period to the nineteenth century. In colonial Massachusetts, there were more crimes of morality, whereas in the nineteenth century crimes were more focused on property or liquor-related offenses.

The citizens of Boston believed that there was a dramatic increase in crime in their city during the 1850s. The Boston city marshall reported an enormous increase in police arrests and complaints, from 3,382 in 1850 to 12,217 in 1854; by 1857 arrests and complaints rose to 19,093 (Boston City Marshall, 1851, 1855, 1858). In less than a decade the number of Boston police arrests or complaints had risen by 465 percent, while the population of that city had grown only about 22 percent (calculated from Warner, 1867).[6]

The involvement of youths in these arrests and complaints fluctuated somewhat, but overall almost one out of five offenses was committed by a minor. The number of police arrests or complaints against minors rose from 622 in 1850 to 2,472 in 1854; by 1857 it had reached 3,244—an increase of 422 percent during a seven-year period (Boston City Marshall, 1851, 1855, 1858). As the Boston chief of police observed in 1857, "The great number of minors, which, it will be seen, have been arrested for various offenses, and affords an ample field of labor for those engaged in moral reform (Boston Chief of Police, 1857: 19). (For a discussion of the rise of juvenile crime in antebellum Boston courts, see Ferdinand [1992].)

There was also growing concern about the problems of juvenile delinquency during the 1850s. Antebellum reformers frequently lamented the increases in troubled youth. They believed that most delinquents displayed flawed characters that resulted from inadequate parenting and disadvantaged backgrounds. As a result, the reformers developed an extensive system of public and private reform schools and stressed teaching morality in public schools to compensate for poor moral training at home (Hawes, 1971; Holloran, 1989; Mennel, 1973; Platt, 1969).

Antebellum reformers made a sharp distinction between male and female delinquents—especially in regard to sexual indiscretions. Although male delinquents were more numerous and problematic, they were also seen as more redeemable. Loring Brace, a prominent mid-nineteenth-century New York reformer who was typical of many child-savers, almost romanticized delinquent boys:

> A girl street-rover is to my mind the most painful figure in all the unfortunate crowd of a large city. With a boy, "Arab of the streets," one always has the consolation that, despite his ragged clothes and bed in a box or hay-barge, he often has a rather good time of it, and enjoys many of the delicious pleasures of a child's roving life, and that a fortunate turn of events may at any time make an honest, industrious fellow of him. At heart we cannot say that he is much corrupted; his sins belong to his ignorance and his condition, and are often easily corrected by a radical change of circumstances. . . . It is true that sometimes the habit of vagrancy and idling may be too deeply worked in him for his character to speedily reform; but, if of tender years, a change of circumstances will nearly always bring a change of character. (Brace, 1872: 114–15)

Brace, like most antebellum reformers, had a very different view of female delinquents. Once they had committed a crime, particularly a sexual one, there was much less chance of saving them because the natural passions of women were regarded as stronger and more indelible than those of men: "With a girl-vagrant it is different. She feels homelessness and friendlessness more; she has more of the feminine dependence on affection; the street-trades, too, are harder for her, and the return at night to some lonely cellar or tenement-room, crowded with dirty people of all ages and sexes, is more dreary. She develops body and mind earlier than the boy, and the habits of vagabondism stamped on her in childhood are more difficult to wear off" (115).[7]

Most nineteenth-century reformers saw boys and girls as biologically different in how they recovered from their wrongdoings. As a result, contemporary observers employed a clear double standard in evaluating the chances of reforming male and female delinquents:

> For there is no reality in the sentimental assertion that the sexual sins of the lad are as degrading as those of the girl. The instinct of the female

is toward the preservation of purity, and therefore her fall is deeper—an instinct grounded in the desire of preserving a stock, or even the necessity of perpetuating our race. . . .

This crime, with the girl, seems to sap and rot the whole nature. She loses self-respect, without which every human being soon sinks to the lowest depths; she loses the habit of industry, and cannot be taught to work. . . . If, in a moment of remorse, she flee away and take honest work, her weakness and bad habits follow her . . . and unless she chance to have a higher moral nature or stronger will than most of her class, or unless Religion should touch even her polluted soul, she soon falls back, and gives one more sad illustration of the immense difficulty of a fallen woman rising again. (Brace, 1872: 115–17)

Most reformers made a sharp distinction between trying to prevent the delinquency or corruption of young females and helping those who had fallen. Everything possible was done to protect the innocence of young girls, but once they had become sexually active, it was felt that there was little hope of reforming them. Indeed, most nineteenth-century reform institutions for destitute or orphaned girls refused to admit anyone who was sexually experienced— particularly as they feared these girls might corrupt the rest of the inmates (Brenzel, 1983; Hobson, 1987; Holloran, 1989; Schneider, 1992; Smith-Rosenberg, 1985).

During the early nineteenth century, concern about increasing juvenile delinquency and the problems created by placing first-time youthful offenders with hardened adult criminals led to efforts to create special institutions for the young—especially the boys. Modeled after comparable institutions in New York and Philadelphia, the Boston House of Reformation for Juvenile Offenders opened in 1826. A few prepubescent girls were admitted among its first inmates, but officials were always concerned that they might corrupt the morals of the delinquent boys—in spite of the fact that strict segregation by sex was maintained (Hawes, 1971; Mennel, 1973).

Although the Boston House of Reformation initially was intended as a humanitarian institution to save impoverished and endangered youth, by the mid-1830s the institution had become a degraded receptacle for hardened delinquents and had gained a reputation as a school for future criminals. Children whose only misfortune was their orphanhood or poverty were now sent to such private institutions as the Protestant Boston Asylum for Indigent Boys, the Boston Farm School, and the Boston Female Asylum, or the Catholic St. Vincent Female Orphan Asylum and the House of the Angel Guardian.[8]

Massachusetts established a state facility for delinquent juvenile boys at Westborough in 1847 (Katz, 1968; Wirkkala, 1973). There was agitation for a comparable institution for girls, but the legislature did not authorize its establishment until 1854. The State Industrial School for Girls opened at Lancaster in 1856. It housed girls in four small cottages rather than in a large building characteristic of most earlier antebellum asylums. The Lancaster school was intended for poor and wayward girls and not those who were sexually depraved or experienced (Brenzel, 1983).[9]

In addition to private and public institutions to house poor and troubled girls, several societies were created to protect female virtue. These reform organizations argued that women were preyed upon by men and accustomed the public to worry about innocent children being seduced (Smith-Rosenberg, 1985). The New England Female Moral Reform Society was founded in 1836 and published a bimonthly magazine, *Friend of Virtue*, which portrayed women as innocent victims seduced and betrayed by unscrupulous males. It particularly emphasized the dangers to young women from the countryside coming to work and live in urban areas, such as Boston, who were then seduced by unprincipled male predators—often disguised as gentlemen (Hobson, 1987). Some of the writings about crime and juvenile delinquency had a strong class dimension to them, with the wealthy and powerful being depicted as the sexual exploiters of the daughters and wives of the poor and the workers (Papke, 1987).

The double standard in dealing with sexual crimes became particularly pronounced in the antebellum period. In early colonial America, both male and female fornicators were exposed and punished, but in the nineteenth century there was increasing attention to only the females. Barbara Hobson's (1987) analysis of Boston prostitutes reveals that while the females faced punishment, their male clients and even their pimps usually went free of any legal prosecution. Similarly, in cases of alleged rape, men were not prosecuted if there was any indication that the women had tempted or cooperated with them (Arnold, 1989; Smith-Rosenberg, 1985).[10] Moreover, although there was growing concern about saving young children in the decades before the Civil War, teenage girls were not accorded special legal protection from sexual molestation. Indeed, Christine Stansell (1986: 182) maintains that "for the men, taboos against sexual involvement with children seems to have been weak; in court they often alluded to their actions as legitimate and benign, if slightly illicit, kind of play."[11]

Thus, there was mounting concern in Boston in the 1850s about the growth of crime and female delinquency, as well as anxiety about whether the public school system could adequately take care of these problems. At the same time, it became very important to determine whether delinquent girls were innocent victims or hardened streetwalkers. If the former, their plight was idealized and every effort was made to rescue them. If the latter, they were often ignored, abandoned, and blamed for their own weaknesses. Moreover, if it were established that the girls were at fault, the men were often absolved of any real crime or responsibility.

"Recent Outrages upon School Girls"

For many students one of the more embarrassing moments in their lives occurs when a teacher intercepts a personal note that they have passed to a friend in class. But few confiscated notes have led to as much notoriety and difficulty as the one whose contents were revealed in November 1856 by a teacher at the Hancock Grammar School for females in Boston's North End (*Boston Pilot*, November 29, 1856). Newspapers throughout the Commonwealth were soon reprinting stories about the "Outrages upon School Girls," and the three businessmen involved were quickly brought before the Boston Police Court (*Boston Daily Evening Transcript*, November 22, 1856).[12] Few, however, anticipated the final outcome of this episode.

The initial response in most newspapers was shocked indignation and a call for the harsh punishment of the businessmen who were assumed to be guilty of corrupting the girls.[13] The *Boston Post* broke the story as:

> "Horrible Depravity among School Children." Circumstances have re-
> cently transpired at one of the public schools in this city whereby it has
> been discovered that six young girls attached to the institution, ranging
> twelve to fifteen years, have for some time been pursuing a path of vice
> that is sickening to contemplate. The accomplices of these children have
> consisted of three *men*, and it seems that frequent and regular visits have
> been paid by these girls to the places of business occupied by the men
> for illicit purposes, and it is to be hoped that those fiends in human
> shape who have thus been instrumental in leading these young creatures
> from the path of virtue to bring eternal ruin upon themselves, and
> shame and misery upon their parents, will be exposed, and made to suf-
> fer the extreme penalty of the law. (November 20, 1856)[14]

The concern was not just for the girls, but also for the implications this had for the quality and perceptions of the much-vaunted Massachusetts public school system and the general moral culture of the North. "This story will be copied all through the Southern States—for Uncle Tom has none surpassing it—and every braggart upstart of slavedom can well tell us to look at home—to find a remedy for our own sins before we offer our services to others. It will be reported all over Europe to our disgrace, Catholics will point to it as the fruits of Protestantism; despots as the work of unbridled license. It will be seized upon by the opponents of free schools, as an argument against the pro-miscuous mixture of our society; and thus we are arming the enemies of free-dom and progress with false weapons" (*Newburyport Herald*, November 22, 1856).

Enemies of the Boston public schools used this incident to raise questions about the effectiveness of these institutions in teaching children proper moral behavior. The *Boston Pilot* lost no time in pointing out the implications of this scandal: "Debauching Children." . . . The case has created considerable excitement. . . . The affair will lead to an extended investigation throughout the schools, there being reason to believe that the evil has not been confined to the parties now in the hands of the law. The boasted purity of our public schools has received a severe shock" (November 29, 1856).

The proponents of public schools did not ignore these attacks. Its defenders pointed to the vigilance of the Hancock Grammar School in apprehending the girls and questioned whether other groups and institutions were not equally responsible for what had transpired. As a letter to the *Boston Journal* put it:

> The school has detected and exposed what the vigilance of parents had not been able to prevent. For months these young girls have been in the habits of meeting these contemptible specimens of masculine humanity, for the disgusting purposes brought to light in recent investigations; the school, under the control of which the children were not, at times when the offenses were committed, put a stop to the evil that other influences failed to arrest. Yet reflections are cast upon the school as though that should take the blame for parents' neglect of their duties! . . .
>
> Does it not speak well for our public schools and the vigilance of their teachers? Why not as well complain of the church, whose peculiar province is to teach virtue, morality and religion? Why not arraign the system of police in whose very eyes these acts have been perpetuated? Why not that laxity of public sentiment that in its pity for the sufferings of parents, will no more sternly rebuke the criminal neglect by which they brought these sufferings upon themselves? Why not mete out its due portion of censure to each of those who have done nothing in this matter, to restrain vice, but administer it all to the school that has done all that has been done? (December 10, 1856)[15]

In spite of the charges and countercharges about which individuals or institutions were responsible for this incident, several newspapers saw this crisis as symptomatic of the broader problems of American society. They idealized the tranquility and stability of the past and used the occasion to call for sweeping societal reforms.

> We say on this matter, that the crime and vice that is increasing in the community, has a deeper seat than most think of; it is in the very basis of our social and family relations. New England, twenty years ago and before, was a model community; and how came it so? It grew out of our model religion—the Puritanism that taught the observance of the Sabbath; that rung the young people home at nine o'clock in the evening; that gave us christian families, where Bibles were read and prayers of-

fered; and gave parents and clergymen who looked closely after the rising generation, that they were not taught to waste and squander money, or follow ridiculous fashions. It is time for us to "progress backwards" a little, for we may rest assured that where the family is what it ought to be, society cannot be bad, and safety will be secured for the children that we should prize higher than life itself. Boston has given us a terrible lesson; it will be well if we do not need a second one for home improvement. (*Newburyport Herald,* November 22, 1856)

One of the surprising aspects of this episode is what happened to the three men accused of seducing the girls. Almost all the newspapers immediately and vociferously condemned them and called for swift and harsh punishment. Yet at their initial arraignment before the police court on November 24, 1856, it was intimated that the girls had been willing accomplices—a theme that the defense was to use repeatedly and effectively against the formal charges brought by the Boston prosecutors.[16] As the *Boston Post* reluctantly admitted immediately after disclosing the supposedly private testimony given before the police court: "These girls it appeared, were in the habit of visiting the stable office . . . and the shops . . . where improper liberties were taken with them, and fruit, ice creams or money was given them as a compensation. The testimony was somewhat contradictory, either through constraint or failure of memory in some cases, or unwillingness to tell the whole truth, and on the part of one or two of the witnesses, the evidence of the others showed that they too willingly submitted themselves to exposure, indicating previous tampering with their morals by others, or a lack of moral training" (November 26, 1856).

After it was learned that the girls might have been willing partners rather than innocent victims, most of the initial sympathy for them faded. Moreover, many newspapers now went out of their way to highlight and even exaggerate their guilt and complicity. When it appeared that the girls may have been consenting partners, most of the newspapers ignored the responsibility of the adult males for mistreating them. Indeed, there was little public concern that the men might escape any punishment whatsoever for their abuse of young children if the girls were judged to have acted immorally.

The hearing before the Boston Police Court on December 4, 1856, revealed the direction of the case. The girls, aided by two of their attorneys, repeated their testimony. The defense lawyer countered with his set of witnesses, who attacked the credibility and morality of the girls.

Judge Thomas Russell, who appears to have been quite concerned about public reaction to his ruling, delivered a lengthy and carefully crafted opinion which was immediately published verbatim in the media.[17] While castigating the improper behavior of the defendants, he cited several English and American legal precedents which stated that if the girls had willingly assented to the advances of the defendants in any of the cases, the defendants could not be convicted for that offense.

> These cases establish the law that if the party assents there is no assault upon her. If there were no precedents, I should certainly be inclined to hold that the party could not assent to a misdemeanor. I should suppose these cases to be like the indictments for prize-fights or mutual assaults, where the assent of the party assaulted does not take away the criminality, the offense being not against the personal rights of the parties, but against the peace and good morals of the community.
>
> But the weight of the authority is decisive in favor of the defendant's view. I do not feel bound to state the offensive details of the evidence on either side; it is sufficient to say that they show such assent as it makes it impossible to convict the defendant of assault and battery.
>
> It is not for me to decide whether he is guilty of any other offense. There are some crimes against good morals, of which the law takes no cognizance, leaving the offender to the punishment of his own conscience. Perhaps this is one of that class. (*Boston Daily Journal*, December 8, 1856)[18]

Based on this reasoning, Judge Russell dismissed the case against one of the defendants but continued the cases against the other two because there was not conclusive evidence that the girls involved had actually assented to the sexual encounters; in fact, there was evidence that some of the girls had resisted the initial advances. Rather than finding the remaining two defendants guilty, however, Judge Russell ruled that "the offense is more aggravated than most, of which this Court usually takes jurisdiction; and it is certainly in our power to send the case to a higher tribunal, where full justice can be done to the offender (*Boston Daily Journal*, December 8, 1856).[19] Moreover, he suggested that the evidence of the immoral behavior of the girls be laid before the commissioner for the Industrial School for possible action.[20]

The girls' situation rapidly deteriorated. Rather than being perceived as innocent victims, they now found themselves accused of immoral behavior (and in one case of assenting to it) and threatened with commitment to the new State Industrial School for Girls at Lancaster. Their misfortunes did not stop there. On hearing of Judge Russell's decision and recommendations, the Boston School Committee took the unusual step of voting to agree with the Hancock School District Committee to expel the girls and then publicized their decision in the newspapers.[21] The stated reasons for the expulsions were the immoral behavior of the girls and the fear they might "vitiate and corrupt the minds and characters of those with whom they may associate, and [be] dangerous to the good morals and well-being of the School" (Boston School Committee, Minutes, December 9, 1856).

After the widespread publicity that was given to Judge Russell's decisions and the actions of the Boston School Committee, the media did not mention this incident for almost a month. Then, in early January, many newspapers ran a short follow-up, which stated that the grand jury of the municipal court had dismissed the charges against the remaining two defendants.[22] None of the newspapers protested that these men, who only two months earlier had been accused of "outrages upon school girls" and faced demands that they be penalized harshly, were now set free. None of the newspapers questioned the grand jury's decision to ignore the complaints against the men from very young girls who had clearly resisted their initial advances. The nineteenth-century biases against prosecuting males who took advantage of females of questionable reputation was evident not only among members of the grand jury, but among almost all of the Massachusetts media.[23]

If the businessmen could not be convicted of rape, why didn't the prosecutor bring new charges of immoral behavior against them? In colonial Massachusetts, individuals accused of rape were often found not guilty of rape because the alleged victim had seemingly consented to earlier sexual advances. But colonial courts sometimes brought new charges of "open gross lewdness and lascivious behavior" against these defendants and successfully prosecuted them (Lindemann, 1984). Certainly that possibility existed in this case, as Judge Russell hinted, but no action was taken. As several scholars (Hindus, 1980; Lindemann, 1984; Nelson, 1975) have noted, by the early nineteenth century the Massachusetts courts were more reluctant to involve themselves in prosecuting cases dealing with private morality—especially when it involved charges against prominent adult males in the community.

Perhaps reflecting their embarrassment about the outcome of this case or concerned about appeals that might be brought by the girls' parents, the Boston School Committee, in another highly unusual action, six months later reinstated three of the girls "to the full privileges of the public schools of this city " (Boston School Committee, Minutes, July 20, 1857). No reason was given for this reversal, and most of the Commonwealth's newspapers did not acknowledge the girls' exoneration, even though earlier they had been so quick to join in their condemnation.[24]

The Response of Massachusetts Educators

The response of Boston educators to the scandal over the Hancock Grammar School girls was conditioned in large part by their earlier concerns about moral training and the arrival of large numbers of Irish immigrants during the previous decade. Boston School Committee members, like many other municipal leaders, feared that the sudden influx of poor Irish immigrants threatened the social and political stability and the well-being of their community. They believed that many, if not most, of these immigrants were uneducated and immoral. Because they felt that most Irish parents were incapable of properly raising their children, they saw the schools as institutions for providing immigrant children with moral training and guidance.

> The tide of pauper emigration to this country, and to this City is of alarming extent. Already whole districts are becoming depopulated of the native inhabitants. . . . This state of things has a most vital bearing upon the Schools. Vast numbers of this foreign population are young children. We cannot keep them from our shores. What are we to do with them? If we let them run wild, we shall feel the effects ten years hence, in the insecurity of property, in the records of our criminal courts, in the expenses of our houses of punishment, and in our taxes for pauperism. We must, if possible, educate and reclaim them. We must open the of our school houses and invite and compel them to come in. There is no other hope for them or for us. At home they have no teacher. . . . In our Schools they must receive moral and religious training, powerful enough if possible to keep them in the right path amid the moral darkness in which is their daily and domestic walk, and if this is not sufficient we must follow and watch over them, as far as is practicable, to their homes. (Boston School Committee, *Annual Examination Subcommittee*, 1849: 29)

At the same time, the Boston School Committee was trying to persuade the more affluent, native-born parents to send their children to the public schools rather than to private ones. To do this they had to convince these more affluent clients that their children would not be corrupted by exposure to the growing numbers of lower-class, immigrant children. One argument in defense of the public schools was that their moral training and discipline was excellent, so that everyone attending, including those from the lower classes, were well-behaved and moral pupils.

> As to morals and manners. No doubt among the great numbers of children who are indiscriminately admitted to the Schools, there will be found many individuals, whose ideas of morals and standards of manners are very low; but this evil must have, of late years been greatly mitigated, by the prepatory training of the Primary Schools. Its amount is very much exaggerated at the present day. We do not think that justice is done to the characters of the *corps instructif* of our Schools, to their efforts or their success. In our examinations and inquiries, both on the Annual and the Sub-Committees, we have been made acquainted with but one instance of crime, during the past year, and have found the general

moral tone of the scholars to be satisfactory. (Boston School Committee, *Annual Examination Subcommittee*, 1848: 37–38)

Many newspapers responded to the Hancock Grammar School incident by questioning the efficacy of moral training in Massachusetts generally and in Boston specifically. The Boston School Committee responded by expelling the girls, stating that their presence might be dangerous to the morals and well-being of the other pupils. The Boston School Committee briefly considered this incident in their annual report, but it did not condemn specifically the quality of moral training the girls had received.

The subject of the moral education of our pupils has recently been brought most painfully before the public. All hearts have been terribly shocked by recent disclosures of depravity in one of our schools, which has exceeded the most fearful imagination. Parents are, with reason, alarmed, and are asking with an emphasis which a parent's heart alone can give, what is the moral training that is given in our schools? What attention is paid to the culture of those principles which govern the conduct and the life, which form and sustain a high and honorable character? They are asking whether, amidst all the labor that is spent to produce good scholars intellectually, anything like a proportionate exertion is made to produce good children morally. It is a question which demands to be eagerly listened to. It is a vital question, and must be answered. It should be a lasting shame to any teacher who cannot answer it with honor upon honor. (Boston School Committee, *Annual Report*, 1856: 25)

The school committee did acknowledge that the quality of moral training in some classrooms often did not meet state and city requirements. Its advice to teachers, however, was not to teach the Ten Commandments mechanically.

There is reason to fear that this most important part of all education is neglected amid the throng of other cares and labors. Too much reliance is placed upon instruction given elsewhere, forgetting that it is by line upon line, and precept upon precept, given everywhere, under every condition in which the child is placed, in the changing circumstances amidst which it is thrown, in the house, in the school, in the playground, when alone, and with companions, that the training of the child to righteousness and holiness must be carried forward. . . . There is one matter, however, which can and ought at once to be broken up; and that is the manner in which the commandments, those holy laws of the Most High God, are recited in some, at least, of our schools. They are repeated in concert, at the top of the voice, with no apparent understanding, and with evident carelessness of the meaning of the solemn words they are uttering. Far better would it be that they were not said at all, if this be the only way in which they can be repeated. Your Committee would urge with all of their power, a more interested attention to this whole subject. (Boston School Committee, *Annual Report*, 1856: 25–27)

The committee's concern about moral training was echoed by John D. Philbrick, who became the superintendent of the Boston public schools in January 1857. Although he felt that the grammar schools were well run, he identified three defects. The third defect appears to have been a direct response to the crisis in moral education triggered by the Hancock Grammar School incident: "The third and last defect which I shall mention, is *the want of a vigorous and efficient system of moral culture*. I need not speak of the importance of this element in every system of instruction for the young. No one will deny or doubt that it should be regarded as the very corner stone. I would not be understood to say that there is not at present any good, healthful moral influence exerted in our Primary Schools; but I feel bound to say that the amount of moral culture and moral training bears no sort of proportion to what it ought to be" (Boston School Committee, *Annual Report*, 1857: 32).

Education officials in other Massachusetts towns and cities also were now given an opportunity to comment on the state of moral training in the public schools. Since 1849, the Massachusetts Board of Education published topical abstracts from the local school reports. Usually these topics were announced the previous year by the secretary of the Board of Education, and local school committees were expected to respond. Interestingly, no questions about moral education were asked before the Hancock Grammar School incident. Indeed, George Boutwell, the secretary of the Massachusetts Board of Education, admitted at the conclusion of his first report that he had omitted one important topic, "*the influence of a system of public instruction upon the morality of a people*; but neither the proper limits of a Report, nor the materials at hand, permit the investigation which the subject requires" (Massachusetts Board of Education, *Annual Report*, 1857: 86). Nevertheless, Boutwell was confident that public education had a positive influence on the morals of the people: "I cannot, however, doubt the benign influence of our system of public instruction upon the morality and virtue of the people. With the increase of knowledge there is an increase of wealth, and as wealth increases the temptations to crime are multiplied; but there is no evidence to show that ignorance is better protected than learning against the allurements of an excitable and prosperous era in human affairs" (86).[25]

In the aftermath of this crisis, the Massachusetts Board of Education requested information about moral education at the local level. A content analysis of the education abstracts about moral education provided some interesting patterns. Overall, responses about moral education were published from eighty-seven communities—or 26.4 percent of Massachusetts towns and cities. There was not much difference by town size in the likelihood of having an abstract about moral education printed, but the larger communities were more likely to discuss this issue in some detail. Communities in central and southern Massachusetts were more likely to have abstracts about moral education published than those from western Massachusetts.

The answers ranged in length from a short paragraph to several pages. The Agawam School Committee had only a very short paragraph about the value of moral education, while the Easton School Committee devoted almost ten pages to that topic (Massachusetts Board of Education, *Abstracts*, 1858: 69, 98–108). The average length of abstracts dealing with moral education was just over one page. About one-third of the abstracts about moral education dealt with the topic only in passing, but the others discussed the issue in some detail.

More than one-third of the abstracts mentioning moral education stated that teachers should be moral, and one-sixth of them expressed concern about the current hiring process for teachers. Teachers and schools were cited in 29 percent of the abstracts for the lack of proper morals among the younger generation, and 32 percent blamed parents and the home. Interestingly, teachers and schools were almost never assigned the primary responsibility for the lack of morals among the young, but nearly one out of five reports dealing with moral education placed the blame upon parents and the home.[26] For example, the Lowell School Committee stated that:

> Teachers cannot make up for the deficiencies of home. Children badly reared at home are troublesome, disobedient and mischievous at school. Bad manners learned at home show themselves in bad conduct at school. A parent, who is vulgar, profane, and indecent, will be very likely to find his vulgarity, profanity and indecency reproduced in his children. . . . It cannot be expected that teachers can remedy such an evil as this; but they can, at least check its progress; and possibly, by the influence of refined manners, of attractive speech, of benignity of character, and the charm of courtesy, or, by the stronger influence of complete manliness and womanliness of character, can effectually neutralize the vicious influence of home training. They can, also, confirm whatever good impressions may have been made at home. (29)

Moreover, in 28 percent of the abstracts dealing with moral education, the local school committees complained about parent-teacher conflicts. In most of these discussions, parents were admonished to support the teacher and to be suspicious of their children's complaints about classroom discipline. The Groton School Committee suggested that: "Family government and school government should help each other. The child who does not learn how to obey, will never really learn how to command. Do not take your child's representation of a difficulty as certainly correct. Go into the school and see for yourself whether the child is in the right or in the wrong before you harbor a feeling of complaint. The teacher should never be unnecessarily disparaged in the hearing of the child" (Massachusetts Board of Education, *Abstracts*, 1858: 22).

Religion and moral education were often explicitly linked in the reports responding to the question about moral education (38 percent of the time). The Palmer School Committee argued that "experience has abundantly shown that religion, (not sectarianism,) and education cannot be safely divorced" (71). Yet direct mentions of using the Bible in the classroom appeared in only 12 percent of these abstracts, and another 14 percent explicitly stated that no sectarianism should be allowed.[27] More than one-fourth of the reports mentioned the state law requiring the teaching of morality in the public schools and frequently quoted from that statute.

Although a few reports mentioning moral training distinguished between proper moral values and bad manners, many simply mentioned these together. Indeed, much of the concern about the lack of moral training appears to have been stimulated by the perceived lack of proper manners and behavior among children. Nearly one out of four of the reports specifically referred to children swearing. Thus, the Lancaster School Board stated that they "would also here call attention, and that of parents in particular, to an increasing prevalence of profane and other not less degrading and corrupting language, not merely among unmannerly and graceless young men in our streets, but among the more juvenile members of our schools" (51–52).

Although these responses clearly reveal the acceptance of the mission of the public schools to provide proper moral training for their pupils and a recognition that this had often been neglected, few of them addressed the issues surrounding the Hancock Grammar School incident. In their discussion of moral education, only about one out of six reports revealed any concern about crime, and fewer than one out of twenty indicated that they thought crime was on the increase. Perhaps most startling of all, given the publicity surrounding the Hancock Grammar School episode, only one report made a specific reference to that event, and only one community mentioned the dangers of early sexual activity.[28] Whereas the controversy over the quality of moral education in public schools stimulated considerable debate in Massachusetts newspapers, educators downplayed the incident and chose to reaffirm their more general support for moral training in the classroom.

The response of George Boutwell was somewhat different from that of the local school committees. While he acknowledged that there was new public concern about moral education, he also denied that many in the Commonwealth questioned the value of public schooling for promoting morality.

The public schools, in their relations to the morals of the pupils and to the morality of the community, are attracting a large share of attention.

In some sections of the country the system is boldly denounced on account of its immoral tendencies; in States where free schools exist there are persons who doubt their utility; and occasionally, partisan or religious leaders appear to deny the existence of any public duty in regard to education, or who assert and maintain the doctrine that free schools are a common danger. As the people of this Commonwealth are not followers of these prophets of evil nor believers in their predictions, there is but slight reason for discussion among us. It is not probable that a large number of the citizens of Massachusetts entertain doubts of the power and value of our institutions of learning, of every grade, to resist evil and promote virtue through the influence they exert. (Massachusetts Board of Education, *Annual Report*, 1858: 59–60)

Despite Boutwell's insistence that there was "slight reason for discussion," he went on at considerable length defending the public school system. He appears to have been rather surprised by the criticisms voiced by the local school committees. Boutwell struggled to justify his optimistic view of the state of contemporary morality by arguing that: "The change in manners cannot be denied, but the alleged change in morals is not sustained by a great amount of positive evidence. The customs of former generations were such that children often manifested in their exterior deportment a deference which they did not feel, while at present there may be more real respect for station, and deference for age and virtue than are exhibited in juvenile life. . . . And notwithstanding the tone of the reports to which I have called attention, and notwithstanding my firm conviction that many moral defects are found in the schools, I am yet confident that their moral progress is appreciable and considerable" (60).

In addition, although five out of six of the local school reports discussing moral education did not mention the issue of crime, Boutwell placed it at the center of his rationale for taxing everyone for supporting public schooling. "On what moral grounds then does the right of taxation for educational objects rest? I answer, first, education diminishes crime" (67). Boutwell demonstrated that education prevented crime, but he drew almost all of his examples from Great Britain—perhaps because it would have been difficult to document that connection in Massachusetts, where the rate of juvenile crimes was increasing at the same time the public schools were expanding.[29] Particularly puzzling from the perspective of the Hancock Grammar School incident is why Boutwell did not comment on the why girls pursued such allegedly immoral activities if education was so effective in preventing criminal behavior.

Although Boutwell devoted considerable space to discussing moral education in the public schools, most of his report focused on defending current practices rather than on suggesting ways of improving them. Compared to his predecessors Horace Mann and Barnas Sears, Boutwell appears to have been less interested or less able to discuss improving teaching practices and more interested in broader policy issues. Both Mann and Sears provided more thorough discussions of moral education, although Boutwell was secretary of the Board of Education at the time of the Hancock Grammar School incident, when it was the subject of public discussion.[30]

The Hancock Grammar School scandal triggered a statewide reexamination of moral education in the public schools, but it did not have much impact on this issue in the long run. Although from time to time educators reaffirmed their commitment to moral training, it usually was not a topic of discussion. When they did refer to the value of education in preventing immorality and crime, they were usually more restrained than Mann had been when he asserted that proper schooling for everyone could eliminate criminal activity.

George Boutwell remained secretary of the Board of Education for another three years. In his annual report of 1859, he ignored the issue of moral education almost entirely. He returned to the topic the following year as part of his concerns about crime and the poor state of education in many manufacturing communities. Whereas in his earlier discussions of crime Boutwell had relied almost exclusively on information from Great Britain, he now presented information on reform schools in Massachusetts to establish that the inmates were not well educated and had often been truants (though again he failed to address the issue that many delinquents were relatively well educated). He concluded that:

> We cannot deny that there exists an intimate connection between ignorance and crime. The nature of this connection it may not be possible always to comprehend and disclose. Often, no doubt, criminal tendencies and criminal habits, early formed, lead to truancy and persistent neglect of the schools; and in such cases the work of reformation is a part of the process of education. In these instances common schools may not always be equal to the work. I am, however, of the opinion that in a number of cases so great, that the exceptions need not be noticed, the criminal character is developed in consequence of neglect of mental and moral training. It cannot be asserted that the schools are always competent to furnish this training; but they are the chief reliance of the public. (Massachusetts Board of Education, *Annual Report*, 1860: 64)

In the same report, Boutwell argued that moral training for factory operatives was of special importance because these people lived in communities that abounded in temptations and were employed in jobs that encouraged dangerous amusements after work:

> If we consider only the pecuniary advantage of education, I know not that any distinction should be made; but, in a moral aspect, we could

regard with comparative complacency a degree of ignorance among farmers which would excite apprehension and alarm, if observed among mechanics and manufacturers. The former are isolated and comparatively free from temptation. They dwell in the country and are subject to the influence of rural scenes which temper and chasten common life. If their labors are not more arduous than those of the mechanic or the manufacturer, their duties are continuous, and they are seldom able to command even a single hour daily of complete relaxation. The laborers in mills and shops usually dwell in large towns and cities. Temptation is on every hand; and he is but a poor observer of the ways of men who does not know that deviations from the path of virtue bear a relation . . . to the opportunities for wrong-doing. There are also two adverse influences always operating upon the laborer in the mills. His vocation during the ten or twelve hours of daily labor requires his undivided attention; this intense mental and physical action is followed by two or four hours of leisure that he is to spend in the midst of excitement and temptation. Under such circumstances he needs all the safeguards which a moral training can furnish, and he needs, moreover, a love of study that shall give occupation and variety for his leisure hours. (Massachusetts Board of Education, *Annual Report*, 1860: 54–55)

Boutwell's last annual report was devoted to an annotated discussion of the current state laws on education and did not pay special attention to the issue of moral education . His successor, Joseph White, ignored the role of moral education almost entirely in the the four annual reports he prepared during the Civil War. In his second report, White did admit that he neglected some important issues such as "the call of our times for a more thorough and systematic moral and religious training," and he promised that they would receive "a more full investigation and discussion at a future time" (Massachusetts Board of Education, *Annual Report*, 1863: 69). But White did not return in any detail to the issue of religious and moral training during the war.

It is hard to know what impact the renewed interest in moral education had on local school committees. It does not appear to have had a major, long-term effect on the Boston School Committee. Concern about the events at the Boston Hancock Grammar School quickly faded, and discussions about moral education in the Boston school reports became relatively infrequent and unimportant. There was a brief mention of the importance of moral education in 1858, but there were almost no references to the issue in the next three years (Boston School Committee, *Annual Reports*, 1858–61).

An exchange between a Boston principal and the superintendent of schools illustrates the gulf between public pronouncements and the practical experiences in the classrooms. At the Massachusetts Teachers' Association meeting in 1858, F. A. Sawyer, principal of the Brimmer School in Boston, lectured on "physical, moral, and intellectual education." He was reported as saying that: "The culture of the moral faculties does not belong peculiarly to the school. It is the great duty and the peculiar privilege of those who assume the parental relation, to the performance of which they are bound. . . . The neglect of parental instruction at home often results from the mistaken notion that the morals of children are sufficiently cared for in the Sabbath School and the Common School. In the meeting-house, ministers often preach over the heads of teachers themselves, and almost always over the heads of children. . . . The amount of intellectual training demanded in our schools was another obstacle to this proper moral training" (*Massachusetts Teacher*, January 1859: 35–36).

John D. Philbrick, superintendent of the Boston Public Schools, objected: "He thought no one in the capacity of a teacher—a public servant—ought to say he had no time to give moral instruction. It is the business of the teacher to do the greatest possible amount of good to the children committed to him. If, by giving a portion of time to inculcating Christian virtue, the children are benefited, more good will be done than if all the time is given to intellectual instruction. The best results will not be attained till teachers feel that moral instruction is of the highest importance, nor toll they keep before them in all their instruction the cultivation of moral character" (*Massachusetts Teacher*, January 1859: 36).

Surprisingly, Sawyer continued to argue against his superintendent by acknowledging that:

> It would be well to have this moral teaching in the public schools if it were possible; but the public expects more of teachers now in their specific line of intellectual training than they are able to accomplish . . . and he protested against its being any more the duty of a teacher of a public school than that of every other citizen. The whole constitution of public schools points to the fact that the teacher is selected for intellectual work. . . . The statute . . . respecting the duty of teaching moral and religious principles is the only one that has no penalty. . . . My only ground of objection to the work is, that the whole labor of the teacher is demanded in a specific line, and therefore it is impossible for him to give moral instruction. It is folly to go on expecting public schools to do what they do not do, and what from common observation we know they cannot do faithfully and well. (*Massachusetts Teacher*, January 1859: 36)

While Sawyer was very unusual in his candor about the actual role of moral training in the classroom, his willingness and ability to state such a radical departure from the orthodox position on moral instruction so soon after the Hancock Grammar School incident suggests that the impact of that event for many instructors was quite short-lived. This exchange also cautions us about accepting at face value the numerous pronouncements on moral training by superintendents and school committee officials as reflecting the actual practices in the classrooms.

An analysis of published local school reports from thirty Essex County communities for 1860–61 does not indicate any heightened concern about moral training in the public schools. Some local school committees, such as the one in Boxford, discussed the importance of moral education on a fairly regular basis. But many others, such as the ones in Beverly and Bradford, did not emphasize the topic in their general remarks about schooling. Although there was a momentary increase in mentions of moral and religious teaching in response to the Hancock Grammar School incident and to the subsequent request for information about moral education from the secretary of the Massachusetts Board of Education, it did not last long. Almost three-fourths of them did not mention moral education at all, while only one in ten discussed the topic at any length (one out of six briefly mentioned moral education).

The crisis about moral instruction in the Boston public schools did stimulate temporarily discussions about this topic in the *Massachusetts Teacher*—the journal for teachers and educators in the Commonwealth.

> It is an omen for good, that the subject of moral instruction has, of late, assumed a degree of prominence that commands a very large share of the attention of the educational public. This prominence is discernible in the well-known fact, that this branch of culture is a leading topic in everything that emanates from the press, the pulpit, and the lecture-room, pertaining to the family circle, home education, and those other influences which do so much to educate the child. It is also to be found upon the programme of almost every teachers' convention; and educational journals, our own included, frequently, almost monthly, discuss the subject in its various relations and bearings. (*Massachusetts Teacher*, February 1858: 65)

This interest in moral education soon faded. Instead of writing "almost monthly" about this topic, the *Massachusetts Teacher* did not publish another essay specifically on moral instruction until 1860, although the journal did report from time to time that moral education was discussed at teacher association meetings throughout the state.

The drift away from explicit concern about moral training in the early 1850s was halted only temporarily by the debates over the incident in Boston. Most educators and other officials appear to have quickly forgotten or ignored the crisis in moral education despite the initial widespread public outrage over the scandal involving the young students from the Hancock Grammar School.

Notes

1. In spite of the widespread publicity this event received, neither historians of female delinquency nor scholars of antebellum education in Massachusetts made note of it and its subsequent impact on moral training. I discovered the episode while reading through issues of the *Newburyport Herald* for the 1850s as part of my analysis of that community.

2. Although most historians today have ignored or downplayed the importance of religious and moral training in nineteenth-century America, an older generation of scholars did not (Culver, 1929; Dunn, 1958; Smith, 1926). For a useful study of Massachusetts schooling that explores the religious dimensions of public education, see Glenn (1988).

3. There was an extensive debate in the 1840s over the exact meaning of the 1827 legislation and its later revisions. Edward Newton, a member of the Massachusetts Board of Education, argued that Horace Mann and his supporters had deliberately distorted its intention by excluding religion from the Massachusetts public schools. Mann replied that while he was opposed to sectarian materials and teachings in the classroom, he was not opposed to moral and religious instruction. For a detailed analysis of this controversy, see Culver (1929), Dunn (1958), and Smith (1926).

4. Sears, for example, felt that the earlier disagreements over the role of religion in the public schools had now been satisfactorily resolved. "It has been found, upon experiment, that religion can be introduced into the schools without polemical theology; that the Christian temper and spirit can be exhibited and inculcated without stirring the bitter waters of strife; and that instruction in religion and religious doctrines can be added to any extent, at home or elsewhere, through some one or more of the numerous provisions which are made for all who desire that instruction. Whatever metaphysical difficulties may encompass the subject in the minds of any, men are pretty well united on the practical question of maintaining our system of free schools as it is, neither surrendering its principle nor relaxing its vigor, and encouraging the conscientious teacher in the use of all proper means necessary to fulfil the provision of the law which requires 'the principles of piety' to be taught in the schools" (Massachusetts Board of Education, *Annual Report*, 1855: 48).

5. In fact, Sears felt that most of the innovations in education had already been discovered and that it was his task to implement them. As he put it, "During the first twelve years of the existence of the Board, the foundations of what is new in our system of popular education were all laid. During the period which has followed, though not many new measures have been introduced, those that were already introduced have been carried out on a much larger scale. It has been a period of growth, rather than of invention; of the application of principles, rather than of discovery. The theory of education had already been amply discussed. What was now most needed, seemed to be practical improvement, carried into all the towns and districts of the Commonwealth" (Massachusetts Board of Education, *Annual Report*, 1855: 46).

6. For an analysis of trends in arrests in nineteenth-century Boston, see Ferdinand (1967) and Lane (1967, 1992). For an interesting contemporary view of crime in Boston from a policeman's perspective, see Savage (1865). There was comparable concern about the increase of crime in New York City in the 1850s. For a discussion of middle-class anxiety about children in the streets, see Stansell (1986).

7. Even nineteenth-century observers who were very sympathetic to the plight of young girls and saw few differences between males and females in terms of intellectual ability and moral responsibility continued to believe it was unlikely that an unmarried woman could be redeemed once she had experienced sexual intercourse. William Hosmer wrote: "The unmarried woman is the future wife, and she ought to possess an honorable character in the estimation of every marriageable man of her acquaintance. This she cannot do without the utmost propriety of conduct. But little can be pardoned to the indiscretion or inexperience of youth, for the unchaste girl will be very likely to make an unchaste wife. The pilfering boy generally proves a dishonest man; unprincipled youth is the too sure precursor of criminal manhood. This is a condition of human nature equally common to both sexes" (1851: 26)

In contrast, Stansell states that in the mid-nineteenth century, "laboring people seem to have made their judgments of female vice and virtue in the context of particular situations rather than by applying absolute moral standards" (1986: 180). She has not developed this claim in her book, however, and so we must await further documentation on how different classes responded to sexual improprieties by women.

8. Probably the best survey of antebellum Boston institutions for wayward children is Holloran (1989). Unlike many accounts, he covers not only the efforts of Yankee Protestant reformers, but also those of Catholics, Jewish, and African-American reformers. Unfortunately, this very useful and comprehensive book is marred by its dated views of family and educational developments in the Commonwealth—particularly in the colonial period. For a useful analysis of juvenile delinquency in antebellum Boston, see Schneider (1992).

9. The Lancaster School for Girls started out as a reform institution for those who were poor and at risk of becoming delinquents, but after the Civil War it became the home for more hardened and difficult girls (Brenzel, 1983; Holloran, 1989; Schneider, 1992).

10. For a discussion of sexual assault in late-eighteenth and early-nineteenth-century England, see Clark (1987).

11. The age for statutory rape in Massachusetts was only ten. This rape statute was enacted in 1669 by the Massachusetts Bay Colony, and it remained in effect, with some revisions, into the antebellum period. In 1852 the Massachusetts General Court passed a revised statute regarding rape that stated: "Every person who shall ravish, and carnally know, any female of the age of ten years or more, by force and against her will; or shall unlawfully and carnally know and abuse any woman child, under the age of ten years, shall be punished by imprisonment in the State Prison for life" (Metcalf, 1854, chap. 259, para. 2: 854).

The meaning of this section was upheld in a Massachusetts Supreme Judicial Court, *Commonwealth v. Sugland*, in 1855, which restated the law as: "By our statutes, the punishment of rape embraces all cases of violation of females of any age. If the party assaulted be

above the age of ten years, then, to constitute the offence of rape, the act must have been committed by force and against her will. But if it be upon a child under the age of ten years, it is alike punishable under the statute, whether committed with the consent or against the will of such female child" (Gray, 1858, 4: 10).

For useful discussions of the colonial rape law and practices in Massachusetts, see Kohler (1980) and Lindemann (1984). In 1893 the age of consent was raised from ten to sixteen (Ferdinand, 1967: 91). I am indebted to Ted MacVeagh and Carl Schneider for assistance in obtaining the information about the legal aspects of statutory rape in antebellum Massachusetts. Although mid-nineteenth-century Americans clearly distinguished between youth and adults, hey did not make a sharp distinction between teenage and adult victims of sexual crimes (Vinovskis, 1988c).

12. Although the names of the girls and the businessmen involved in this incident were widely publicized in the local newspapers and are also available through the court records, in the interests of their privacy there is no reason to publish them here. For a useful discussion of access to Massachusetts criminal records and the issue of privacy, see Abrashkin and Winsor (1989).

13. Some contemporaries made a distinction between adult women and young girls being seduced or raped by males. For example, Ball Fenner expressed little sympathy for adult women who claimed they were seduced or raped by men. "I hardly believe such a thing to be possible as the commission of the crime of rape upon an adult female, who is in perfect possession of health, and those faculties which a benign and beneficent Creator has bestowed upon all His Children. . . . I am slow to believe that the female . . . is not endowed with sufficient strength and power to resist all amatory advances of the opposite sex, after they have come to the years of maturity. . . . In the case of a child, I grant that this is far different. To those brutes (and there are many that exist who would, and do commit such crimes upon them) I should say that the punishment awarded by Chinese laws to the parricide, would be altogether too mild" (Fenner, 1856: 264).

14. Not all Boston newspapers discussed this incident. For example, the *Boston Daily Advertiser* ignored the scandal. Initially, some newspapers (*Boston Daily Bee*, Nov. 21, 1856) were concerned that an effort was underway to hush up the matter.

15. The *Massachusetts Teacher* (December 1857: 547), the journal for educators, acknowledged the complaints against the schools for failing to teach moral education properly but defended the schools by pointing out that "the accountability of parents is far greater than that of the schools, and ever must be. If the boys and girls of today are less reverent, more profane and vicious, than were those of former times, the fault falls more upon parents than upon the schools."

The *Boston Investigator* (Nov. 26, 1856), a spiritualist-oriented newspaper, observed that this scandal occurred "in the Puritan city of a hundred churches," but it did not go on to develop the responsibility of the churches for this incident. Almost all of the other newspapers ignored or minimized the responsibility of churches for the behavior of the men and the girls.

16. For a useful, though idiosyncratic, contemporary description of the Boston Police Court system, see Fenner (1856). For a more detailed analysis of the functioning of the Boston Police Court and the Boston Municipal Court before 1850, see Ferdinand (1992).

17. Judge Thomas Russell was appointed to the Boston Police Court in 1852 at the young age of twenty-six. Apparently he had a reputation for "decisions hastily made, and many persons think, ill-timed." Yet he was also regarded "by the community at large to be an upright magistrate, and an impartial dispenser of the law" (Fenner, 1856: 26, 100).

18. I have checked four of the legal precedents cited by Judge Russell, and it appears that he was correctly interpreting them.

19. Judge Russell's contention that the more serious cases—like an alleged rape— would be sent to a higher court appears to be correct. A detailed analysis of the Newburyport Police Court records in the late 1850s and early 1860s provides numerous examples of more serious crimes that were referred to a higher court.

20. Judge Thomas Russell had a reputation for being hard upon any witnesses whom he suspected of wrongdoing. "When Justice Russell is upon the Bench, witnesses should be exceedingly careful how they testify. If they come with a lie in their mouths, the chances are that they will become prisoners, instead of witnesses, and be sent up to a higher court, indicted for perjury" (Fenner, 1856: 100).

21. Expelling someone from a public school was not unusual. What was unusual was the involvement of the Boston School Committee in this process.

22. An extensive search of the Boston Municipal Court records at the Massachusetts State Archives did not yield much information about these two defendants. The two cases are recorded as docket numbers 47 and 48 for the Boston Municipal Court in 1857. There is, however, only some scattered information about summoning principals and the bond for the defendants are in these files. None of the more detailed discussion of the cases could be found, although I went through the extensive set of records for that year to see if it may have been misfiled. I am indebted to Elizabeth Bouvier of the Massachusetts Supreme Judicial Court Archives and Records Preservation for assistance. For a useful discussion of the organization of the Massachusetts court system and its records, see Menand (1987).

23. Most of the newspapers examined were from Boston as they contained the most complete accounts of this incident. Out-of-town newspapers tended to reprint stories from the Boston newspapers, although they sometimes added editorial comments. The out-of-town coverage was erratic. Some papers, like the *Newburyport Herald*, devoted considerable attention to it while others, like the *Essex County Mercury, Salem Gazette, Salem Observer,* or *Salem Register,* did not even mention it.

24. An interesting question is whether the socioeconomic or ethnic characteristics of the girls affected how they were ultimately treated by the courts and the school system. Unfortunately, no information on the personal characteristics of the girls was available in the court records or the newspapers. Therefore, a search of the manuscript Massachusetts state census of 1855 for Boston was undertaken to locate

these girls and their families. All the inhabitants in wards 1, 3, 4, 5 and 6 were carefully examined (about 60,000 individuals altogether).

All six girls were located in the census (the identification seems certain in five of the six cases—in one the age of the girl may be one or two years younger than I had anticipated, but this might be due to a census error). In almost all of the cases, the combination of the full name, including a middle initial, and the approximate age were enough to make an unambiguous identification.

The findings are very informative. The girls lived in wards 1 and 3 in which about one-third of the inhabitants had been born in Ireland. Yet all six girls were born in Massachusetts. Five of them lived with both parents, and one lived with only her mother. Of the five couples, two of the parents were native-born, two of mixed marriages (native-born husband, Swedish wife; Irish husband, native-born wife), and one of foreign-parentage (English husband, wife from Nova Scotia). The single mother was from Ireland. Most of the fathers worked in blue-collar occupations, but one was a policeman.

In other words, while the media and Protestant reformers were complaining of the proclivity of immigrant children toward vice and crime, these girls did not fit that stereotype—indeed one was the daughter of a native-born Boston policeman. None of the discussions in the media mentioned the girls' backgrounds—perhaps because the personal characteristics of those involved did not fit the existing stereotypes of troubled girls. Moreover, the fact that these girls were not immediately sent to a reform school and that three of them were reinstated in the schools may also have something to do with their ethnicity.

I am indebted to Stephen Frank for searching through the manuscript census of wards 1, 3, and 4 and to Andris Vinovskis for searching through the manuscript census of wards 5 and 6 for this information.

25. Boutwell completed his first report on December 31, 1856—just in time to be aware of the Hancock Grammar School incident, but probably too late to rewrite substantially his lengthy report (Massachusetts Board of Education, *Annual Report*, 1857: 86).

26. I noted in chap. 1 the Puritan assumption that the family had chief responsibility for education of the young and that the state would intervene only when the family failed. The emphasis of the school committees on the primacy of the family reflected the persistence of this thinking.

27. The explicit statements against sectarianism were almost always made after the local school committee had praised the value of religious training or the use of the Bible in the classroom. Cautions against sectarianism were not meant as an argument against religion in the classroom. For example, the Ashby School Committee noted that "from a fear that sectarian religious influence should be exerted, the common principles of morality have been too much neglected" (Massachusetts Board of Education, *Abstract*, 1858: 18).

The lack of discussion about the use of Bibles in the public schools was somewhat surprising. A Massachusetts law of 1855 stated: "the school committee shall require the daily reading of some portion of the Bible in the common English version; but shall never direct any school books calculated to favor the tenets of any particular sect of Christians to be purchased or used in any of the town schools" (Massachusetts Board of Education, *Annual Report*, 1861: 104).

28. The allusion to the Hancock Grammar School incident was in the Boston School Committee report. The mention of the dangers of sexual activity by girls came in the Lowell School Committee report, which warned against the neglect of parental responsibility. "What is before the boy, but a career of iniquity and crime? What is before the girl but a fate worse than death itself? It is terrible to think of the vast influence exerted for evil upon all ranks of society, when the passions and vice which are dreadful even in childhood, shall have grown into a beastly manhood and an infamous womanhood" (Massachusetts Board of Education, *Abstracts*, 1858: 3–4, 27).

29. Boutwell did mention the fact that of the 1,909 boys admitted to the Massachusetts State Reform School, 1,334 were known to have been truants (Massachusetts Board of Education, *Annual Report*, 1858: 69). Yet this did not address the question of why crime

rates had been increasing at the same time as public schooling grew.

30. In general it appears that Boutwell was less interested in the specifics of educational practices than his two predecessors. In his two volumes of reminiscences written many years later, Boutwell does not devote much space or attention to his five-year tenure as the secretary of the Massachusetts Board of Education (Boutwell, 1902, 1:256–61).

All societies are confronted with the problem of working with poor children. Often this means finding ways to overcome or compensate for their disadvantaged backgrounds. A common response among developed nations is to work through the educational system to provide these children with the skills and values they will need to function effectively in society. Indeed, concern for disadvantaged children in the United States today has led many policy makers (Bennett, 1988) to look to the schools for assistance.

In spite of a strong and persistent belief in the importance of education in preparing future citizens, not everyone agrees that American schools are designed or prepared to help disadvantaged children. Some contend that family background is the main determinant of student achievement and subsequent job placement (Jencks, 1972, 1979). Although these scholars acknowledge that the total amount of education received matters, they argue that the years of schooling completed is more dependent upon a child's home environment than on the quality of the school. Other analysts have gone further and argued that public schools in nineteenth-century America were deliberately designed to perpetuate the existing inequalities within the expanding capitalist economy (Bowles and Gintis, 1976; Katz, 1975; Spring, 1972). These critics argue that school systems were created in large part to allow middle- or upper-class parents to help their children while ensuring that those from disadvantaged backgrounds would not advance.

In this chapter I shall investigate the relation between schooling and poor children historically by examining the origins and development of nineteenth-century education in the United States, with particular attention to whether or not schools helped poor children obtain better jobs.[1] In the first section I shall analyze the establishment and expansion of schools in the early nineteenth century. Next, contemporary views of schooling and poor children will be noted and their ideas about the relation between education and economic productivity explored. A look at three antebellum educational reforms intended to help poor children—monitorial charity schools, Sunday schools, and infant schools—will allow me to assess the extent to which early-nineteenth-century Americans were interested in the problems and needs of poor children. Next I shall investigate school attendance among poor children to see if they were excluded from these new institutions as some historians have claimed. Finally, the important question of whether or not schooling actually fostered occupational mobility among poor children will be addressed.

By examining the development of schooling and its impact on poor children, I shall ascertain the intentions and evaluate the achievements of early efforts to help disadvantaged children. Furthermore, investigating the different ways school reformers tried to alleviate the problems associated with poverty will place current educational reforms in a broader historical perspective.

Expansion of Schooling in the Nineteenth Century

Schools have not always been the primary institutions for socializing and training children. In colonial New England, for example, the household had the primary responsibility for educating children and servants (Bailyn, 1960). Ministers and churches provided some assistance since the goals of education were primarily religious (Axtell, 1974). Initially, the father was entrusted with the education and catechizing of the children. Only after the mid-seventeenth century, when males stopped joining the New England churches, did Puritans slowly and reluctantly turn to women as the chief agents for home education (Moran and Vinovskis, 1986).

Although parents were expected to educate their children and servants, they sometimes made use of schools. Older women, often widows, set up dame schools to educate young children (Cremin, 1970). In some communities, private elementary schools were created for parents who did not want to educate their children at home (Murphy, 1960). The few children who continued their education beyond the rudiments of reading and writing went to grammar schools that were established in larger communities (Vinovskis, 1987). Increasingly during the colonial period, parents placed their children in private or public schools whenever they became available, but at least one scholar (Sheldon S. Cohen, 1974) argues that opportunities for formal education may have actually declined in the eighteenth century.

One of the major changes in nineteenth-century American life was the development of mass public elementary or common schools. There is considerable disagreement on when or why this occurred. In the 1960s and 1970s a group of scholars, sharply critical of the existing educational system, reexamined the origins of American schooling and concluded that common schools were established as a response to industrialization (Bowles and Gintis, 1976; Field, 1974; Katz, 1968). These historians, often designated as "revisionists," argued that manufacturers and merchants spearheaded public school expansion and reforms in order to instill in future workers the respect for law and authority necessary in the newly emerging capitalist economy. As Samuel Bowles and Herbert Gintis put it:

> There can be little doubt that the educational reform and expansion in the nineteenth century [were] associated with the growing ascendancy of the capitalist mode of production. Particularly striking is the recurring pattern of capital accumulation in the dynamic advanced sectors of the economy, the resulting integration of new workers into the wage-labor system, the expansion of the proletariat and the reserve army, social unrest and the emergence of political protest movements, and the development of movements for educational expansion and reform. We also find a recurring pattern of political and financial support for educational change. While the impetus for educational reform sometimes came from disgruntled farmers or workers, the leadership of the movements—which succeeded in stamping its unmistakable imprint on the form and direction of the educational innovation—was without exception in the hands of a coalition of professionals and capitalists from the leading sectors of the economy. (Bowles and Gintis, 1976: 178–79)

The revisionists' particular focus on Massachusetts parallels the concentration of other scholarship on the educational and economic developments in that state. This is significant because the Commonwealth was not only a leader in educational changes, but also in the forefront of urban and industrial development. The revisionists date the emergence of public schooling to the two decades before the Civil War and use the appointment of Horace Mann as the secretary of the Massachusetts Board of Education in 1837 as a starting date: "The growth in attendance paralleled these dramatic changes in the legal, financial, and social structure of U.S. education. Twenty years before the Civil War, just under 38 percent of white children aged five–nineteen were attending schools. By 1860, the figure had risen to 59 percent. Thus Mann's ascendancy to the newly created Massachusetts State Board of Education in 1837, marked a major turning point in U.S. social history" (Bowles and Gintis, 1976: 154). There are numerous problems with the revisionist interpretation of the development of mass education and school reforms in nineteenth-century America. For one thing, it equates the movement for public school reforms in the 1840s and 1850s with the expansion of mass education and does not look at developments outside of Massachusetts.

Yet mass literacy and education in Massachusetts occurred well before the 1840s and 1850s. Kenneth Lockridge (1974) has documented that about 90 percent of men and 60 percent of New England women were literate by 1790.[2] According to the census figures on literacy, only 1.1 percent of the white population aged twenty and above in Massachusetts in 1840 were illiterate (Vinovskis, 1989). In addition, estimates of Massachusetts school attendance indicate that it was already high in 1800 and gradually increased over the next four decades. Contrary to the interpretations of the revisionists, the percentage of children in Massachusetts schools actually decreased slightly from 1840 to 1860 (Kaestle and Vinovskis, 1980).[3]

There were important changes in some aspects of Massachusetts education in the two decades before the Civil War, such as the shift from private to public schools and the establishment of public high schools. But even here one needs to acknowledge that some of these changes were a continuation of earlier trends. For example, the proportion of children in school receiving at least some private education dropped from 18.7 percent in 1840 to 8.0 percent in 1860. Nevertheless, more than four out five students were already going to a public school in 1840; therefore, the major changes from private to public schooling occurred earlier.[4]

Another reason why the revisionist equation of the rise of mass education with industrialization is incorrect is because most of the expansion in schooling in the antebellum period occurred in areas that were predominantly rural. The largest increases in the percentage of white children attending school and in the total number of new students between 1840 and 1860 was not in New England or in the Middle Atlantic states, but in the North Central region (Fishlow, 1976). The percentage of whites under twenty attending school in the largely agricultural North Central states rose from 29.0 percent in 1840 to 70.3 percent in 1860, while the percentage in the more industrial New England states declined from 81.8 percent to 73.8 percent (Vinovskis, 1985).

If the revisionists exaggerated the causal relation between the rise of mass education and industrialization, they overestimated the role of the manufacturers and merchants in achieving educational reforms (Bowles and Gintis, 1976; Field, 1974; Katz, 1968). Although both of these groups generally supported the public school movement, they were less important than others, such as clergymen at the local level (Vinovskis, 1985a). In addition, school reformers were active not only in the more industrialized states, such as Massachusetts, but also in agricultural states, such as Michigan and Ohio. Nor were school reformers restricted to urban areas, as the revisionists imply; they were also present in rural communities—though in those communities they often faced a different set of problems. Finally, rather than seeing education imposed on an indifferent or hostile working class, as many revisionists believe, there is considerable evidence of widespread public support for education—including strong enthusiasm among northern workers for common school education (Kaestle, 1983; Katznelson and Weir, 1985).

Instead of seeing mass education as the result of mid-nineteenth-century industrial development, it is more accurate to view it as a continuation of the colonial Puritan activities to ensure that everyone was able to read the Bible. This religious enthusiasm for education was reinforced by the establishment of the United States in the late eighteenth century and the extension of suffrage to almost all white adult males in the early nineteenth century. Given the perceived fragility of the early republic, public schools were seen as essential—not only as a means of promoting widespread literacy, but also as a way of preserving moral values. As mothers were now regarded as the natural educators of the next generation, women received the access to public schooling that had been denied to most of them in the colonial period. Add to this a growing recognition in the 1840s and 1850s that education fosters social mobility and stimulates economic development, and it is not surprising that mass public schooling for whites expanded rapidly in all regions of the United States except the South, where geographic and social conditions limited the establishment and maintenance of common schools (Kaestle, 1983; Vinovskis, 1994).

Antebellum Views of Poverty and Education

Concern about poverty and disadvantaged children does not necessarily imply support for mass education. In early nineteenth-century England—a rapidly industrializing nation beset by problems of poverty and social unrest—calls for mass education encountered strong opposition. English opponents of education for the poor argued that schooling would encourage unrealistic occupational aspirations and lead to discontent among children of common laborers. They also feared that education would facilitate the dissemination of dangerous ideas against religion and civic authority. As a result, while individual English philanthropists pioneered many of the educational programs for the urban poor in the late eighteenth and early nineteenth centuries, their efforts also stimulated strong opposition from conservatives that delayed mass public education in England (Silver, 1965).

There was almost no opposition to the education of poor whites in the United States. Given the creation of the republic and the need for an educated electorate, conservatives supported schooling as a means of instilling proper values (Kaestle, 1976). The Free-School Society for the Education of Poor Children in New York City petitioned the New York legislature in 1805 to help poor children because:

The condition of this class [of children of the poor] is deplorable indeed; reared up by parents who, from a variety of concurring circumstances, are become either indifferent to the best interests of their offspring, or, through intemperate lives, are rendered unable to defray the expense of their instruction, these miserable and almost friendless objects are ushered upon the stage of life, inheriting those vices which idleness and the bad example of their parents naturally produce. The consequences of this neglect of education are ignorance and vice, and all those manifold evils resulting from every species of immorality, by which public hospitals and alms-houses are filled with objects of disease and poverty, and society burthened with taxes for their support. In addition to these melancholy facts, it is to be feared that the laboring class in the community is becoming less industrious, less moral, and less careful to lay up the fruit of their earnings. (quoted in Sol Cohen, 1974: 983)

Although there was strong and widespread support for educating poor children in the United States, it was usually justified in terms of protecting society rather than of helping individuals get ahead. The value of education, according to most commentators, was to improve the moral character of the poor rather than to enhance their occupational skills or to foster individual social mobility. In part this orientation was due to the expectation that workers would acquire their specific job skills through apprenticeship instead of schooling (Rorabaugh, 1986).

Eighteenth- and nineteenth-century British classical economists did not emphasize education as a key to individual or even societal economic productivity (Blaug, 1986; Johnson, 1964; Vaizey, 1962). Adam Smith, for example, briefly acknowledged that monetary rewards should compensate workers for acquiring skills, but he did not elaborate on the important implications of this insight. Instead, his brief discussion of education focused on its value for controlling workers who might otherwise cause social and political unrest during periods of rapid economic change. Most early-nineteenth-century American political economists agreed—though some placed a little more emphasis on the benefits of education than did their British counterparts (Phillips, 1828; Wayland, 1843).

The leaders of the American workers in the 1820s and 1830s stressed the importance of universal common school education (Carlton, 1908). But they also paid scant attention to the value of education for enhancing economic productivity or fostering social mobility (Kaestle, 1983; Vinovskis, 1994). Instead, they saw in schooling a means of educating workers to recognize and protect their rights through the political process (Luther, 1832; Simpson, 1831).

The one person who did stress the economic productivity of education was Horace Mann.[5] Responding to the legislative efforts to abolish the Massachusetts State Board of Education in 1840, Mann sought to broaden the support for public education by demonstrating its economic value to the state economy and to the individual in his *Fifth Annual Report* (Massachusetts Secretary of the Board of Education, 1842). Based on a flawed, but seemingly objective, survey of textile mill managers in Lowell, he argued that educated workers earned about 50 percent more than uneducated ones. Although Mann's estimate of the value of antebellum education is clearly exaggerated and based on faulty data and reasoning, it appeared scientific and plausible to his contemporaries.

Thanks to the work of Mann and his supporters the economic productivity of elementary education was recognized and praised by the time of Civil War. This reinforced the growing belief that the children of the poor could escape poverty through education. Education became even more highly valued as an alternate means of occupational mobility when other ways of training young people, such as apprenticeship, declined in early-nineteenth-century America (Vinovskis, 1994).

Antebellum Programs for Educating Poor Children

Did nineteenth-century Americans develop special educational programs to help poor children? And if programs for poor children were set up, were they altered over time to adjust to the development and changes in the common schools? To answer these and other related questions I shall look at three antebellum educational programs: monitorial charity schools, Sunday schools, and infant schools. Although these programs were not the only or even the most typical of antebellum efforts to educate children, they illustrate how concerns about poverty and disadvantaged children were translated into special educational programs.

In the late eighteenth and early nineteenth centuries, efforts were made to establish charity schools for poor children in American cities. These institutions were intended for children whose parents were either incapable of educating them at home or unable to enroll them in a private school. Many of these schools were sponsored and funded by religious groups, and they catered not only to poor white children, but also to free African-American children (Cremin, 1970). (For a discussion of the changing attitudes and practices toward the poor in late eighteenth-century and early-nineteenth-century New England, see Wright [1992]. For comparable material on England, see Cunningham [1991].)

Lancasterian Schools   It was expensive to establish and maintain charity schools, and their philanthropic sponsors looked for ways to economize. One of the most promising and innovative approaches was to adopt the ideas and organization of Joseph Lancaster, a young English teacher who established monitorial (Lancasterian) schools for poor children in London and other British communities in the early nineteenth century. Lancasterian schools emphasized memorization and recitation and used older students to oversee and monitor the progress of younger ones. Having older students help the teacher was not a new idea, but Lancaster perfected the technique with his standardized and simplified rules and detailed curriculum instructions. One teacher could supervise up to five hundred students and thereby greatly reduce the cost of education. The appeal of monitorial schools went well beyond economics. By encouraging competitive group activities, such as reading and spelling, Lancasterian schools often were more exciting than traditional schools, which emphasized individual memorization and recitation (Kaestle, 1973b).

Lancasterian schools spread to the major urban areas in the United States in the 1810s and 1820s. Voluntary societies in large cities adopted them, as well as those in smaller communities, such as Alexandria, Detroit, and Richmond. The schools were efficient, economical and usually organized on a nonsectarian basis. Students were allowed to progress at their own pace, and large numbers of poor children received their education in them. Although American educators were at first enthusiastic about Lancasterian schools, complaints about the rote memorization and the impersonal education surfaced. As American school reformers of the 1830s and 1840s were exposed to the ideas of Johann Pestalozzi (Barlow, 1977), who stressed the need for more individual attention and for a close emotional relationship between the teacher and the pupil, the Lancasterian approach gradually fell out of favor and use.[6]

The movement away from monitorial schools was reinforced by the growth of public schools and by efforts to make them attractive for children of middle-class families. While the highly regimented and inexpensive Lancasterian schools were seen as adequate for poor children, they were viewed as inappropriate for middle-class children, whose parents demanded a better education (Kaestle, 1973b). Poor children, in turn, benefited because they were then able to enroll in one of the smaller classes in public schools. Nevertheless, for a few decades in the early nineteenth century, monitorial schools provided education for many disadvantaged children who otherwise might not have received any schooling. Furthermore, by stressing nonsectarian training and emphasizing the need to educate everyone, Lancasterian schools helped to pave the way for the public common school reforms of the 1840s and 1850s.

Sunday Schools Sunday schools were another educational innovation borrowed from England and intended for helping the poor. Robert Raikes, a middle-class philanthropist, is often credited with creating the first Sunday school in England in 1780, but similar institutions had been established decades earlier. Some saw in Sunday schools a way to rescue poor children from their immoral and corrupt parents. Others viewed them as a means of spreading religion—both to the poor children and through them to their parents. The Sunday school movement was encouraged by the optimistic and romantic views of children in the late eighteenth and early nineteenth centuries. As English reformers despaired of influencing adults who were set in their ways, they turned to children, who were regarded as more pliable and receptive to educational and religious improvements (Laqueur, 1976).

Sunday schools were popular in England and spread rapidly. In spite of their image as an urban institution, they were as common in rural areas as in the cities. In fact, London trailed other communities in the percentage of children attending a Sunday school. Although many Sunday schools were established and maintained by middle-class benefactors, others had a working-class origin, and children in all of these institutions were usually instructed by members of their own class. Evangelicals were particularly active in the Sunday school movement. In the early nineteenth century, nearly every working-class child in England outside of London attended a Sunday school for an average of four years (Laqueur, 1976).

Sunday schools were introduced into the United States in the 1790s and proved to be equally popular here. Some of the first Sunday schools were set up in factory towns by industrialists, such as Samuel Slater, who wanted to provide schooling and religious training for poor children working in their textile mills (Tucker, 1984). As in England, religious activists played a key role in establishing Sunday schools in the larger cities, but initially these institutions were not controlled by or oriented toward a single religious denomination (Rice, 1917).

At first, Sunday schools emphasized teaching both poor children and illiterate adults to read and encouraged the memorization of long passages from the Bible. Sunday schools often provided a basic education for those who were denied one elsewhere. Not surprisingly, many African-Americans in northern cities received their limited education in them. In New York City, nearly 25 percent of the pupils in the Sunday School Union Society's institutions were African-Americans (Boylan, 1988).

As public common schools became more available and adult illiteracy declined, Sunday schools changed their clientele and goals. Fewer illiterate adults attended, and increasingly middle-class children joined the children of the poor in Sunday school classes. Since reading and writing were now taught in the public schools, it was no longer necessary to teach literacy in the Sunday schools. By the 1830s, Sunday schools emphasized evangelical training and became a religious complement to the public schools. Large numbers of children in antebellum America attended both institutions, and Sunday schools were seen as essential for all Protestant children because public schools were becoming more nonsectarian. At the same time, Sunday schools moved away from their interdenominational origins toward becoming auxiliary institutions for specific Protestant religious sects (Boylan 1988; Rice, 1917).

Infant Schools Whereas monitorial and Sunday schools sought to educate poor children of all ages, infant schools were especially designed for young children (see chapter 2). Based on the pedagogical ideas of Johann Pestalozzi and on Robert Owen's model infant school at New Lanark, Scotland, these institutions spread rapidly throughout Europe and America in the 1820s and early 1830s. Much of their popularity stemmed from the belief that by reaching disadvantaged children at the ages of two or three, it was possible to save them from the harmful habits and dangerous values of their impoverished environment (Owen, 1920; Salmon and Hindshaw, 1904; Whitbread, 1972).

Early-nineteenth-century Americans believed that children were capable of intellectual development at an early age, and so the idea of special schools for children of poor parents seemed reasonable and natural. The educational practices in infant schools ranged from allowing the children to play to teaching them to read, but there was widespread agreement that educating poor young children helped to overcome their disadvantaged backgrounds (Dean and Vinovskis, 1977).

Infant schools initially were intended for poor children, but before long middle-class parents wanted these institutions made available to all children. As a result, infant schools and early childhood education spread rapidly in the United States. At first infant schools were set up only in larger urban areas, but soon many rural communities established them as well. In 1840 approximately 40 percent of all three-year-olds in Massachusetts were enrolled either in a special infant school or in a regular common school (Kaestle and Vinovskis, 1978).

In spite of the initial enthusiasm for infant schools by parents and educators, they did not last long. In 1833, Amariah Brigham, a prominent physician, argued that early intellectual activity among children weakens the development of the brain and eventually may lead to insanity. Brigham's ideas, based on the best medical and scientific thinking of the day, were widely disseminated through popular magazines. Support for infant schools and early childhood education quickly faded, and by 1860 there were almost no children younger than five in Massachusetts public schools (Dean and Vinovskis, 1977). What had started out as a means of helping poor children was now seen as detrimental to any young child. Middle-class parents were more likely than lower-class ones to withdraw their children from the infant schools—partly because they were more likely to read the popular magazines and advice books. When philanthropic support and public funds were withheld from the infant schools and educational authorities barred very young children from entering public schools, early schooling in America collapsed (Kaestle and Vinovskis, 1978).

It is clear that antebellum Americans did set up special educational programs for disadvantaged children. Their motivations were mixed. Some feared the social and economic disruptions caused by urbanization and industrialization and believed that educating poor children would help minimize these difficulties. Others were more concerned about political stability and felt that an educated electorate was essential in the new republic. Many philanthropists and educational reformers were genuinely concerned about the well-being of disadvantaged children and felt it was their religious duty to help the less fortunate.

Many of the educational efforts aimed at poor children originated abroad and came to the United States from Great Britain. Historians have often ignored or minimized the importance of this transmission of ideas and institutions by viewing American developments in isolation. In the United States, however, the establishment and growth of educational institutions for the poor was not identical to that of comparable programs in Great Britain. As there was virtually no opposition to the education of poor whites in nineteenth-century America, it was much easier to promote such innovations here than in England, where strong opposition to mass public education persisted.

In the United States, educational programs for the poor frequently began as private, charitable efforts, but they quickly sought and received public funding. One of the interesting characteristics of many of these programs is that they shifted from efforts aimed exclusively at poor and disadvantaged children to ones intended for everyone. There were many advantages to having educational programs designed for the poor expanded to include all children. The stigma attached to attending private charity schools was largely eliminated when these institutions became public schools intended for middle-class as well as lower-class children. The quality of the education often improved because middle-class parents insisted on better facilities and teachers. But there were also some disadvantages for poor children that did not receive much attention at the time. Once schools were intended for everyone, nineteenth-century reformers usually assumed that disadvantaged children in the public common schools did not need any special help. Indeed, in the case of infant schools, there was concern among middle-class parents that any special efforts on behalf of the poor might disadvantage their own children. As a result, the focus of much nineteenth-century educational reform was on getting poor children into public common schools rather than on looking for ways of helping poor children after they had enrolled.

Although there was little distinction by gender, the special educational programs for poor children in antebellum America were intended mainly for whites. African-American children usually did not receive equal access either to these special programs or to public common schools. Sometimes separate monitorial charity schools, Sunday schools, or infant schools were established in large cities for African-American children, but not often. In the North, African-American children faced strong racial prejudices and often segregated schools that limited their education. With the increased fear of abolitionists and slave revolts in the 1830s and 1840s, southern states tried to restrict education for slaves. As a result, African-American children, who were clearly among the most disadvantaged individuals, did not receive equal access to schooling.

Poor Children and School Attendance in 1860

Despite the availability of public common schools, especially in the Northeast and the Midwest, were most poor children forced into the labor force because of poverty? Most analysts agree that by 1860 almost every child in Massachusetts, including those from poor or working-class families, received some common school education. During their teens, however, these children were more likely to drop out of school than those from wealthy or middle-class families (Katz, 1987; Katznelson and Weir, 1985; Soltow and Stevens, 1981). The classic and most frequently cited study of school attendance of poor children in antebellum America is Stephan Thernstrom's analysis of Newburyport, Massachusetts. He analyzed the lives of common laborers in that community in 1860 and concluded that poverty forced almost all of their children to drop out of school at an early age: "The relentless pressure of poverty—stemming from the depressed age level for common labor and from sharp seasonal fluctuations in employment opportunities—forced the children of Newburyport's laborers into the job market at an early age. Sometimes a laborer went several weeks without earning a cent; then the four dollars a week his twelve-year-old son earned as a bobbin boy was the family's sole source of support. Opportunities for formal education past the age of ten or eleven, as a result, were effectively nil for working class children" (Thernstrom, 1964: 22–23).

Thernstrom's pessimistic portrayal of school attendance among children of the working class in antebellum Newburyport is exaggerated and incorrect. A more detailed statistical manuscript census analysis of all 13,000 residents of Newburyport in 1860, rather than of the 400 common laborers in Thernstrom's study, demonstrates that lower-class children received more schooling in that community than Thernstrom believed (Vinovskis, 1985b). Thernstrom said that the chances of school attendance of an eleven- or twelve-year-old whose father was a common laborer were nil, but our statistical reexamination found that more than 90 percent of these children were still in school. Indeed, 41.1 percent of all children ages thirteen to nineteen whose fathers were common laborers were in school, compared to 51.4 percent of those whose fathers were in high white-collar occupations. Or, 40.9 percent of all children ages thirteen to nineteen whose family had less than $100 worth of assets were in school, compared to 57.3 percent of those whose families had over $5,000. Thus, although Thernstrom was correct to point out that poor children were less likely to remain in school as teenagers than wealthy ones, that differential was much less than suggested and seriously underestimated the extent of school attendance by children of working-class parents (Vinovskis, 1985b).

Were the patterns of school attendance in Newburyport similar to those in other Massachusetts communities? Another individual-level manuscript census study of Lawrence, Lynn, Salem, and five smaller communities in Essex County in 1860 produced similar results—though a somewhat lower overall rate of school attendance. For children ages thirteen to nineteen whose fathers were in an unskilled or semi-unskilled occupation, 30.0 percent were in school, compared to 56.8 percent of those whose fathers were in either a professional or semiprofessional occupation (Kaestle and Vinovskis, 1980).

If most antebellum poor children in Massachusetts received at least some common school education, and many remained in school as teenagers, did they also have access to the newly created public high schools? Again, the consensus among historians was that few public high schools existed in the nineteenth century, and the small number that were established served almost entirely children from the middle or upper classes. Overall, only a tiny minority of children ever attended a public high school and working-class parents either did not want to or could not afford to send any of their children to one of them (Krug, 1969; Peterson, 1985).

Public high schools were certainly rare in antebellum America, but in some areas of the country, such as Massachusetts, they were more commonplace. Nor were high schools confined only to large urban cities; they existed in smaller communities as well. In most large cities, there was only one high school, so that only a small percentage of children could attend. In smaller communities with high schools, however, a much higher proportion of children enrolled. An analysis of high school attendance in Essex County, Massachusetts, in 1860 found that a substantial minority of youth passed through such an institution (see chapter 5). Combining both public high schools and comparable private academies, 19.0 percent of Essex County children received at least some high school education. Most students entering high school did not stay long enough to complete the degree, however, and so it is not clear exactly what benefits, if any, came from a limited exposure to secondary schooling (Vinovskis, 1988).

Were children of working-class families in effect excluded from public high school education, as some historians have argued? Not entirely. Although children whose parents were wealthier and in white-collar occupations were more likely to attend high school, some children from poor families also enrolled. In

Newburyport, almost a third of all children in 1860 enrolled at some time in one of the local public or private high schools, and 30.8 percent of those who attended graduated. Whereas two-thirds of the children whose fathers were in high white-collar occupations attended high school, about one-third of those whose fathers were in skilled occupations and one-sixth of those whose fathers were in unskilled occupations also enrolled (Vinovskis, 1985). Thus, although children of poor and working-class families were less likely to enroll in a high school, the institution was not entirely beyond their reach in communities such as Newburyport.

This examination of the patterns of elementary and secondary school attendance has been confined to Massachusetts, a state with well-developed common and high schools. Although the overall levels of antebellum school attendance is somewhat lower in the Midwest, the same general patterns appear. Only in the South, where the common schools were slow in developing, might one anticipate much lower rates of school attendance and perhaps more of a differential in education between children from poor and more affluent families. Finally, while many poor white children had considerable access to public and private schooling, the same was not true for African-American children (Kaestle, 1983).

Education and Social Mobility among Poor Children

In nineteenth-century America, according to popular thought, everyone had an opportunity to get ahead through hard work and some luck. Education was not always seen as a key factor in social mobility, but good habits and character were considered essential (Burns, 1976; Cawelti, 1965; Wyllie, 1954). But was there real social mobility for nineteenth-century Americans if we look at their behavior rather than their beliefs? This is a very complicated issue because it depends on the definition of social mobility and which particular case studies are used. Most historians have subdivided nineteenth-century occupations into five broad categories: (1) high white-collar, (2) low white-collar, (3) skilled, (4) semiskilled, and (5) unskilled. Social mobility is usually defined as movement from manual or blue-collar occupations (skilled, semiskilled, or unskilled) to nonmanual or white-collar occupations (high white-collar or low white-collar). Sometimes social mobility is also measured in terms of movements from one of the five occupational groupings to another one (for example, from unskilled to semiskilled). Others define social mobility differently altogether, by not looking at occupational changes but at acquisition of property and wealth—particularly, the ability to own a home. There are also differences in what is used as the basis for the comparison. Some social mobility studies look at the intergenerational mobility between fathers and sons while others focus only on the career mobility of individuals.

The findings of social mobility studies of nineteenth-century Americans are mixed when we look at those near the bottom of the occupation structure (unskilled or semiskilled). Overall, it appears that most unskilled or semiskilled workers or their children were able to improve slightly their occupational standing or to purchase their own home. It was much less likely, however, that either unskilled or semiskilled workers would move directly into high or low white-collar positions, although their children were more likely to do so. Surprisingly, there was little difference between America and Europe in regard to overall career mobility, but there was slightly more upward mobility among unskilled workers in the United States than in Europe (Kaeble, 1985).

But was education a key factor in fostering social mobility among unskilled or semiskilled workers and their children? According to most revisionists, the answer is a clear no. Based on a study of three nineteenth-century Canadian cities, Harvey Graff concludes:

> Social thought and social ideals have, for the past two centuries, stressed the preemption of ascription by achievement as the basis of success and mobility, and the importance of education and literacy in overcoming disadvantages deriving from social origins. In the three cities, in 1861, however, ascription remained dominant. Only rarely was the achievement of literacy sufficient to counteract the depressing effects of inherited characteristics, of ethnicity, race, and sex. The process of stratification, with its basis in rigid social inequality, ordered the illiterates as it did those who were educated. Only at the level of skilled work and its rewards did literacy carry a meaningful influence. Literacy, overall, did not have an independent impact on the social structure. (1979: 114–15)

Similarly, Michael Katz and his colleagues examined the impact of school attendance on social mobility in Hamilton, Ontario, in 1861 and also concluded that education was not an important factor: "School attendance itself, it is important to stress, did virtually nothing to promote occupational mobility. With other factors held constant, school attendance exerted no influence on the occupation of young men traced from one decade to another" (Katz, Doucet, and Stern, 1982: 275).

In contrast, such scholars as Thernstrom have implicitly assumed in their studies that education was a major factor in social mobility in the nineteenth century. Unfortunately, most of the early studies of the relation between education and social mobility in nineteenth-century America are so flawed methodologically that one cannot draw any reliable conclusions from them (Vinovskis, 1994).

Several studies have appeared recently, including some by a conceptually and methodologically more sophisticated generation of revisionist scholars, that address this question. Whereas earlier scholars, such as Bowles and Gintis (1976), argued that schools simply reproduced the existing capitalist structure by excluding children of working-class families from them and then discriminating against the few who did enter, David Labaree's study of the Central High School of Philadelphia found that: "Students obtained admission to the school through a mixture of class background and academic ability. However, once admitted, they found themselves in a model meritocracy where academic performance was the only characteristic that determined who would receive the school's valuable diploma. Therefore, although middle-class students were still the primary beneficiaries of the high school, since they constituted the majority of those admitted, this class effect was mediated through a form of meritocracy that held all students to the same rigorous academic standard" (Labaree, 1988: 37).

If Labaree's study demonstrates that working-class children, once admitted to a high school, could do just as well as middle-class children, what about their subsequent occupation mobility? The study of Central High School did not trace the students to their jobs; but an analysis of the intergenerational mobility of grammar and high school students in Somerville, Massachusetts, in the second half of the nineteenth century did. Reed Ueda discovered that: "The blue-collar son who was raised in the suburb and obtained the high school credential had powerful advantages over the average blue-collar son in Boston in obtaining white-collar employment. Blue-collar sons who went to high school in Somerville achieved a higher and faster rate of entry into the white-collar field than blue-collar sons in Boston of all levels of schooling" (1987: 179).

The most sophisticated study of late-nineteenth- and early-twentieth-century social mobility is Joel Perlmann's logit analysis of schooling and occupational achievement in Providence, Rhode Island, between 1880 and 1935. Even after controlling for the effects of family background, for most children some high school education (but not necessarily having graduated) was a great advantage occupationally: "The suspicion that secondary schooling did not help working-class boys, or immigrant working-class boys, who received it cannot be sustained. Education did not merely reflect the advantages of birth. Immigrant working-class boys who reached high school entered much more attractive occupations than others of similar social backgrounds" (1988: 38).

A high school education was not equally useful for everyone in Providence. Perlmann found that while white children of poor and immigrant parents benefited from entering high school, African-American children who received some high school education still faced almost insurmountable racial job discrimination. As a result, although many African-American children in Providence attended the high school and did well academically, education by itself was not sufficient to overcome the racial barriers to their social mobility.

Conclusion

Americans have always been concerned about disadvantaged children, but the ways they have tried to help them has varied considerably. Part of the nineteenth-century concern about poor children stemmed from a fear of what would happen to society if the next generation did not share its elders' values and goals, and part grew out of Christian benevolence toward the less fortunate . Whatever the source of that concern—and it was complex and mixed—there was general agreement that it was easier to change the child than to reform the adult. Most nineteenth-century Americans also saw education as an effective means for guiding and controlling the development of disadvantaged children into productive citizens.

Colonial and nineteenth-century Americans believed that the primary responsibility for education rested with the parents. Over time private and public schools were acknowledged as substitutes for inadequate training at home, but these institutions were never seen as a total replacement for the family. In the nineteenth century, the family and the schools were each expected to play an important role in the upbringing of the child.

We need to return to this idea—that both the family and the schools have an important responsibility in the education of children. Compared to colonial or nineteenth-century Americans, most parents today neglect their role as educators in the home. Although we should not idealize parental involvement in education in the past, at least it was a goal commonly accepted by nineteenth-century Americans.

Nineteenth-century Americans also established special educational programs for poor children. Monitorial charity schools, Sunday schools, and infant schools were designed to help poor children overcome their disadvantaged family backgrounds. Efforts were later made to integrate poor and middle-class children in public schools. Although we should not always applaud the results of their efforts (especially in those cases of late-nineteenth-century tracking, where poor children were systematically excluded from more academically oriented training), on the whole children from poor and disadvantaged backgrounds often received classroom education roughly comparable to their more fortunate compatriots—especially since the more rigid neighborhood segregation by class and wealth occurred only after the Civil War.

Nineteenth-century Americans were open to innovative programs to help educate poor children and frequently borrowed ideas and models from other countries. We need to recapture that openness and experiment more with alternative ways of helping disadvantaged children through our schools. We also need more awareness of comparable educational efforts in other countries, such as Japan and Germany, and a willingness to learn from their educational programs. We cannot afford to be as insular in our educational knowledge and policies as we have been.

Most nineteenth-century Americans believed that those who were hard working—even if they came from disadvantaged backgrounds—could succeed. Although their faith in the openness of their society was exaggerated and did not pay enough attention to the structural components of inequality, it did foster a climate of opinion in which individuals were led to believe that everyone could succeed through his or her own efforts. Today, while acknowledging and working to eliminate the structural impediments to social mobility, we also must stress the importance of individual and family efforts in getting ahead. The recent educational successes of the children of the boat people provide testimony to the role of family and cultural values in motivating disadvantaged students to excel in schools.

Surprisingly, most early nineteenth-century Americans did not emphasize education as a key to either individual success or economic growth. The notion that education is central to economic growth was explored and publicized only after the efforts of Horace Mann and others in the 1840s and 1850s. But earlier Americans did recognize the importance of moral development in building good citizens and workers. Today, in our discussions of the economic productivity of education, we often fail to acknowledge the importance that values and character play in preparing the next generation.

Contrary to the strong and often-cited claims of the revisionists of the 1960s and 1970s, it does appear that schooling in nineteenth-century America promoted individual social mobility. Although so far we have few methodologically sound studies on this issue and almost all of them are confined to students who entered high schools, the weight of the evidence suggests that schooling did matter. This is not to imply that children of poor parents were not disadvantaged—they clearly were. Nor does it imply that schools could overcome all of the disadvantages of poverty for the individual. But it does suggest that schools did more than just reproduce the existing capitalist structure—they also provided some real opportunities for advancement.

Finally, schooling by itself is of limited value if society refuses to acknowledge and reward those with better educational preparation and training. Unless successful students in school have equal or near-equal access to better jobs and other material rewards, any advantages conferred by further schooling will be quickly lost. African-Americans in the nineteenth century not only faced discrimination in schooling, but even those who were educated could not compete effectively with whites in the labor force. As a result, the great enthusiasm and interest in public schooling among African-Americans after the Civil War began to wane by the early twentieth century when they realized that education had little impact on their subsequent occupational opportunities. Therefore, current educational campaigns to help poor and disadvantaged students must be accompanied by serious and sustained efforts to eliminate any remaining discrimination in our society on the basis of class, ethnicity, race, or gender.

Although this review of nineteenth-century efforts to help poor and disadvantaged children through schooling does not and cannot lead to any simple or mechanical prescription for how to organize or implement comparable programs today, it should reinforce our commitment to helping disadvantaged children through schools. In the past, education has played an important complementary role in efforts to help poor children have equal access to the full range of opportunities in society, and I think it can continue to do so today.

Notes

This chapter appeared in an earlier form in *American Behavioral Scientist* 35, no. 3 (Jan./ Feb. 1992): 313–31. Reprinted by permission of Sage Publications, Inc.

1. For an overview of seventeenth-century educational developments, see also chap. 1.

2. See also chap. 1 for a discussion of more recent studies of literacy that find a higher rate of female literacy than Lockridge's estimate.

3. Trends in antebellum high school attendance are discussed in chap. 8.

4. See chap. 11.

5. See chap. 5 for an in-depth discussion of Mann's beliefs about the economic value of education.

6. Pestalozzi's work was also enormously influential in the infant school movement as discussed in chap. 2.

Chapter 5 / *Horace Mann on the Economic Productivity of Education*

During the past decade economists have become increasingly aware of the economic value of educational improvements. Although there is no consensus on the rate of return to investments in education, most economists agree that education is one of the major factors in economic growth (Bowman, 1966; Schultz, 1961a). Historians have also begun to investigate the role of education in America's past. Some economic historians have tried to assess the contribution of education to the economic growth of nineteenth-century America (Fishlow, 1966; Solomon, 1969). Others have reexamined the works of writers who stressed the importance of investments in human resources (Carlton, 1908).[1] Educational historians have focused on the economic arguments used by nineteenth-century Americans to justify larger and better public school systems (Curti, 1965; Katz, 1968; Kendall, 1968). Yet, since few investigators have attempted to explore in depth the origins of this economic rationale, considerable ambiguity continues to persist about the actual motives of the early school reformers.

Horace Mann is a pivotal figure in these discussions of the pecuniary value of education.[2] In his famous *Fifth Annual Report* he tried to estimate the economic value of education, and as a result he was to a large degree responsible for popularizing the view that education was an economic benefit to the entire community.[3] Unfortunately, the educational historians who have discussed Mann's economic ideas have neither analyzed them sufficiently nor considered the reasons why he chose to emphasize them in his *Report*. Economic historians, by contrast, have either ignored Mann's contributions, or they have dealt with them casually.

In this chapter I shall explain why Mann waited until his *Fifth Annual Report* to stress the economic value of education. In addition, I shall examine Mann's methodology for estimating the economic productivity of education to determine the validity of his procedures. Finally, I shall attempt to assess his contributions as an innovator and as a champion of this view.

Evaluating Mann's reasons for advocating educational reforms is complicated by the fact that he resorted to many different justifications and modes of presenting his views. Some scholars have exaggerated a particular aspect of his efforts and ignored the general framework of his ideas, concentrating only on those selections that support their interpretation.

There have been many attempts to categorize Mann's arguments for education. One useful summary presents the following seven categories: (1) education is necessary for the preservation of a republic, (2) it helps to prevent class differentiation, (3) it tends to diminish crime, (4) it reduces the amount of poverty and distress in society, (5) it increases production, (6) it is the natural right of all individuals, and (7) it rectifies false values prevalent in society.[4] In his twelve years as the secretary of the Massachusetts Board of Education, Horace Mann had ample opportunity to resort to all of these arguments. He tended to favor those rooted in moral principles or civic virtues rather than the appeals based on economic self-interest. Nevertheless, it was often necessary for Mann to appeal to the self-interest of his audiences to achieve his goals.

Merle Curti has asserted that Horace Mann was always trying to demonstrate the economic value of education: "Thus we find him constantly endeavoring to prove that universal education would promote prosperity. As his experience in the temperance movement had taught him, it was well to appeal to self-interest; and this conviction was strengthened by the emphasis that phrenology placed on the basic importance of the propensity of acquisitiveness" (1965: 112).[5] A closer examination of Mann's career leads to a somewhat different conclusion. Although he was always aware of the economic considerations, he was not constantly trying to stress the profitability of the educational system.

Before becoming an educational reformer, Mann was active crusading for the abolition of imprisonment for debt, the establishment of an insane asylum, the support of a school for the blind, and the temperance movement.[6] Although his motivation in each instance was humanitarian, he gained statewide prominence in the temperance movement by his economic analysis of the benefits of temperance to grocers and retailers (Mann, 1834). In his early annual reports, he displayed an interest in calculating the costs of alternative types of school reforms (MBE 1, 1838: 30–31), and there is scattered evidence in his writings before 1841 that he was aware of a relation between education and economic prosperity (MBE 1, 1838: 56; 3, 1840: 85–87, 96).

Yet Horace Mann did not emphasize the economic value of education until his *Fifth Annual Report*. His previous remarks on the subject were more in the nature of asides rather than direct appeals to self-interest. His reluctance to stress the economic value of education must be seen in the context of the directives from the Board of Education, his views on the role of economics in society, and the political situation confronting the Board of Education.

Although Horace Mann and the board were eager to undertake the task of "awakening a new interest in the cause of school education" through the annual reports, county conventions of educators, and the *Common School Journal*, they were reluctant to resort to outright propaganda in the annual reports (MBE 1, 1838: 7–8). The directive to the secretary of the Board of Education called for a much narrower and more objective role (MBE 1, 1838: 21). Consequently, in his first four annual reports, Mann focused more on specific educational issues than on a general defense of the program from an economic point of view. In his lectures before the county conventions, where he discussed the value of a universal educational system, he concentrated on the importance of education for teaching moral values and for preserving a republican form of government. Although he mentioned the connection between education and prosperity, he did not pursue this in detail.[7] Mann minimized economic values because he regarded this appeal as less desirable than those based on loftier principles (Mann and Mann, 1891: 2:152–54; MBE 3, 1840: 92).

Mann recognized that certain minimal physical needs had to be satisfied before the development of higher powers could be pursued (MBE 5, 1842: 82–83), but he also felt that these animal appetites had to be continually curbed (Mann and Mann, 1891: 2:144, 149–50, 163–67). In Mann's view, the problem in contemporary society was that people were pursuing their narrowly selfish interests to the detriment of themselves and their community (Mann and Mann, 1891: 2:159, 177–78). The role of education was to prevent these unfortunate developments from occurring in the next generation (Mann and Mann, 1891: 2:80).

Horace Mann was pragmatic enough to know when to compromise his principles. Thus he advocated the use of the state school fund as a pecuniary inducement for the creation of more school libraries and the election of more conscientious school committeemen (MBE 1, 1838: 46; 3, 1840: 98–100). He regretted these deviations from moral appeals because he believed that people motivated by altruistic motives worked harder and more efficiently than those pursuing material interests (MBE 1, 1838: 46; Mann and Mann, 1891: 2:171). Whenever possible, Mann appealed to people's nobler instincts because he felt calls to economic self-interest would only encourage the very evils he hoped to eliminate through educational reforms (Mann, *Journal*, June 9, 1838). Besides, such tactics seemed unnecessary in his early years as secretary when Mann was confident that enlightening the public would lead to reforms in the school system.

Mann was not a naive idealist. He recognized the formidable obstacles facing any attempt to reform the existing system. Most people were apathetic about the schools, and the legislature had created the Board of Education without giving it any coercive powers over the locally controlled schools (Mann, *Journal*, Aug. 19, Sept. 11, 24, 1838; Sept. 15, 1840). He was confident, however, that his reform efforts would eventually triumph as more and more people recognized the importance of properly educating the young (Mann, *Journal*, June 30, 1837; Oct. 10, 1838). Although he encountered numerous discouraging setbacks in his trips across the state, there were also signs of progress in many towns (MBE 2, 1839: 29–31, 33; 3, 1840: 35–39; 4, 1841: 10–13; Mann, *Journal*, Sept. 4, 29, 1838). The political situation in the state also seemed favorable for the future of school reforms. Although the Massachusetts legislature had left the Board of Education only the power of persuasion, many of the board's recommendations had been enacted into law.[8] Furthermore, Mann's successful career in the legislature had earned him many friends on whom he could count for further assistance.[9]

Thus, Horace Mann in his first years as secretary of the board saw neither the need for, nor the value of, justifying his educational crusade from an economic point of view. By the time of the *Fifth Annual Report*, however, unexpected developments in the state and the legislature convinced him to defend the school reforms as an economic benefit. First, it became increasingly apparent that many of the towns in the Commonwealth simply were not interested in better schools. Appeals to their moral principles had had little effect; perhaps they would welcome change if it were demonstrated that reforms were economically profitable.[10]

Another factor was the economic depression of 1839–43. During the period of expansive growth in the 1800s, Massachusetts leaders listened sympathetically to demands for financial aid to alleviate inequities within the state. At the local level, taxpayers were willing to vote increased expenditures for a variety of projects, including education. The Panic of 1837, caused by a temporary maladjustment in the internal monetary situation and a sharp drop in cotton prices on the world market, interrupted this prosperity. There was a slight recovery in 1838, but by 1839 the depression gripped the nation with a severity comparable to that of the depression of 1929 (McGrane, 1924; North, 1961). The depression was less severe in New England, but Massachusetts suffered as the demand for manufactured goods and agricultural produce declined. Throughout the state there were efforts to cut back on all nonessential expenditures. Reformers now faced hostile taxpayers who were no longer satisfied by discussions based merely on moral principles.

The third and major factor that caused Mann to change his approach was the threatening political situation in 1840–41. Although it is difficult to assess the relative importance of the motivations of the opponents of the board, there were five main points of dissatisfaction: religious, political, organizational, economic, and personal.

Certain religious leaders had opposed the board from its inception because it had refused to sanction the use of religious books in the classroom. These opponents were mainly orthodox Calvinists who felt that Mann was destroying the vital connection between religion and education. However, some prominent clergymen, such as Thomas Robbins, supported Mann throughout the ensuing controversy (Culver, 1929: 41–110, 127–62).[11]

The Board of Education also faced political opposition. Although the board had tried to avoid partisan politics, its opponents remembered that it had been created by the previous Whig administration. Orestes Brownson, editor of the *Boston Quarterly Review* and a prominent Democrat, felt that the board was an instrument for spreading Whig ideology. This partisan hostility was weakened by the fact that a few members of the board, such as Robert Rantoul, Jr., were Democrats. Furthermore, although there was a Democratic governor in 1840, the main challenge came from the legislature, which was firmly controlled by the Whigs (Culver, 1929: 127–31).[12]

Opponents of a centralized school system formed a third group that was dissatisfied with the board. They feared that the present board was slowly extending its authority in order to imitate the highly centralized Prussian school system. Many prominent Democrats, such as Governor Marcus Morton, were in this category.[13]

Some legislators felt that the additional expenses accrued by the Board of Education and the normal schools were fiscally unsound in a depression. During 1840–41 members of both parties were trying to establish themselves as the champions of retrenchment by eliminating unnecessary expenditures. In 1841, the House Committee on Retrenchment requested that the Committee on Education reexamine the necessity of continuing the Board of Education (Culver, 1929: 152–53).[14]

Finally, there were individuals whose opposition was the result of personal conflicts. For example, Frederick Emerson of Boston opposed the board because he had been excluded from membership and because his books had been rejected for use in school libraries (Culver, 1929: 145–49).

Although these groups were active in 1840–41, the continuation of the board did not become an important statewide political issue during that year (Culver, 1929: 130–31; Darling, 1925: 239–42).[15] Instead, the challenge was concentrated in the legislature where a small, dedicated band of opponents attempted to form a broad coalition against Horace Mann and his supporters. Most members of the legislature were rather indifferent on the question of the

Board of Education; however, many legislators were determined to eliminate any unnecessary spending, and the religious opponents of the board sought to exploit this sentiment. Thus, the opponents tried to demonstrate that the Board of Education and the normal schools that trained teachers were not only economically wasteful, but morally dangerous to the Commonwealth.[16]

Horace Mann recognized this political danger as he "welcomed" the new year in his diary: "I enter upon another year—not without some gloom and apprehension—for political madmen are raising voices and are against the board" (Mann, *Journal*, Jan. 5, 1840). His fears were soon confirmed.

Marcus Morton, the newly elected Democratic governor, favored the cause of public education but doubted whether the Board of Education was a necessary part of it (Mass., House, *Document*, 9: 29–30). On March 7, 1840, the House Committee on Education proposed a bill to abolish the board and the normal schools. Four days later, a minority of that committee replied by issuing a report defending the board and the normal schools as essential to the educational system of Massachusetts (Mass., House, *Document*, 49, 53). When the bill to abolish the board and the normal schools reached the floor of the House, it was defeated 182–245 (Culver, 1929: 140–44). Horace Mann was overjoyed by this victory and the subsequent defeat of Governor Morton in the fall of 1840.

But Mann rejoiced too soon. The new Whig governor, John Davis, proved to be mainly interested in his own popularity and felt that defending educational reforms was a political liability. The same forces that had opposed the board the previous year once again attempted to abolish it (Culver, 1929: 152–53; Mann, *Journal*, Nov. 29, 1840; Dec. 12, 1841). The supporters of the board were in control of the House Committee on Education in 1841; the minority of that committee proposed a bill to abolish the Board of Education. The opponents postponed action on the bill until the closing days of the legislative session when many of Mann's supporters had already returned home. Yet the continued existence of the Board of Education was upheld by a vote of 131 to 114 (Mann and Mann, 1891: 1:150–51). Horace Mann was shaken by the unexpected weakness of his position. A switch of only nine votes would have destroyed the work he had so diligently labored to promote.

Instead of despairing, Mann reaffirmed his dedication and resolved not to rest until he had convinced the legislature and the people of the Commonwealth of the need for continued school reforms. If this meant altering his tactics, he would do so: "People will bear truths if expressed in one way, but they will crucify one for expressing in another; and I have to select the way, if possible, that does not lead to crucification;—not so much, however, as I believe on my own account as on account of the cause" (Mann, *Journal*, May 24, 1841).

Horace Mann realized that it was now necessary to demonstrate to the legislature and to the citizens of Massachusetts that education was a sound economic investment. The first indication of his decision to stress the connection between education and economic prosperity is revealed in his diary, where he recorded his intention to go to Lowell to interview several factory managers (Mann, *Journal*, Sept. 12, 1841).[17] After this interview, he noted that: "Questions founded on these views I have put to them, and they have answered in a way attesting the value of education beyond my expectations" (Mann, *Journal*, Sept. 14, 1841). Confirmed in his views and hopes, Mann now set about writing his famous *Fifth Annual Report*.

Mann's thesis in the *Fifth Annual Report* was that education was the most productive enterprise an individual or a community could undertake: "They [his evidence] seem to prove incontestibly that education is not only a moral renovator, and a multiplier of intellectual power, but that it is also the most prolific parent of material riches. It has a right, therefore, not only to be included in the grand inventory of a nation's resources, but to be placed at the very head of the inventory. It is not only the most honest and honorable, but the surest means of amassing property" (MBE 5, 1842: 100–101).[18]

He arrived at this conclusion by noting that some areas with few natural resources are often more prosperous than those possessing them in abundance. Massachusetts, which was relatively poor in minerals and good soil, produced more wealth than most other states in the Union. Hence the key to prosperity was not natural resources, but an educated populace (MBE 5, 1842: 104–5). Similarly, Massachusetts, with its large percentage of educated citizens, had been able to overcome its numerous disadvantages in order to compete successfully with industries in England:

> It is a fact of universal notoriety, that the manufacturing population of England, as a class, work for half, or less than half the wages of our own. The cost of machinery there, also, is but about half as much as the cost of the same articles with us; while our capital when loaned, produces nearly double the rate of English interest. Yet, against these grand adverse circumstances, our manufacturers, with a small percentage of tariff successfully compete with English capitalists, in many branches of manufacturing business. No explanation can be given of this extraordinary fact, which does not take into account, the difference of education between the operatives in the two countries. (MBE 5, 1842: 110–11)[19]

Education benefited the economy in several different ways. It was essential for rational decision making and long-range planning: "Education is an antecedent agency, for it must enlighten mankind in the choice of pursuits, it must guide them in the selection and use of the most appropriate means, it must impart that confidence and steadiness of purpose which results from comprehending the connections of a long train of events and seeing the end from the beginning, or all enterprises will terminate in ruin" (MBE 5, 1842: 101).

In addition, educated workers were more punctual and reliable in their work. Furthermore, the habits of industry and frugality would make them more useful citizens in the community (MBE 5, 1842: 85).[20] Whereas the uneducated laborer had to be told what to do at every step in the operation of a machine, the educated worker could perform his duties without constant supervision. As the machinery in factories became more complex and required more skill in operating them, the educated worker was less likely to damage expensive equipment (MBE 5, 1842: 85). Education also provided the knowledge necessary to use the best available techniques of production. Thus the educated farmer would rely on chemical fertilizers and crop rotation to preserve the fertility of the soil (MBE 5, 1842: 102–3).

New labor-saving inventions resulted in a tremendous increase in production during this period. Mann noted that education provided workers with the background knowledge and proper attitude to encourage them to seek more efficient methods. This "inventiveness" distinguished American workers from their English counterparts (MBE 5, 1842: 104–6). The advantages of an education made it increasingly difficult for uneducated workers to earn a living. This was evidenced by the higher wages and more rapid promotions that workers with a common school background received (MBE 5, 1842: 85–86).

To prove his assertions, Horace Mann attempted to gather statistical evidence by sending questionnaires to businessmen who employed large numbers of workers. He felt their replies would be the most useful for assessing the difference in productivity between literate and illiterate workers because: (1) their contact with large numbers of workers would enable them to decide how much of the productive differences between workers was the result of educational background rather than differences in natural ability, and (2) in large manufacturing establishments "the absurd and adventitious distinctions of society do not intrude"—that is, factories tend to hire and promote on the basis of economic value rather than personal connections (MBE 5, 1842: 83–85).[21]

In making his calculations of the economic value of education, Mann should be commended for trying to select a sample in which differences due to innate ability or favoritism would be minimized. Unfortunately, by concentrating on large-scale manufacturing operations, he was unable to discern the differences in the economic value of education for agriculture, industry, and commerce. Furthermore, the rates of return might have been quite different for any of the numerous smaller manufacturing establishments in Massachusetts.[22]

A more serious and unnecessary weakness was the manner in which he posed his questions. Throughout the questionnaire and in his correspondence with the businessmen, Mann clearly suggested the answers he expected to receive. For example, he concluded his letter to them with this observation: "I am aware, my Dear Sir, that to every intelligent and reflecting man, these inquiries will seem superfluous and nugatory; and your first impulse may be, to put some such interrogatory to me in reply, as whether the sun has any influence on vegetable growth, or whether it is expedient to have windows in our houses for the admission of light. I acknowledge the close analogy of the cases in point of self-evidence" (MBE 5, 1842: 89). This weakness was compounded by the fact that in several cases Mann sent questionnaires to businessmen only after he had discussed the subject with them and knew that they would confirm his conclusions.[23]

As a result, the responses to the questionnaire were hopelessly biased. Nevertheless, these questions and their answers are useful in that they reveal how some Massachusetts businessmen viewed the economic value of education. In presenting the results of this survey, Mann simply reprinted four replies that he asserted were representative of the letters he had received.[24] Needless to say, each of the four correspondents enthusiastically confirmed Mann's assumptions about the economic value of education. Several interesting aspects of the replies are worth noting.

Although each of the respondents mentioned the ability of educated workers to work more efficiently than others, none of them emphasized the importance of the "inventiveness" that Mann stressed throughout the *Fifth Annual Report*. Instead, they tended to concentrate on the fact that these workers were able to follow directions better, were more punctual and reliable, and were less likely to be unreasonable during periods of labor turmoil. This last point seemed to be particularly significant to businessmen who feared that uneducated workers would resort to violence during labor disputes; they pointed out that educated workers had a soothing effect on the more rowdy ones (MBE 5, 1842: 90–100).

Two respondents tried to estimate the actual economic value of education in terms of higher wages. J. K. Mills noted that literate workers earned on the average about 27 percent more than illiterate ones; J. Clark arrived at a figure of 18.5 percent. They then calculated the wage differential between the highest-paid literate workers and the lowest-paid illiterate workers. Mills found that this difference was 66 percent, whereas Clark put it at 40 percent (MBE 5, 1842: 91, 98).

Throughout the *Fifth Annual Report*, Mann referred to these replies as conclusive evidence in support of his views, but this evidence was more impressionistic than statistical. He felt it was "practicable to determine with arithmetical exactness, the productions of one individual and one class as compared with those of another individual and another class" (MBE 5, 1842: 84). Nevertheless his own discussions of the rate of return to primary education tended to be vague and rhetorical. The only explicit calculation that Mann made yielded a result of about 50 percent. This was apparently a rough average of the results obtained from the two respondents noted above: "From the facts stated in the letters of Messrs. Mills and Clark . . . , it appears that there is a difference of not less than fifty percent between the earnings of the least educated and of the best educated operatives,—between those who make their marks, instead of writing their names, and those who have been acceptably employed in schoolkeeping" (MBE 5, 1842: 111–12).

There are problems with both Mann's method of reaching his figure of 50 percent and his application of that result. In making his calculations, Mann uses figures based on the *extremes* of the literate and illiterate workers rather than on the *averages* of those two groups. He was looking at the unusual cases rather than the typical ones. If he had used the average wage earned in each group, his estimate of the return to education would have been about 23 percent (MBE 5, 1842: 91, 98). Furthermore, when he tried to ascertain the increase in production as a result of educated female workers, he became hopelessly confused (MBE 5, 1842: 111–12).

Mann made many other mistakes in his estimate of the productivity of the common schools. For instance, he asked the businessmen to distinguish between the productivity of literate and illiterate workers. Yet the problem for Mann was not to demonstrate that everyone should have enough schooling to be literate. Most people in Massachusetts agreed with that view. He needed to prove that additional education was economically profitable; but he did not address his questions to that issue. Using figures applying to the extremes of literate and illiterate workers was no solution because it exaggerated the value of education to the typical wage earner. The question he should have asked was: are workers with twelve years of common school education more productive than those with only five years of schooling.[25]

Mann also equated the rate of return from education to parents with its value to the community. This fails to recognize that the rate of return to parents will be always higher because the cost of education is shared among all the taxpayers. In other words, the return to a family is increased because it does not bear the full cost of the education although it receives all the benefits of that training.[26]

Using wages to measure the productivity of education is probably the most practical method for purposes of calculation. This, however, fails to take note of the imperfections in the labor market. Wages are often the result of the relative bargaining power of the employer and the employee rather than the productive contribution of the worker (Leibenstein, 1965). Another flaw is that Mann did not calculate the additional cost of education that resulted from income lost because children in school are unable to work. This was particularly important during the 1840s when many children worked in factories from the age of ten.[27] Furthermore, in comparing the wages of workers, Mann should have considered their ages. Less educated workers tend to reach their maximum level of earning earlier in life than those with more education (Becker, 1964).

As a result of these and other errors in the methodology, Mann's estimate must be viewed as an educated guess rather than a scientific calculation. The manner in which the data are summarized in the *Fifth Annual Report* made it impossible to recalculate the economic productivity of education. It is difficult to make adjustments for Mann's various mistakes because some of them would increase his estimate while others would decrease it. At the same time, there is no other information with which to compare Mann's conclusions. It is likely, however, that Mann's figure of 50 percent for primary education greatly exaggerates the actual productivity of education during that period. A much more likely estimate would be in the range of 10 to 20 percent.

Horace Mann devoted a large part of the *Fifth Annual Report* to a discussion of the economic productivity of education because he saw this as necessary to winning additional support at a time when the Board of Education was facing an increasingly hostile legislature. He expressed the hope that the report would be popular: "I have got out my Fifth Annual Report. It is mainly addressed to the organ of acquisitiveness and therefore stands some chance of being popular" (Mann and Mann, 1891: 1:162). His prediction of the success of that report was quickly confirmed. The *Report* was hailed throughout the nation and abroad as evidence of the importance of further school reforms. The New York legislature ordered 18,000 copies to be printed. Mann's work was also distributed overseas and even translated into German.

Although there were other factors involved, Mann's demonstration of the economic value of education was one of the main reasons for the increased popularity of the Board of Education among the lawmakers. Whereas a defense of the board had been a definite political risk in 1841, by 1843 the board had acquired such wide support that most politicians were no longer willing to seriously consider abolishing it (Culver, 1929: 163–80). Mann's decision to justify the expenditure of public funds for education on the basis of its economic profitability proved to be a successful tactic.

During the 1820s and 1830s some educators and political leaders had tried to point out the economic value of education, but their discussions tended to be rhetorical rather than analytical; Horace Mann's writings on this subject before 1841 fit into this category (Curti, 1965: 50–100). When Mann wrote the *Fifth Annual Report,* he claimed originality for his hypothesis that education was the most productive factor in the economy (MBE 5, 1842: 111). In fact, he chided statesmen and political economists for totally neglecting education in their discussions of the American economy. Although Mann was correct in charging that most scholars and politicians had ignored the importance of education, he exaggerated the complete lack of information on this subject. For example, Willard Phillips, a prominent Boston economist, had noted the economic importance of education in his treatise on the American economy in 1828.[28]

Although a few economists and educators had recognized the connection between education and prosperity, Horace Mann popularized the idea; this fact was acknowledged by many of his contemporaries. A group of prominent Boston businessmen praised his achievements in 1845: "You have demonstrated that the arm of industry is served, and the wealth of the country is augmented, in proportion to the diffusion of knowledge, so that each humble school-house is to be regarded, not only as a nursery of souls, but a mine of riches" (letter to Horace Mann, 1845). And John D. Philbrick, a distinguished educator, recalled in 1863 that the *Fifth Annual Report* had "probably done more than all other publications written within the past twenty-five years to convince capitalists of the value of elementary instruction as a means of increasing the value of labor" (quoted in Curti, 1965: 113). Even more significant was the fact that Horace Mann was one of the first to try to calculate the actual value of education. Although his analysis lacked the methodological rigor of today's surveys, it was a commendable effort to quantify what had hitherto been mere speculation.

The great success of the *Report* induced Horace Mann to continue to mention the economic value of education in his later writings, but he did not introduce any new concepts or data.[29] As far as Mann was concerned, he had already conclusively demonstrated the profitability of education in 1842, and he saw no need to muster more evidence.

Yet Mann never forgot that the appeals based on the economic advantages of education were inferior to those derived from loftier principles. He closed his *Fifth Annual Report* with the following reminder: "But, notwithstanding all I have said of the value of education, in a pecuniary sense, and of its power to improve and elevate the outward domestic and social condition of all men, yet, in closing this report, I should do injustice to my feelings, did I abstain from declaring that to my own mind, this tribute to its worth, however well deserved, is still the faintest note of praise which can be uttered, in honor of so noble a theme;—and that, however deserving of attention may be the *economical* view of the subject which I have endeavored to present, yet it is one that dwindles into insignificance when compared with those loftier and more scared attributes of the cause" (MBE 5, 1842: 120).

Whether Horace Mann's hypothesis of the importance of education to the development of the nineteenth-century economy will prove to be correct or not must await further research by economic historians. But there can be no doubt of his important pioneering efforts and his significant contribution to spreading that idea throughout the country.

Notes

This chapter appeared in an earlier form in *New England Quarterly* 43, no.4 (December 1970): 550–71. Reprinted with permission.

1. Although Carlton (1908) discussed the ideas of educators and politicians on this issue, he ignored the writings of political economists. Some of the articles on European economists also provide useful information on education and productivity (Johnson, 1964; Kiker, 1966; West, 1964).

2. For a discussion of Mann's views on the moral and social value of education, see chap. 3.

3. Massachusetts Board of Education, *Fifth Annual Report of the Board of Education Together with the Fifth Annual Report of the Secretary of the Board* (Boston, 1842). Hereafter cited as MBE 5, 1842.

4. Adopted with some minor revisions from Carlton (1908: 45). When Mann discussed the economic productivity of education he focused on the fifth category. I will also focus on this issue here because it coincides with the practice of most modern economists. It must be remembered, however, reducing crime and poverty has a positive effect on the total wealth of the community. For Mann's analysis of these factors, see *Annual Report* (MBE 11, 1848: 39–135; 12, 1849: 53–63). For a modern attempt to deal with the benefits of reducing crime through education, see Weisbrod (1962).

5. Most scholars disagree on the significance of Mann's discussions of the economic value of education, but they have accepted Curti's contention that these appeals were relatively constant throughout Mann's career as secretary of the Board of Education (Kendall, 1968; Messerli, 1965).

6. For an excellent summary of Horace Mann's early career, see Messerli (1963).

7. Mann's 1838 lecture "The Necessity of Education in a Republican Government" was one of his longest early discussions of the value of education. In it he made only a brief mention of the economic value of education (Mann and Mann, 1891: 2:143–88).

8. One of the main criticisms of the board in 1840 was that the legislature accepted its recommendations almost automatically (Mass. House, *Document*, 49: 3). Although this criticism exaggerates the willingness of the legislature to follow the advice of the board, it is true that many of the board's recommendations were followed.

9. The only major threat to the Board of Education in this early period was the controversy over the use of religious materials in the schools. For an excellent discussion of this, see Culver (1929: 41–110). The supporters of educational reform did not feel that this challenge had damaged the board (see letter by Rev. Jacob Abbott, Dec. 7, 1839 [quoted by Culver, 1929: 132]), but as the events of 1840–41 demonstrated, this optimism was mistaken.

10. This was a very important consideration for Mann. He prefaced his discussion of the productivity of education by stating that the towns of the Commonwealth would increase their school appropriations if it were demonstrated to them that schools are economically profitable (MBE 5, 1842: 81).

11. Culver (1929) provides the best analysis of the crisis of the Board of Education in 1840–41. His stress on the importance of religious opposition is correct.

12. For a detailed examination of the complex political situation in Massachusetts during this period, see Darling (1925). For Mann's mention of the partisan attack on the Board, see Mann (*Journal*, Feb. 2, 1840).

13. Fear of a highly centralized school system is evident in the report of the House Committee on Education to abolish the board and the normal schools (Mass. House, *Document*, 49: 4–5).

14. Culver (1929: 152–53) asserts that the stress on economy meausures came in the 1841 legislature. But in a letter to George Combe on Feb. 22, 1840, Mann emphasized the importance of this issue (Mann and Mann, 1891: 1:123).

15. In fact, Mann doubted if the new governor even knew of the existence of the Board of Education (Mann, *Journal*, Jan. 26, 1840).

16. For Mann to overcome the political danger from this coalition, he had to demonstrate that education was a valuable and an essential service for the citizens of the Commonwealth. As many of these legislators were concerned about the expenses of the state, Mann emphasized the economic value of

his reforms to meet their objections to school reforms.

17. In his *Fifth Annual Report*, Mann mentioned that he had begun to collect data on this question only during the past year (MBE 5, 1842: 83).

18. Unfortunately, most historians have accepted Mann's statistical work without critically analyzing its methodology or assumptions (Curti, 1965: 112–13; Hinsdale, 1913: 168–69; Williams, 1937: 160–61).

19. For an analysis of the differences between British and American development, see Habakkuk (1962).

20. Mann did not go into a discussion of the importance of education for health in the *Fifth Annual Report* because he was saving that aspect for a later report. For his detailed analysis of the health question, see (MBE 6, 1843: 56–160).

21. Mann could have gone one step further by recognizing that the educational system tends to select and encourage individuals with higher I.Q.'s to continue their education. Becker (1960) has tried to calculate this effect by standardizing his data for differences among college and noncollege workers on the basis of test scores. He found that adjusting for differential ability reduces the rate of return on college education from 11 to 9 percent.

22. In calculating the rates of return to education, Mann was comparing the wages of educated and uneducated workers. Modern economists who calculate the direct rate of return to education usually compare lifetime earnings. Much of the methodological weakness of Mann's approach is due to his failure to recognize the importance of distinguishing between differences as measured by current wages rather than lifetime earnings. For the problems of calculating direct rates of return, see Hansen (1963).

23. Mann noted that he visited J. K. Mills and J. Clark in Lowell in September (Mann, *Journal*, Sept. 14, 1841), yet the replies of these two businessmen to Mann's questionnaire were dated December 3 and 5, 1841 (MBE 5, 1842: 90, 97).

24. It is unlikely that Mann had received many more letters than the four he printed. In his analysis of crime in the *Eleventh Annual Report* (MBE 11, 1848: 49–85), he sent out only eight questionnaires.

25. Mann never addressed the problem of different rates of return to education at the various levels of education. For instance, Hansen (1963) calculated that the rate of return for the first two years of education in 1950 was 8.9 percent, whereas it was 29.2 percent for the seventh and eighth year and 13.7 percent for the eleventh and twelfth year.

26. There is an additional factor that must be considered—the tax structure. If there is a progressive tax system, the difference between the private and the social rate of return to education will be diminished because an increasingly large share of the additional income will be regained by the state. However, in the nineteenth century, Massachusetts had a tax structure that was not very progressive, so this factor would be relatively unimportant in this case.

27. Opportunity costs are a major part of the total expenses of education. For a useful discussion of this topic, see Schultz (1961b).

28. For a good background on the economic ideas of Americans during this period, see Dorfman (1946, 1967).

29. The Mann Papers at the Massachusetts Historical Society contain abundant references to the *Fifth Annual Report*; for his fullest summary of the importance of education to prosperity, see *Twelfth Annual Report* (MBE 12, 1849: 53–75).

Chapter 6 / *Immigrants and Schooling*

Most Americans are either immigrants or the descendants of immigrants. As successive waves of immigrants came to the New World, they and their children encountered problems in adapting to a different environment. Many scholars, as well as the public, believe that schools played a key role in that transition, by either facilitating or hindering the immigrants' assimilation into American life.

In this chapter I shall explore the relation between immigrants and schools in four different time periods: colonial America, antebellum America, the late nineteenth and early twentieth centuries, and the post–World War II period. The relation between immigrants and schools varied considerably, not only by the characteristics of different groups of immigrants, but also by the changing nature of the American society and economy when they arrived. Much of the general education of immigrants often occurred outside formal institutions in such areas as neighborhoods and workplaces. Nevertheless, by seeing the changing role of schooling on the lives of immigrants over time, we can develop a better appreciation of the diversity of immigrant experiences in the settling of America.

Immigrants and Schools in Colonial America

For many analysts immigration is almost exclusively a nineteenth- or twentieth-century phenomenon. This is unfortunate because individual and societal responses to colonial America provide a useful context for understanding the experiences of later immigrants.

In his classic analysis of the relation between immigrants and schools in colonial America (1960), Bernard Bailyn portrayed the English family as stable, extended, and patriarchal. Children received almost all of their education in the household, and the rest was supplied by their neighbors. There was little opportunity or need for formal schooling, except for the small minority pursuing professional training.

The early English settlers brought with them the expectation that children and servants would be educated at home. But, according to Bailyn, the colonial family was fragmented and disrupted by the wilderness. The extended family gave way to a nuclear family in which parents experienced great difficulty in mastering the multitude of tasks before them without the assistance of established, stable institutions. Children in some ways proved more adept in coping with these problems, and they challenged their parents' authority and ignored or rejected the traditional restraints placed on them by the church and the local community. With the collapse of traditional sources of authority and the failure of household education, the colonial authorities—particularly in Puritan New England—demanded the creation and maintenance of schools to educate and discipline the next generation. Although most efforts to establish a network of schools failed because of the dispersed population and the lack of adequate wealth, the idea of schools as a major component of education was established in principle if not in fact.

Bailyn's provocative statements about the immense problems facing the first immigrants and their frantic attempts to create schools have not gone unchallenged. Recent studies of sixteenth- and seventeenth-century English families conclude that they were more nuclear and less geographically stable than had been suggested (Laslett, 1965). Similarly, the extent of schools in England appears to have been underestimated (O'Day, 1982; Stone, 1964). Nevertheless, Bailyn's emphasis on the importance of household education has been sustained (Houlbrooke, 1984).

Just as English families were more nuclear and geographically mobile than Bailyn envisioned, so too New England families were more stable and cohesive. Indeed, American demographic historians portray New England families as more prosperous and less endangered than their English counterparts (Greven, 1970; Lockridge, 1970). Thus, the desperation and rationale for building primary schools in the New World now appears less compelling than previously thought. Furthermore, other immigrants, such as the Pilgrims, never shared the Puritan obsession with education although they presumably experienced the same rigors of the trans-Atlantic crossing and making a living in the wilderness as their northern neighbors (Demos, 1980). Finally, the settlers of the Chesapeake, who faced the most severe and disruptive demographic conditions, also do not appear to have placed as much emphasis on providing schooling for their children as the New England Puritans (Rutman and Rutman, 1984).

If Bailyn exaggerated the demographic and geographic disruptions of New England family life, he did not overstate their anxiety about socializing the next generation. Concern about perpetuating their religious ideals and doubts about the ability of the households to catechize children and servants encouraged greater reliance on schools and churches. As a result, the ideal of an educated citizenry and the responsibility of the local communities for helping to achieve it became an accepted part of the New England heritage (Vinovskis, 1987).

Although there is little evidence so far that the schools played a major role in socializing the children of the immigrants throughout most of the colonies, in the North, at least, they complemented the efforts of families and churches. In such colonies as New York and Pennsylvania, where the population was much more ethnically and religiously heterogeneous than in either New England or the Chesapeake, schools were not frequently or extensively used as major instruments for assimilating immigrants or helping them to preserve their cultural heritage.[1] Instead, most immigrants received their education and guidance in their households, churches, and local communities, with only limited exposure to formal schooling (Cremin, 1970). Furthermore, schools played no part in helping the large numbers of African slaves who were brought to the New World cope with their destinies (Boles, 1983).

Immigrants and Schools in Antebellum America

By the mid-nineteenth century, American society differed considerably from its colonial heritage. Major changes after the American Revolution in the economy, political system, immigration, and schools transformed the experiences of newcomers in the antebellum period. During the colonial period, most Americans were either farmers or closely tied to agriculture. Almost everyone lived on a farm or in a rural community. Children anticipated following in the occupational footsteps of their fathers, and most of them saw little need for education or training away from the home. The first half of the nineteenth century witnessed changes in where many Americans lived and worked. The percentage living in towns of more than 2,500 people rose from 5.1 percent in 1790 to 19.8 percent in 1860.[2] More significant was the increase in nonagricultural workers, from 28.1 percent of the labor force in 1820 to 41.0 percent in 1860.[3] While only a small proportion of the increase in nonagricultural occupations was caused by industrialization, the general commercialization of the economy forced more Americans to look beyond their local community. Antebellum children increasingly faced more occupational choices than their colonial predecessors.

As the economy expanded, the relation between the employer and the employee was altered. Particularly significant was the demise in the early nineteenth century of the apprenticeship system, which had provided some colonial youth with the training and experiences necessary to become skilled artisans and craftsmen (Rorabaugh, 1986). In the 1820s and 1830s, workers were gradually forced to seek additional schooling for their children to prepare them for the new employment opportunities because apprenticeship was no longer a viable alternative.[4]

Change in the political system coincided with these economic developments. Following the American Revolution and the ratification of the U.S. Constitution, an increasingly large proportion of the white male electorate became enfranchised and politically active. As a result, while many political conservatives in England questioned the wisdom of schooling for workers, there was a growing consensus in the United States that education was essential as a means of preserving the Republic from mobs and political demagogues. Indeed, much of the widespread support for the expansion of schooling in the first half of the nineteenth century rested on the perceived need for an educated electorate (Kaestle, 1983; Kaestle and Vinovskis, 1980).

About 5 million people moved to the United States between 1820 and 1860. Antebellum migration reached its peak in the 1840s and 1850s, with approximately 4.3 million immigrants arriving mainly from Ireland and the German-speaking states of Central Europe. Most of these immigrants were poor and desperate and competed with native workers for unskilled and semiskilled jobs. Whereas the German-speaking immigrants were more likely to settle in rural areas and the Midwest, the Irish were more likely to remain in urban areas and in the Northeast. Because a large proportion of these immigrants were Catholic, many native Protestants saw them as a threat to the existing political and social order. Not surprisingly, schools were often enlisted in the attempt to change the religion and culture of the children of these immigrants (Taylor, 1971).

Whereas relatively few elementary schools existed in seventeenth-century America, by the mid-nineteenth century schools became commonplace throughout the North. Although the so-called revisionist scholars argue that the rise of mass schooling in the 1830s and 1840s was the direct result of the activities of capitalists and manufacturers who created these institutions to foster a more docile workforce, these schools were developed in the late eighteenth and early nineteenth centuries—well before industrialization had occurred in the United States.[5] Furthermore, the greatest increases in school attendance in the 1830s and 1840s was not in the more industrialized and urbanized Northeast, but in the more rural and agricultural Midwest. Although eastern school reformers, like Horace Mann in Massachusetts, sought to replace private schools with public ones and to professionalize and centralize the control of local schools, they did not increase significantly the percentage of school-age children attending these institutions (Vinovskis, 1983b).[6]

But did schooling really help individuals in antebellum America to succeed economically? And did the children of immigrants attend these new schools, or were they forced by poverty to enter the labor force prematurely? There is little consensus among historians on these important questions.

Nineteenth-century Americans agreed on the importance of education in general, but they did not always associate it with economic success and mobility. Classical British economists like Adam Smith mentioned the value of schooling, but mainly as a means of promoting social stability and harmony rather than fostering occupational mobility (Blaug, 1986). Similarly, American antebellum political economists praised the value of education for enhancing the political and social well-being of the nation, but they also did not emphasize the role of schooling in promoting social mobility (Phillips, 1828). In part this was because most occupational training and advancement was associated with the practice of apprenticeship in the early nineteenth century.

As we have seen in chapter 5, the one person who did the most to link schooling with an increases in economic productivity was Horace Mann. If nineteenth-century educators like Mann saw a strong causal relation between schooling and occupational attainment, the recent revisionist scholars deny it altogether or see schools as a deliberate impediment to social mobility. Harvey Graff (1979), for example, argues that literacy was not an important skill for nineteenth-century workers. Michael Katz (1975) adds that schooling did little to promote antebellum social mobility because poor immigrants could not afford to send their children to school. Furthermore, many of these scholars (Bowles and Gintis, 1976) question the existence of social mobility in American society and see the schools as institutions designed to promote and justify the existing capitalist system.

As I noted in chapter 4, there are very few methodologically sound studies of antebellum occupational mobility, and most of these do not address directly the importance of education. Stephan Thernstrom's classic study of social mobility in mid-nineteenth-century Newburyport, Massachusetts, found modest gains in occupational status or property acquisition among the children of unskilled laborers. The Irish were particularly disadvantaged because they removed their children from school by the age of ten, and this presumably contributed to their lower rate of upward mobility.

Studies of other antebellum communities, such as Poughkeepsie, New York, found somewhat greater upward social mobility than in Newburyport but confirmed Thernstrom's observation that the children of immigrants were particularly disadvantaged (Kaeble, 1985). Most of these studies failed to test explicitly the relation between schooling and subsequent mobility. Indeed, even Thernstrom's assumption that the children of unskilled parents had only limited occupational mobility because of their lack of education needs to be re-examined as it appears he underestimated the amount of education they received (Vinovskis, 1985b).

If there is little agreement on just how important schooling was in fostering social mobility, everyone agrees that that public schools were perceived and used as a means of acculturating Irish and German immigrants. Before the development of large-scale parochial school systems after the Civil War, most Catholic children attended public schools, which tried to inculcate them with middle-class Protestant values (Jorgenson, 1987). In some areas, such as St. Louis, public schools found it necessary politically to offer German-language instruction, but most immigrant students attended English-speaking classes (Troen, 1975).

Although much has been written about the intentions of public school officials in trying to assimilate antebellum immigrants or of the immigrants' resistance to these efforts, there is little systematic evidence of the cultural impact of the schools on the children of the newcomers. Perhaps their acceptance and partial assimilation into antebellum society was influenced more by their neighborhood and work experiences than by the training and socialization they received in school. Certainly the Civil War may have played an important role in integrating immigrants into northern society, and it reduced, at least temporarily, the nativist attempts of the 1850s to use public schools to recast the immigrant population into a middle-class Protestant mold (Higham, 1955; Jones, 1960).

The relation between immigrants and schools in antebellum society was more complex than it was in colonial America, where schools were scarce and rarely intended to assimilate immigrants. Although the scholarly literature on the effects of schools on immigrants is mixed and inconclusive, my suspicion is that schools contributed to the limited occupational mobility of their students and helped to expose them to prevailing cultural norms. Nevertheless, this process of adjustment and partial assimilation was moderated by the local control of public schools, which allowed certain large immigrant groups—such as the Irish and Germans—to exercise some control over the education of their children, and was cut short by the Civil War. While free blacks migrating to the North gained some access to public schooling, the strong racial prejudice and discrimination against them probably meant that their newly acquired education had less of an economic value than that received by the children of either native-born whites or immigrants (Horton and Horton, 1979).

Immigrants and Schools in the Late Nineteenth and Early Twentieth Centuries

Social and economic changes continued unabated in the period after the Civil War (Vinovskis, 1989). The urbanization of the population increased steadily. In 1880 28.2 percent of the people lived in communities of 2,500 or more individuals, and 40 years later that proportion had risen to 51.2 percent. By

1920 almost one out of every ten Americans lived in a city with over a million inhabitants (U.S. Bureau of Census, 1975, pt. 1: ser. A57, A69). The percentage of the labor force in nonagricultural work rose from 48.7 percent in 1880 to 74.1 percent in 1920. Part of this shift was due to the increase in the percentage of workers engaged in manufacturing, from 18.3 percent in 1880 to 26.9 percent in 1920 (Lebergott, 1964: 510). Thus, the United States was becoming a more urbanized and industrialized nation with an increasingly small minority of its population living on farms or engaged in agricultural tasks.

The growth of the American economy attracted large numbers of immigrants. Nearly 24 million immigrants came to the United States between 1880 and 1920—although many of them eventually returned home. The characteristics of the immigrants changed as the proportion from Northern and Western Europe declined while those from Southern, Central, and Eastern Europe increased. At the height of immigration in 1907, approximately three-fourths of the immigrants came from Austria-Hungary, the Balkans, Italy, or Russia (Taylor, 1971: 63). Many of these immigrants were either Jewish or Catholic, and most of them did not speak English. Most of them settled in cities. By 1920 one out of five urban residents was foreign-born, and three out of ten were second-generation Americans (Lieberson, 1980: 23). Concerns about their social and political behavior led to efforts to assimilate them through the public schools.

The public schools underwent significant changes in the late nineteenth and early twentieth centuries. Urban school systems expanded rapidly, and the schools became increasingly specialized, age-graded, and centrally controlled by professional educators and local politicians (Cremin, 1988). The proportion of five- to seventeen-year-olds in schools nationally rose slightly from 78.1 percent in 1890 to 83.2 percent in 1920 in spite of the great influx of immigrants (U.S. Bureau of Census, 1975, pt. 1: ser. H419). A sizable minority of immigrant children attended private schools that tried to preserve their ethnic and religious heritage (Olneck and Lazerson, 1980; Sanders, 1976). More important in the long run was the growth in high school attendance. Although high schools existed in some parts of antebellum New England, they now became commonplace in other areas of the country, and efforts were made to attract students who did not plan to go on to college (Vinovskis, 1988b). The percentage of seventeen-year-olds who graduated from high school rose from 2.5 percent in 1880 to 16.3 percent in 1920 (U.S. Bureau of Census, 1975, pt. 1: ser. H599).

Nativist fear of the new immigrants prompted efforts to assimilate their children through Americanization programs both within and outside the public schools. But did the children of immigrants attend public schools and did that experience have any impact on them? Earlier social historians, such as Thernstrom (1973), saw the schools as an important factor in helping immigrant children succeed in America. But the revisionist education historians reject this positive interpretation. Colin Greer, for example, argues that schools deliberately frustrated and failed immigrant children in order to reproduce the existing social order. Public schools were not designed to help lower-class children, but to control them: "The assumption that extended schooling promotes greater academic achievement or social mobility is, however, entirely fallacious. School performance seems consistently dependent upon the socioeconomic position of the pupil's family" (1972: 109).

During the period 1880 to 1920, there was great variation in the school attendance pattern of immigrant and second-generation children. In general, immigrant children received much less education than those of the second generation (Angus and Mirel, 1985; Olneck and Lazerson, 1974). Some immigrant parents, such as those from southern Italy or Hungary, did not place much value on extended schooling, and therefore their children did not receive as much education as others (Barton, 1975; LaGumina, 1982; Stolarik, 1977). Jewish immigrants, in contrast, stressed education, and their children stayed in school much longer (Dinnerstein, 1982). Compared to the children of native-born whites in the North, second-generation children generally attended less school. That difference, however, was not very large and decreased over time. Indeed, since white children in the South were disadvantaged educationally, the overall educational attainment of many groups of second-generation children equaled or sometimes even exceeded that of children of native white parents. Thus, while immigrant children were clearly disadvantaged educationally in the United States, many of those in the second generation were able to be competitive if not equal to the children of the native-born population (Lieberson, 1980).

Even if second-generation children attended public schools, it does not mean that they were treated equally. Several revisionist scholars contend that these children were denied opportunities for advancement within the schools. Unfortunately, we do not have any detailed statistical studies of the classroom experiences of immigrant children in elementary schools, but a recent analysis of the Central High School in Philadelphia suggests that students from disadvantaged backgrounds could compete with those from middle-class families (Labaree, 1988; Perlmann, 1985b).

But did a high school education provide social mobility for immigrant and second-generation children? Until now most scholars have been forced to speculate on the basis of indirect evidence—usually from data on the occupational mobility of immigrants but without any direct information on their schooling. Reed Ueda's (1987) analysis of intergenerational mobility in late-nineteenth-century Somerville, Massachusetts, found that sons of blue-collar workers who attended high school were more successful in attaining white-collar employment than those who did not attend high school. Similarly, Joel Perlmann's (1988) detailed study of secondary schooling in Providence, Rhode Island, between

1880 and 1925 found that high school attendance greatly increased one's chances for upward occupational mobility—even after controlling for the effects of family background.

Whereas second-generation immigrants were able to use their high school training to get ahead, the severe discrimination, even in the North, against blacks greatly diminished the value of any additional schooling for them. Thus, American-born children of immigrants to the United States were able to use education to improve their occupational status, but the children of black migrants to northern cities were unable to capitalize on their educational investment. Over time, this differential in the rates of return to education between blacks and second-generation Americans contributed to a growing gap between the two groups in the amount of education they sought for themselves and their children (Lieberson, 1980).

Recent studies seem to suggest a positive role for schooling in helping the children of immigrants, but what about cultural changes? Did the Americanization programs in the public schools help assimilate the children of immigrants into American society? Most studies of the Americanization efforts have focused on the attempt to influence adult immigrants through special programs rather than on activities directed at their children. Adult Americanization programs flourished particularly after World War I, as native Americans became anxious about the perceived threats posed by unassimilated immigrants. Public schools were frequently used as sites for adult citizenship classes, and about 750 to 1,000 communities participated in the early 1920s with at least one million immigrants enrolled in formal Americanization classes. What impact these classes actually had on the adult immigrants is still open to debate and only a small, though significant, proportion of all immigrants ever attended one. In addition, less than half of those who enrolled actually completed the course, and there was little agreement among educators on how to teach these courses. Nevertheless, many adult immigrants received at least some exposure to the English language and to white Protestant middle-class values, even if most immigrants were unprepared to repudiate their old-world heritage (McClymer, 1982).

Some have argued that the Americanization programs emphasized conformity above all else, but Michael Olneck (1989) sees their importance more in terms of the symbolic reconfiguration of American civic culture, with an emphasis on individualism and a delegitimation of collective ethnic identity. Although he is skeptical of the impact of these programs on individual consciousness, he stresses their importance in fixing the public meanings of what constitutes a "good" American citizen.

Unfortunately, we do not have any detailed analyses of the impact of schools on the assimilation of immigrant or second-generation children.[7] Certainly over time the educational level of more recent European immigrants has become almost indistinguishable from the rest of the white population, and

schools obviously played a key role in this change. Changes in education probably also helped to decrease any occupational or income differences between
these groups. Fertility levels of the more recent European immigrant groups
and their descendants now approximate that of the general white population,
but it is not clear if schools played a key role in this particular aspect of assimilation. Similarly, although intermarriage rates among white ethnics have steadily declined and a sizable proportion of the white population in 1980 no longer
remembered or seemed to care about its specific ethnic heritage, it is not clear
what role, if any, schools played in this process (Lieberson and Waters, 1988).

Socioeconomic and cultural differences diminished significantly between
the children of the late-nineteenth and early-twentieth-century European immigrants and the rest of the white population, but even today there remains a
sizable gap between the white and black populations on a variety of indices.
Although the children of black migrants to the North also partook of the improved educational opportunities there, they faced severe racial discrimination
in the labor force and in the housing market. Public schools may have exposed
blacks to white middle-class Protestant values, but white society refused to
accept them as equals. In the South blacks faced even more discrimination in
the schools and were further handicapped by the overall inadequate educational
facilities and offerings (Kusmer, 1976; Lane, 1986; Perlmann, 1988).

Thus, while the European immigrants and their children who came to the
United States between 1880 and 1920 faced substantial discrimination and hard-
ship, their descendants were able to better themselves economically. Schools
appear to have played a key role in their upward social mobility, but without
the economic opportunities available to them, the additional education would
have been much less useful. The children of black migrants to the North significantly improved their education without reaping the same occupational or
income rewards. As a result, the value of increased schooling became more
apparent over time to the descendants of European immigrants, but among
disadvantaged minorities like blacks it was not always clear that further education was worth the personal effort and family sacrifices that had to be made.
Therefore, the gap in schooling between the descendants of late-nineteenth and
early-twentieth-century European immigrants and black migrants to the North
increased and continues to disadvantage the latter group today.

Recent Immigrants and the Schools

The situation in the United States has changed since the early twentieth century. Almost three-fourths of the population in 1980 lived in communities of
2,500 or more people, although the proportion living in cities of one million or
more was only about 8 percent (U.S. Bureau of Census, 1989: tables 18, 38).
The percentage of the labor force in nonagricultural work had risen to 97

percent, with 19 percent in manufacturing and 32 percent in services (U.S. Bureau of Census, 1989: table 645). Increasingly workers are in jobs that require considerable education—often at least some college training. In 1987, 25 percent of the labor force were in managerial or professional jobs, and 31 percent were in technical, sales, or administrative support jobs (U.S. Bureau of Census, 1989: tables 642–43).

The distribution of the sources of immigration to the United States has also changed dramatically. Approximately 600,000 legal immigrants entered the United States in 1987, but only 10 percent of them were from Europe. The bulk of legal immigrants came from Asia (43 percent), the Caribbean (17 percent), Mexico (12 percent), South America (7 percent), and Central America (5 percent) (U.S. Bureau of Census, 1989: table 7). The number of illegal immigrants crossing the southern border is estimated to be about 200,000—though a sizable proportion of these people will eventually return or be returned.[8] Most legal and illegal immigrants to the United States today are from non-European countries, often do not speak English, and usually are poor.

Large changes have also occurred in schooling. The median years of education for the population ages twenty-five to twenty-nine years old rose from 10.3 years in 1940 to 12.8 years in 1987. The percentage who had graduated from high school increased from 38.1 percent in 1940 to 86.0 percent in 1987; the percentage with at least four years of college rose from 5.9 percent in 1940 to 22.0 percent in 1987 (U.S. Bureau of Census, 1989: table 211).

There were some differences in educational attainment by race, with the median years of school completed in 1987 for those twenty-five to twenty-nine years old being 12.8 years overall, 12.7 years for blacks, and 12.3 years for Hispanics. Since minority children, especially among the Hispanics, were likely to be in grades below those expected for their ages, the differences in the percentage of those ages twenty-five to twenty-nine who had graduated from high school were greater: 85.9 percent overall, 83.4 percent for blacks, and 59.8 percent for Hispanics (U.S. Bureau of Census, 1989: table 213).

As schools were used by more children, they were also better funded, larger, and more age-segregated by classrooms (Cremin, 1988). Federally funded programs, such as Headstart and bilingual education, were introduced in order to help disadvantaged children.[9] Efforts were made to introduce more information about minorities into the curriculum.[10] In recent years, however, there has been growing concern that the quality of public education has deteriorated even though the dollar amounts spent per pupil have increased substantially (Chubb, 1988; Ravitch, 1983).

The bulk of immigrants today are either Asians or Hispanic and are seen as minority members of our society. Therefore, we need to consider how minority children in general have fared in American schools in order to ascertain how recent immigrants, in particular, are faring. Some minority children, like blacks, continue to be disadvantaged in terms of school attendance or high school completion, but recently they have made sizable gains in closing some of the educational gap between themselves and the white native-born population (Farley and Allen, 1987). Others, like the second-generation children of Japanese or Chinese parents, have excelled educationally and often do better in American schools than the rest of the population (Hsia, 1988). Overall, Hispanic children have not done as well educationally, but there are significant differences among them. Cuban-American children, for example, do relatively well educationally compared to Puerto Rican or Mexican-American children (Bean and Tienda, 1987).

Various theories have been advanced to explain the difficulties many minority children encounter in American schools. Four of the more prominent are: biological determinism; cultural deprivation; discontinuity between the minority and majority culture; and psychosocial explanations (Suarez-Orozco, 1989).

Although the attempts at a biological explanation attracted considerable attention in the late 1960s and early 1970s, these studies have been largely discredited as inadequate (Gould, 1981; Jensen, 1969). Likewise, the argument that the inadequacies of the cultural background of minority children could explain their problems in school flourished in the 1960s, but it has few advocates today (Bloom, 1965; Ogbu, 1978). A more recent and persistent explanation for the problems of minority youth is the "cultural conflict" or "discontinuities" between the minority student and the school environment, which reflects the dominant culture (Johnson, 1970). Nevertheless, critics of this approach point out that some children from very different and distinct cultures, such as second-generation Japanese or Chinese, have done remarkably well in American schools (Hsia, 1988).

Perhaps the most popular explanations for the difficulties of minority students are psychosocial ones, which stress that educational deficits are only a reflection of larger problems facing these minorities. John Ogbu (1986) argues that castelike minorities, such as blacks, Puerto Ricans, and Mexican-Americans, fare much worse educationally than the rest of the population because they were incorporated into the United States against their will and have faced a job ceiling regardless of individual talents or school achievements. As a result, there is little incentive among castelike minority youth for further education—especially when schooling becomes identified with the majority, hostile culture.[11]

Other psychosocial explanations focus on problems of the family, which are particularly severe among many minority populations. Some studies have suggested that even after controlling for socioeconomic factors, children from single-parent homes do worse in school than those from two-parent families (McLanahan and Bumpus, 1988). Although some scholars dismiss the importance of the family as a factor in educational attainment, much of the literature on schooling suggests that the role of parents is crucial in predicting the amount of schooling their children receive (Coleman, Hoffer, and Kilgore, 1982; Featherman and Hauser, 1978).

Given the diversity among immigrants today, one would expect considerable variety in the adjustment of their children to American schools. One might hypothesize that immigrant children whose parents were relatively affluent and well educated would fare reasonably well in the public schools. Those whose parents were poor and uneducated, however, might be expected to do less well— particularly if they were members of nonwhite minorities. Studies of recent immigrants and schooling in the United States challenge this conventional wisdom.

An anthropological study of Central American legal and illegal refugees in two inner-city high schools in California found that notwithstanding their impoverished condition, the El Salvadorian, Guatemalan, and Nicaraguan youth studied did surprisingly well academically. Although confronted with violence and hostility in these two heavily minority high schools, the immigrant children were more successful than many of the other minority children. The author pointed out that despite the obvious handicaps faced by these non-English speaking students, they succeeded in large part because of their particular cultural and familial situation. Having escaped from the terror and poverty of their homelands, these immigrants saw the United States as a land of unlimited opportunity for those with education and personal drive. In addition, the sacrifices made by their parents encouraged these youth to succeed in school as a means of repaying those who had helped them. Furthermore, even when conditions in the United States did not live up to their expectations, the situation in their homelands was even worse and therefore not a viable alternative (Suarez-Orozco, 1989).

Another larger and more detailed statistical, five-site study of the Indochinese boat people suggests that the children do well in the public schools despite the seemingly insurmountable odds against them. Although many of the parents of these children were able to find employment, the jobs were low-skilled with little prospect for upward mobility. Yet they sent their children to the public schools and encouraged them to get ahead by acquiring a good education. Although the children initially were not literate in English, they eventually managed to earn decent overall grade point averages and score highly on the California Achievement Test (Caplan, Whitmore, and Choy, 1989).

In trying to explain the unexpected academic success of the children of the boat people, the authors concluded that it was not due to the quality of the public schools, which were not very good, nor to the special English-language classes. They point, instead, to the cultural and familial values that encouraged academic achievement. The parents, having accepted limited occupation mobility for themselves in the United States, placed their hopes on improving the situation of their children through education. As a result, in spite of the relatively poor quality of the schools and the hostility the Indochinese children frequently encountered both within and outside those schools, they excelled academically because they were highly motivated to learn. The authors suggest that: "We have probably gone too far, however, in the direction of believing that low-SES, single-parent homes with large numbers of children cannot succeed in school. The critical issue is not the number and relationship of the adults in the household to the children but rather what dominates and who determines the nature and character of the milieu, its beliefs and behaviors. It means that the values and aspirations linked to student learning have to be instilled early and that an environment promotive of learning must be supported by families in a society concerned with the well-being of all of its members" (Caplan, Whitmore, and Choy, 1989: 176).

Although many of the Central American and Indochinese immigrant children appear to be succeeding in school, the children of undocumented aliens from Mexico are not faring as well (Suarez-Orozco, 1987). Many immigrant children may do well in elementary or secondary school, but they may lack access to higher education because of inadequate financial resources, lack of knowledge about higher education, or fear that undocumented aliens cannot attend a college or university. A high school education is no longer adequate for the best jobs in this country, and so the long-term occupational mobility of these seemingly successful immigrant children may be in jeopardy.[12] In addition, if the immigrant children are unable to translate their education into better jobs and higher incomes because of discrimination, their own children may be discouraged from pursuing more schooling.[13] Finally, successful students appear to have become only partially assimilated into American society—accepting the American values of hard work and education yet rejecting the strong individualism and materialism that characterizes many of their native-born classmates. If they or their offspring adopt the more individualistic and consumer-oriented ways of American society, perhaps some of their comparative advantages will disappear.

Conclusion

The role of the schools in the integration and assimilation of immigrants varies greatly over time and is conditioned by the nature of the society and of the educational system in any given period. In colonial America, the family was the central institution for educating children, and the few primary schools that existed were intended only as a supplement to those efforts. In spite of concerns about immigration, colonial communities did not turn to schools as a means of socializing and assimilating immigrants. Since most of the population was engaged in farming or related agricultural activities, extensive schooling was not viewed as essential for most children.

In antebellum America, the importance of formal education increased as the number of schools multiplied and as schools were seen as a means of preparing children for the growing diversity of employment opportunities. As apprenticeship declined, education was increasingly viewed as necessary for upward social mobility. The influx of Irish and German immigrants before the Civil War led to nativist efforts to use public schools to assimilate these newcomers to white Protestant middle-class values and practices. Although there are no adequate studies of the actual impact of schools on the subsequent life course of their students, it appears that they helped foster at least some limited social mobility.

In the late nineteenth and early twentieth centuries, American society became more urbanized and industrialized and public schools more centralized and professionalized. The new wave of immigrants from Southern, Eastern, and Central Europe alarmed many of the native-born population and led to a sense of urgency in the promotion of Americanization programs both within and outside public schools. Most European immigrant and second-generation children seemed to benefit from the education they received and improved their position in society; today it is hard to distinguish occupationally or educationally among the descendants of these immigrants. Severe racial discrimination, however, prevented black migrants to the North from effectively utilizing schools and contributed to the growing educational gap between blacks and white immigrants in the first half of the twentieth century.

Today, immigrants to the United states are predominantly from Asia or Latin and Central America. Although many of them are disadvantaged in terms of their socioeconomic backgrounds and personal resources in the United States, many of their children are doing surprisingly well in school. Particularly interesting is the important role that familial and cultural values seem to play in facilitating the acquisition of schooling by these recent immigrants. Whether this pattern of school achievement will continue and whether the educated children will be given full and equal access to good job opportunities remains to be seen.

Overall, schooling in the nineteenth and twentieth centuries has provided many immigrant and second-generation children with the skills and credentials necessary for success in America. Although many European immigrants and their descendants initially faced substantial hostility and discrimination from the native population, over time much of that has disappeared. Unfortunately, for many minority populations, such as blacks and Mexican-Americans, that discrimination was more severe, and to some degree it continues to deny their children equal access to advancement. Thus, whereas schooling can and has contributed to the gradual integration and partial assimilation of immigrants into American society, it cannot succeed without the concomitant acceptance of newcomers by the larger society. Furthermore, although schools are essential for providing the training and credentialing necessary for advancement, they cannot accomplish their tasks without the active support and encouragement of the family and local community.

Notes

Reprinted with permission from *Immigrants in Two Democracies: French and American Experience,* ed. Donald Horowitz and Gerard Noiriel (New York: New York University Press, 1992), 127–47.

1. In their efforts to Anglicanize the Dutch population in early-eighteenth-century New York, the Society for the Propagation of the Gospel established English schools in some communities like Albany and New York City. Nevertheless, the extent of their school building appears to have been limited, especially in the countryside, and was only a small, though important, part of the overall efforts to convert the inhabitants to Anglicanism (Balmer, 1989).

2. Calculated from U.S. Bureau of the Census, 1975, pt. 1: ser. A57, A69.

3. Calculated from U.S. Bureau of Census, 1975, pt. 1: ser. D152-D166.

4. Whereas apprenticeship declined sharply in the United States in the nineteenth century, it endured longer in Britain because of its economic advantages and because British traditions favored training certification for job entry into skilled positions (Elbaum, 1989: 337–49).

5. For a discussion of the revisionist debate, see chap. 7.

6. The demise of the infant school movement contributed to stable or even declining enrollment rates during Mann's tenure as secretary of the Board of Education. See chap. 2.

7. For a useful discussion of efforts to Americanize children in the public schools, see Mohl (1981).

8. The commissioner of the Immigration and Naturalization Service estimated that the number of illegal immigrants entering each year is between 1.7 million and 2.5 million. This figure seems much too high compared to most other estimates (*New York Times,* June 18, 1989: 1).

9. There is a great debate over the value of bilingual education in helping disadvantaged students. Some scholars (Glazer, 1981) question the wisdom of emphasizing bilingual education at the expense of giving immigrant children more exposure to English-language training. A multivariate analysis of Hispanic grade delays and high school dropout rates based on the 1980 federal census found that the language spoken at home had little adverse effect on school outcomes after controlling for the effects of the socioeconomic background of the parents (Bean and Tienda, 1987). For a review of the literature on bilingual education from the perspective of child development, see Hakuta and Garcia (1989).

10. Although some initially questioned the introduction of ethnic materials into the curriculum, most have now accepted its value (Glazer, 1988). The debate is now, however, over whether or not courses on ethnic differences and racism should be mandated for all students.

11. Ogbu (1986) sees immigrant children faring better than the castelike minorities, but he underestimates the fact that many of the recent nonwhite immigrants to the United States also face racial opposition (Spener, 1988).

12. Nevertheless, a high school education still provides a substantial advantage over those who have dropped out of high school. For an estimate of the rates of return to schooling in 1962 and 1973, see Olneck and Kim (1975).

13. Some scholars maintain that the current educational system relegates immigrants to only low-paying jobs (Spener, 1988; Bowles and Gintis, 1976). If this were so, one would not expect any real upward mobility for the recent immigrants in spite of their efforts in school. I do not find this line of reasoning persuasive even though minority adults appear to continue to receive fewer rewards for their education than the rest of the population (Olneck and Kim, 1975).

Part Two / *Attendance, Institutional Arrangements, and Social Support for Education*

The essays below continue a debate that began with the publication of *The Irony of Early School Reform: Educational Innovation in Mid-Nineteenth Century Massachusetts* by Michael B. Katz. One celebrated part of this important work was a study of the controversy over the public high school in Beverly, Massachusetts, including a close analysis of the vote in 1860 to abolish the school. These essays originally appeared in *History of Education Quarterly* (vol. 27, no. 2 [summer 1987]: 241–58) on the occasion of the publication of *The Origins of Public High Schools: A Reexamination of the Beverly High School Controversy* by Maris A. Vinovskis. The first essay is a review of the Vinovskis study by Katz, now a professor of history at the University of Pennsylvania; the second is a review by Edward Stevens, Jr., professor of education at Ohio University; the third is a response to these reviews by Vinovskis.

by Michael B. Katz

I approached Maris Vinovskis's book on Beverly with both pleasure and trepidation. Nearly twenty years after the publication of my *Irony of Early School Reform* a talented scholar had devoted an entire book, based on extensive research, to testing my interpretation of one incident. What greater compliment could there be? But what might someone far more sophisticated in quantitative methods than I ever was find out? After all, the research Vinovskis reexamined had been done in 1963 or 1964 when I was a graduate student inexperienced in, and terrified by, any form of complex counting. My first reaction on reading his book, therefore, was immense relief. With only small variations easily accounted for by the imperfections of historical sources our numbers were almost identical. Clearly, my novice coding, record linking, and occupational classifying had been better than I had feared. My sense of relief expanded as I thought more about Vinovskis's conclusions. Although he feels they revise my interpretation of events, they seem to me to deepen and supplement them. In fact, I find nothing in the book that contradicts my essential arguments, and I am left wondering why he tries so hard to distance himself from my interpretation by trying to turn a series of modest adjustments into substantial differences?

For readers unfamiliar with the issue, the event in question is the vote to abolish the Beverly (Massachusetts) high school at a town meeting on March 14, 1860. The event is noteworthy because the town clerk recorded the name of every voter and how he voted. No one has been able to locate a similar nominal level record of voting on another nineteenth-century educational issue. The vote took place in a highly charged atmosphere: the great shoemakers' strike in Essex County, where Beverly is located. Most of the shoemakers and other working-class voters cast their votes against the high school; professionals and businessmen more often supported it. The question is why? More precisely, to what extent was the vote a question of class? My interpretation gave class a prominent place. Vinovskis says I exaggerated.

For the record, it should be noted that *Irony* is about much more than Beverly. The Beverly case occupies 28 of 101 pages (27.8 percent) of the first part of the book or 13.5 percent of the book's text (not a third as Vinovskis says), excluding appendices and notes. The section of *Irony* of which the Beverly case forms a part analyzes high schools and some other key educational reforms of the antebellum period. It sets the Beverly incident in the context of a detailed exposition of the arguments made for high schools; it also contains a case study of Groton, chosen to illustrate the importance of sectional tensions within towns and conflicts between private and public schools, and one of Lawrence, an especially clear example of the social role assigned to education in an industrializing city.

Vinovskis tries to show that social class was not as important a factor in the Beverly vote as I maintained. He emphasizes the role of the town's geography and ongoing local controversies over the politics of education, which were played out in the high school vote. He combines a detailed narrative history of the town's educational politics (based on impressive and thorough research in local primary sources whose discovery required ingenuity and perseverance) with several statistical studies, the most important of which for his purposes was a multivariate analysis of the vote on the high school issue.

Vinovskis has studied educational developments in antebellum Massachusetts, especially Essex County, for several years. Together with various collaborators he has made a number of discoveries, of which the most important are: the high rate of school attendance in Massachusetts before the common school movement; the rise and fall of early childhood education; the extraordinary proportion of native white women who taught school; the important distinctions among measures of educational effort (expenses, length of school year, and attendance) and between urban and rural areas; temporal and local variations in tax burdens imposed by education; the complexity of local educational politics; and the important role of ministers as promoters of educational reform and school board members. Although in a short comment I cannot discuss the significance of these discoveries, which inform his analysis of Beverly, they should remain permanent and important additions to educational historiography.

How does his research in this book relate to my conclusions in *Irony?* First, he contradicts none of my findings, which were based on descriptive rather than multivariate statistics. Rather, he reorders their importance. He argues that geography, that is, the part of the town in which voters lived, was exceptionally important. Wealth also was critical. Occupation worked in the way I predicted, but in his multiple classification analysis (MCA) it had a much lower influence (as measured by its beta weight). Age and family size were reasonably close to what could be expected from my results. Despite his attempt to distance himself from my argument (and his assertions that he succeeded), Vinovskis writes, "Overall the MCA results confirm Katz's findings" (95).

Vinovskis points out that a small minority of Beverly's residents continuously pushed educational reforms through town meetings. If not the richest people in town, they did include many professionals, including ministers (whose actions, he shows, were by no means always supported by their parishioners). Vinovskis repeatedly uses the word "imposition" to describe their reform style. ("Imposition," of course, is the one word for which I have been most criticized over the years, although the critics have neglected the content of my argument, which was not that working people were passive, or that struggles did not take place, but the stronger side had the resources to win.) Vinovskis argues that the majority of Beverly's citizens did not want a high school and voted for it only because they were forced to by state law. He comments on the "anger felt by many voters toward the imposition of an expensive and seemingly unnecessary institution by a determined minority using the threat of a court indictment against the town" (107), and of "the tremendous amount of bitterness that must have been generated by the imposition of this institution on the citizenry" (77). But what were the social sources of this bitterness? The problem here is that, despite his attention to the history of town politics, Vinovskis's account floats in a curious contextual vacuum, and his book lacks a systematic account of the town's economic development and a delineation of its social structure. Without a social and economic context, Vinovskis is unable to explain his major findings in a coherent way. He cannot account for the interest in education he documents or tell readers why some reformers wanted a high school. Indeed, he does not systematically lay out (as does *Irony*) the pro–high school case. Nor is he able to account for reformers' passionate hostility to the district system (also a theme of *Irony* that he does not acknowledge) or to interpret one of his most perceptive observations: namely, that the argument in Beverly was about priorities. How much money should be spent on common schools, and how much on a high school? Although the issue polarized the town, he does not explore its social roots or sources. If he had, questions of class would have been hard to avoid.

Despite Vinovskis's MCA analysis, no one can deny that over 70 percent of voting farmers, mariners, and shoemakers and all the voting laborers (not placed in a separate category by Vinovskis) cast their votes against the high school. Vinovskis attempts to mute the influence of working-class opposition to the high school by arguing that not all mariners, shoemakers, artisans, and farmers opposed it. However, most analysts consider a 70 percent or 80 percent vote by a group reasonable evidence of the attitude of its members. In fact, Vinovskis describes a Beverly filled with tension, conflict, and bitterness. He shows in far more detail than did I how conflicts and animosities shaped educational politics.

As in an earlier book, Vinovskis does not succeed in his larger project: to reduce the influence of social class in antebellum American history. In the earlier book, as I showed at length elsewhere (Katz, 1980), he accomplished his goal only by a methodological maneuver—primarily, the merging of artisans and white collar workers into one meaningless occupational category—that predetermined his results. Here, he ignores the recent, exciting literature on class formation in the period (for instance, Sean Wilentz's brilliant *Chants Democratic*), despite its great implications for understanding the development of education. Notwithstanding age and imperfections, *Irony* is closer than Vinovskis to contemporary currents in historiography, which put the development of a working class at the center of antebellum social history.

None of Vinovskis's attempts to diminish the importance of class are convincing. For example, he argues that the great Essex County shoemakers' strike wasn't very important to the high school story because the Beverly shoemakers joined it a couple of weeks after it had started in Lynn, but he gives no convincing reason why the date they joined is evidence of lukewarm support or less class tension in Beverly. Throughout Essex County, public discourse about the strike was full of class-related themes, and it stretches the imagination to suppose the strike did not color the way working people thought about public questions, including a high school. Nor is Vinovskis persuasive when he argues that the vote on the high school did not reflect working-class sentiments because only a minority of shoemakers, mariners, artisans, and laborers voted. The vote took place during the day when many probably could not afford to stay away from work, and fewer may have voted in the afternoon than in the morning because they could not stay away from their jobs for a whole day. Certainly this interpretation is as likely an explanation as apathy, and it is not inconsistent with Vinovskis's emphasis on hostility to increased taxes and the priority that many residents placed on common schools over a high school.

Vinovskis's presentation of his quantitative analysis left me with some questions about his methods, which he kindly answered by letter. I shall incorporate his answers into my comments. His occupation variable in the MCA analysis might not fully reflect occupation's influence. One other variable—town office holding—is weighted by the importance of office, which in turn is estimated by the occupation of officeholders. So occupation is introduced twice. (Vinovskis reports this makes little practical difference in the outcome of the analysis.) In the same way, wealth cannot be completely separated from occupation, and Vinovskis reports there was some statistical interaction between the two. For instance, no shoemakers had $5,000 or more in property. Also, the occupational scale contains a residual category, "other," with 90 members, or about 25 percent of the total, making it the second largest category. Vinovskis created this large residual category to reduce the number of degrees of freedom in the analysis by eliminating small groups. The category includes laborers, non-shoemaker artisans, and others. It, too, might reduce the summary weighting of occupation. I would find interesting alternative groupings of occupations, combinations of occupation with income, and a division by classes.

The more serious issue, I think, is conceptual. The argument in favor of multivariate analysis is that it enables one to sort out the relative influence of various factors on a dependent variable. Especially as applied to persons, multivariate analysis, when not used sensitively, can create arbitrary and meaningless distinctions because identity has multiple, overlapping, and inseparable components. Vinovskis found poor, working-class men, often from the town's outlying districts, opposing the high school. Do his statistics automatically and irrefutably tell us that one factor alone dominated their vote? How would these voters have identified themselves? Would they, for instance, have separated out their income from their occupation from their residence and told an interviewer, "I really voted against the high school, not because I'm a mariner, but, first, because I live in an outlying district and, second, because I'm poor"? (The same difficulty bedevils attempts to sort out occupation and ethnicity in discussions of the American working class whose ethnic affiliations have been part of its class definition.) By implication, Vinovskis defines class as a wooden, static variable whose influence in American history hinges on a beta weight. In the process, he ignores the direction of contemporary work on antebellum America, which considers class a social relation and searches for ways to discover and portray its shifting forms and meanings.

Nor does Vinovskis explore the social meaning of Beverly's geography. The most interesting recent scholarship (I think of Manuel Castells and others creating a new urban studies rooted in the political economy of cities) stresses that space is not neutral; it is, rather, a social construction, often fiercely contested.

Location, that is, has social meanings. To leave it simply a neutral setting or backdrop is, I think, to overlook another important axis of social differentiation and substitute a mechanical category for a complex, dynamic process.

My intent in this comment has not been to deny that *Irony* has some problems. There is not space here to discuss them, and they are different, I think, than the ones Vinovskis identifies. I do, though, want to point out some places where he does not represent *Irony* wholly accurately. First, I was aware of the influence of geography on the vote and noted its geographical distribution (54–55). I did not, as Vinovskis implies, argue that only manufacturers supported the high school or that its supporters represented only the industrialists in the town. Rather, I pointed out that support came from well-to-do civic leaders and, probably, from parents who otherwise would have paid tuition to private schools for secondary education. Nor, as Vinovskis implies repeatedly, have I ever argued that most working-class people opposed education. Vinovskis produces no evidence on this point because there is none. My contention always has been that working people often had different priorities and sometimes opposed specific innovations, which, at other times, they might support.

A few other points: page 22 misrepresents my position about the relation of education and mobility; page 157, footnote 43, seriously distorts the position my colleagues and I took in f332 in *The Social Organization of Early Industrial Capitalism* (1982). Vinovskis is correct to observe that I carelessly handled farmers differently in the analysis of Beverly from the analysis of high school attendance in Somerville and Chelsea. In practical terms, it didn't matter because the number of farmers' children attending high school in the two cities at the time of my analysis (as the tables in *Irony* clearly show) was negligible in one and 0 in the other.

Vinovskis objects to the tenor of recent debates on educational historiography. He dislikes the strident political attacks on those historians inaccurately lumped together as "revisionists," and he thinks angry responses are inappropriate. Instead, he calls for a "scholarly and objective" reexamination of important issues (119–20), to which, presumably, he hopes his book contributes. But politics cannot be divorced from scholarship, and numbers are no more neutral than words. Vinovskis is as partisan as the rest of us. I mean this as no criticism. Rather, I only wish he would make his assumptions and commitments more explicit and drop the fiction of neutrality. For history, after all, is about questions that matter.

by Edward Stevens, Jr.

The Origins of Public High Schools by Maris A. Vinovskis is both a reanalysis of the Beverly High School controversy and a broader challenge to revisionist history. The Beverly controversy comprised only a small part of Katz's seminal study of nineteenth-century school reform, yet it was an important part of Katz's argument that educational innovation involved two "distinct clusters of antagonists": "prominent, prestigious leaders and a working class" (Katz, 1968: 86).

In his reassessment of the dynamics of educational reform, Vinovskis joins the issue over both methodological and substantive dimensions. *The Origins of Public High Schools* illustrates the increasing methodological sophistication that has helped the subdiscipline of history of education move toward greater integration with social science history. It views critically the ideological assumptions made by revisionist historians and recasts our understanding of educational reform in the mold of "pluralism" rather than "class." Pluralism in this case means to attend less to reform by imposition and more to the influence of partisan politics and local agendas for reform. It means to view reform from a developmental perspective and to place the dynamics of educational reform *within* communities in mid-nineteenth-century America.

Vinovskis's statistical analysis is more sophisticated than that published in 1968 by Katz. Like regression analysis in general, MCA, is a far better tool to assess the relative importance of independent variables to predicting dependent ones. But it is also subject to certain weaknesses. The additive model used in such analyses is insensitive to interactions, and the iterative process used to solve the equations is dependent on the weighted average of other coefficients (Andrews et al., 1973). While excellent for assessing the relative importance of variables, the rankings may change depending upon the number and order of entry of the variables into the equation.

Vinovskis's reanalysis of the vote to abolish Beverly High School does not wholly undermine Katz's analysis. It confirms the importance of wealth as an important predictor of voting behavior on the high school though, unlike Katz's analysis, occupation is a very poor predictor. Vinovskis also takes exception (95) to Katz's claim that "citizens of least wealth and least occupational prestige successfully opposed the high school" (Katz, 1968: 80). How literally Katz meant this statement is uncertain because his own figures show that it was those in the total estate wealth category of $1,000–4,999 who most opposed the high school (278).

In Vinovskis's analysis the three most important predictors of voting behavior are, in rank order: geographic area, town office holding, and wealth. Judging from the tables and R^2s presented by the author, a regression equation written with these three predictors only (the six others being eliminated) would be the most elegant, statistically speaking. It could also alter the magnitude of the beta weights and *reorder* the ranking of the predictors themselves. Vinovskis discusses the effect on R^2 and the variables of wealth and office holding of removing geographic area as an independent variable. Whether or not there is a relative shift in beta weights if only the three variables are used is not clear.

He notes, however, that the removal of geographic area as an independent variable does not "greatly enhance the importance of either wealth or occupation" (161n).

Two of Vinovskis's top three predictors—geography and office holding—deserve further comment because they are the foundation for his most direct challenge to Katz's interpretations. Geography (outlying districts versus those closer to town) was the "single best predictor of a voter's position on the high school" (104). Vinovskis's criticism of Katz for not paying enough attention to this variable seems fair enough. But Vinovskis's explanation of its importance is only partly satisfying. *Persistent* differences seem to be a factor. Location of the high school is rejected as an explanation because it was located in the outlying West Farms district which had rejected "efforts to move it elsewhere" (104). The most plausible explanation is that outlying areas resented their tax dollars being spent on an "expensive and underutilized public high school" and feared centralization and consolidation (104).

The argument, as far as it goes, seems plausible. But why did farmers not see the utility of the high school? I think two additional reasons might be supplied. The curriculum of the Beverly High School had little to offer a farmer's son or sons of a shoemaker, mariner, or fisherman in the way of technical knowledge to improve occupational skills. The language-centered curriculum of high schools might serve as a gateway to higher-status occupations in the urban sector, but for farmers to accept this "opportunity" would have been to reject much of their cherished agricultural heritage. In short, the "tax dollar" argument could be buttressed with further arguments about utility and ideology and thus could address more directly the central question of why or why not a high school was seen as valuable to different "interested" parties.

Vinovskis's analysis of previous officeholders presents certain conceptual and interpretative problems. Using the six years between 1854 and 1860 to identify this voter attribute does raise some question about comparability of data. It would seem reasonable to bring the office-holding variable into line with the year of the other variables.

The office-holding variable presents more problems of interpretation than most of the other variables. Vinovskis accedes to the difficulty of interpreting this variable and notes the plausibility of alternative explanations for its importance (103). Perhaps the variable itself is a surrogate for civic commitment. One suspects, however, that office holding is a mix of several factors and may in fact have a large overlap with other variables in the equation. While it is a variable with good predictive power, its explanatory value is very limited.

In general Vinovskis shifts the ground for interpreting the Beverly High School controversy toward matters of personal and community finance (taxation) and away from ideology. This is an important shift and goes beyond the presentation of figures showing inequalities of wealth between the outlying districts of Beverly and those in the center of town. In fact, the dynamics of educational reform appear quite different in Vinovskis's account from that in *The Irony of Early School Reform* because the dynamics of human behavior and their relations to inequality are seen differently.

In both *The Origins of Public High Schools* and *The Irony of Early School Reform* disputes are settled in the political arena and people behave in their own best interest—or seemingly so. Yet there is an important difference. In Katz's version the intervening link between individual behavior and social structure is ideology. Decisions are not simply decisions carried out by rational calculations of benefits and risks. They are colored by ideological imperatives embedded in the very structure of institutions themselves. Democratic processes of decision making are severely threatened.

It seems to me that in *The Origins of Public High Schools* the actors respond in a relatively free, rational way, taking into account their own best interests while working within the restrictions of certain (mostly economic and legal) structural constraints. They are relatively free from the subtleties of ideology though they resent overt imposition. "In the final analysis," "the vote on the Beverly High School was . . . a local political decision made at the town meeting" (101). As such it was subject to all the local animosities and short-term maneuvering characteristic of local politics. Though it does testify to the importance of local idiosyncrasies in determining the outcomes of decision-making processes, the larger meaning of the vote is also less clear. Plurality replaces class not only in fact, but also in interpretation. It is this very plurality that will probably help set a new research agenda for historians of education.

by Maris A. Vinovskis

Michael Katz and Edward Stevens provide some thoughtful and useful comments on my reanalysis of the Beverly High School controversy. They also reveal a fundamental difference of opinion about the framework and analyses set forth in my book. Whereas Stevens sees the book as shifting "the ground for interpreting the Beverly High School controversy toward matters of personal and community finance (taxation) and away from ideology," Katz believes that "nothing in the book . . . contradicts [his] essential arguments" and is puzzled why I seem to try so hard to distance myself from his original work.

As I frequently mentioned throughout the book, I am indebted to Katz for his pioneering analysis of the Beverly High School controversy and accept his interpretations of some of the specific variables used in his cross-sectional analysis of the vote to abolish the high school. I also agree that the high school was imposed upon the citizens of Beverly who clearly did not favor it (and not just upon the working class as Katz emphasized). I strongly disagree, however, with his account of the origin of the Beverly High School and his explanation of its demise in 1860. Only by quoting my statement that "overall the MCA results confirm Katz's findings" completely out of context (95) does he seem to support his case. The quotation in question clearly refers only to the relation of taxable wealth to the vote on the high school and not to the analysis as a whole. Indeed, I conclude the discussion of the chapter on the pattern of voting by reminding the reader that my analyses using "improved techniques have produced results that are very different from those of Katz" (107).

Katz claims that my analysis "floats in a curious contextual vacuum" and does not examine the "social roots or sources" for the division over "how much money should be spent on common schools, and how much on a high school?" Not only do I disagree with his observations, but I think they are misapplied. Indeed, it is Katz who failed to provide an adequate contextual setting for the establishment of a public high school. Katz concentrated almost exclusively upon the abolition of the high school and simply assumed that those who favored its continuance in 1860 were the ones who sought to establish it in the 1850s. He links the establishment of the high school to the growing economic and social tensions in that community in the 1850s. What he failed to realize is that the effort to create a public high school started in the 1840s rather than the 1850s—at a time when the socioeconomic conditions did not resemble those described by Katz for the 1850s.

Whereas Katz discussed the creation of a public high school in isolation from other educational developments in Beverly, I analyzed in great detail changes in public and private schools in antebellum Beverly. Rather than portraying the creation of a high school as the central educational reform in that community, I see it as only one of many educational innovations and certainly not the top priority in the two decades before the Civil War. As I indicated in the book, Beverly residents were divided between those who lived in the center of the township and those in the outlying areas over the importance of establishing a public high school rather than improving the common schools—a division that reflected in large measure the conditions of education in their respective sections. Missing entirely from Katz's account is any analysis of cost of education or of the ability and willingness of taxpayers to finance additional municipal expenditures. Katz was not even aware that several times Beverly citizens made a trade-off between funding their common schools and establishing a high school. As Stevens correctly notes, my book "means to view reform from a developmental perspective and to place the dynamics of educational reform *within* communities in antebellum America." In short, the book hardly "floats in a curious contextual vacuum" as Katz asserts.

Katz's discussion of the motives of the proponents of the high school in Beverly also is limited because he did not identify or consider its most persistent and ardent supporters. Katz focused on Robert Rantoul, Sr. (who probably did not even participate in the important deliberations in the early 1850s) and alluded to William Thorndike (who died in 1835) as some of the prominent education reformers, but he did not even mention any of the clergymen who dominated the school committees and who were identified by their contemporaries as the most important education leaders in Beverly. Thus, my account, which analyzes in detail the composition of the local educational leadership and discusses their motivations and orientation, seems more relevant and accurate for understanding the establishment of the Beverly High School than Katz's more general, though useful, discussions of the value of secondary education in other communities.

My disagreements with Katz over the origins of the Beverly High School are important because they point to different interpretations of the tensions within that community. Katz stresses the class divisions over the high school whereas I emphasize the sectional differences and the bitterness that arose from having a small minority of the town meeting impose such an expensive institution upon taxpayers. Katz failed to emphasize in his book that a majority of the citizens of Beverly never willingly voted for a public high school. Instead, they agreed in 1857 to comply with the state law requiring them to have a public high school. As a result, one cannot interpret the votes for or against the high school in 1857 or 1860 as an accurate reflection of whether or not someone favored that institution; many residents undoubtedly agreed only reluctantly to a high school in order to escape the threatened substantial fine against the community.

In analyzing the vote to abolish the Beverly High School, I employed more sophisticated statistical techniques than were available to Katz in the 1960s and added some new variables such as town office holding, political affiliation, and church membership. These new variables are important because they significantly enhance the analysis both conceptually and in terms of predictive power. Katz and Stevens are correct, as I acknowledged in the book, that I do not depart much from Katz's original interpretation of some specific variables such as age or children in the household. My analysis did discover, however, a very different pattern of ordering the importance of the independent variables—a fact that Katz acknowledges but then seems to downplay in his review.

Katz complains that I failed to note that he was aware of the influence of geography on the vote to abolish the Beverly High School. Not so. I acknowledged that Katz considered geography as one of his explanatory variables (Vinovskis, 1985a: 86) but pointed out that he did not consider it one of the three most important factors. Katz also dismissed the importance of geography in explaining the vote when comparing events in Beverly and Groton: "In Groton as in Beverly the fight for a high school reflected a deep communal division. But in Groton the greatest tension was not between social classes but between sections of the town" (Katz, 1968: 79).

My analysis of the vote on the Beverly High School demonstrates that where one lived is a much better predictor of how one voted than an individual's occupation. This should not be too surprising since 94 percent of the voters in the Cove and 87 percent of those in the Bald Hill, East Farm, or West Farm areas opposed the high school. The overwhelming opposition to the high school from these outlying areas persisted even after controlling for the effects of the other independent variables including the occupation of the individual.

Katz claims that I "did not explore the social meaning of Beverly's geography" and that I left this variable simply as "a neutral setting or backdrop." The lengthy discussions about school developments in the different sections of the community as well as a detailed analysis of their wealth and expenditures demonstrate otherwise. Unlike Katz, who was not aware of the earlier sectional conflicts over school expenditures, I have shown how the outlying areas frequently challenged the educational priorities of those who lived in the central grammar school district.

Stevens is more accurate in his discussion of my use of geographic location. He acknowledges my arguments that the outlying areas resented spending their tax dollars on a high school rather than on their common schools and that they feared school district centralization and consolidation. He suggests, however, that I should have gone one step further because the "language-centered curriculum of high school" had "little to offer a farmer's son or sons of a shoemaker, mariner, or fisherman in the way of technical knowledge to improve occupational skills" and that for farmers to accept a high school "would have been to reject much of their cherished agricultural heritage."

The points raised by Stevens are important and intriguing. I continue to believe that the residents of the outlying areas rejected the high school mainly as too expensive and unnecessary—especially since their children at the time were not receiving even an adequate common school education. Undoubtedly some parents did question the relevance or usefulness of high school education altogether. Yet New England farmers increasingly did not want all or even most of their children to pursue careers in agriculture because opportunities seemed much more attractive elsewhere. In addition, not all parents in skilled or unskilled occupations rejected a high school education in principle. My recent work on Newburyport, Massachusetts, at the time just before the Civil war shows that while children of parents from these occupations were less likely to attend one of the local high schools, 37 percent of children whose parents were unskilled attended high school. In addition, some working-class parents may have favored a high school education but simply could not afford to send their older children to school. Thus, the suggestion by Stevens that we should explore further the meaning of a high school education for rural and working-class Americans is a good one, but it probably was not a very compelling consideration for most voters deciding on the Beverly High School.

The second best predictor of the vote is a weighted index of town office holding. Both Katz and Stevens raise questions about the construction and meaning of that variable. Katz says that my weighting scheme for the town officeholders "is estimated by the occupation of the officeholders" so that "occupation is introduced twice" in the MCA. This is incorrect. As I stated in the book, "the scale was constructed on the basis of an estimate of the prestige and importance attached to these offices by contemporaries" (161n). The occupation of the officeholders was never used to make those inferences—though there is of course some overlap between office holding and one's occupation. The amount of overlap between this and the other independent variables, however, was not large enough to distort the analysis. For example, with town office holding removed from the MCA, geography continues to be a much more important factor than occupation in explaining the vote on the high school.

Stevens questions "using the six years between 1854 and 1860 to identify this voter attribute" and argues that it "would seem more reasonable to bring the office-holding variable into line with the year of the other variables." He also says that since "office holding is a mix of several factors and may in fact have a large overlap with other variables in the equation . . . its explanatory value is very limited." One could legitimately adopt Steven's suggestion and only use the list of town officeholders in 1860 to construct this variable. This would miss, however, the importance of a life course approach that sees individuals affected by their prior experiences. In other words, someone who was a former school committee member or former alderman in Beverly probably viewed his responsibility toward the town and the high school issue somewhat differently than an individual who had never held any local office. Stevens is correct, of course, to point out that my interpretation of the meaning of town office holding is complex because several different factors are reflected by this variable. This does not, however, eliminate the explanatory value of the variable, but only limits its conceptual clarity. I also wonder if some of the other variables we routinely employ such as wealth, occupation, and ethnicity are really any less complex in how they describe individual attitudes and behavior? While we need indices as unambiguous and straightforward as possible, in practice many of the socioeconomic factors used in historical analyses have multiple and complex meanings.

Although Katz insists that my results are not very different from his, the statistical analyses suggest otherwise. To compare the differences between our approaches, I ran two additional MCAs: one using his three best predictors (occupation, wealth, and children in household), and the other using my three best predictors (geographic location, town office holding, and wealth). As reported in the book (107), my set of variables accounts for 29.4 percent of the total variance while Katz's variables only explain 9.6 percent. Stevens correctly points out that the rank ordering of my variables may have changed when I used three instead of nine independent variables. It turns out, however, that the rank order of geographic location (beta = .3793), town office holding (beta = .3190), and wealth (beta = .2072) remains the same.

Given the additional information that now has been uncovered about the controversy over the Beverly High School as well as the MCA runs reported in my book, it is not surprising that my interpretation of events in that community differs from Katz's original study. What is puzzling is that Katz continues to defend unequivocally his previous class explanation and especially his linkage of the shoemakers' strike to the vote against the high school. Quite frankly, I simply do not think that he has sufficient evidence to warrant such an interpretation.

The vote on the high school did not reveal clear-cut divisions along occupational lines. While two-thirds of the voters in professional and white-collar occupations favored retaining the high school, only half of the manufacturers endorsed it. While most farmers, shoemakers, and mariners opposed that institution, more than one-fourth of them did support it. Katz is correct to see differences among these occupational groups, but at the same time he should acknowledge that the town was hardly as polarized along class lines on this issue as he suggests. Furthermore, and perhaps most important of all, controlling for the effects of the other independent variables in the MCA, occupation is only the eighth best predictor of a voter's position on the high school among the nine independent variables. Even removing geographic location, which Katz sees overlapping so much with occupation, does not help his argument much as occupation is then only the sixth best predictor among the eight independent variables.

Katz's efforts to counter my reservations about his class interpretation are imaginative, but not convincing. He does not understand why the fact that the Beverly shoemakers joined the strike "only" three weeks after it started (and two weeks after an estimated 20,000 shoe workers in twenty-five towns went on strike) might raise questions about the extent of class antagonisms in Beverly. Since the shoe strikers in Lynn pleaded with their brethren in other towns to join the strike immediately, the unusually lengthy delay among Beverly workers may indicate less conflict within Beverly than elsewhere and less solidarity with their counterparts in other communities—especially because strikers wanted everyone to join quickly as many antebellum strikes could not last very long if they did not have widespread support immediately.

If the vote against the high school was regarded by workers as an important opportunity to strike back at representatives of manufacturers and commercial interests, as Katz believes, then one might expect an unusually large turnout at the town meeting by the workers. Yet the turnout among workers was much lower than in state or national elections and lower than among the more propertied citizens. Katz suggests that since "the vote took place during the day

when many probably could not afford to stay away from work," it is not surprising that workers did not participate in larger numbers. Yet if class tensions
were as high in Beverly as Katz asserts and opposition to the high school seen
as an important symbol, perhaps more workers would have sacrificed one day's
wages. Besides, since the shoe strike in Beverly started on March 13 but the
vote on the high school did not occur until March 14, most shoe workers
presumably did not have to worry about working that day. In addition, if opposition to the high school was so important to the strikers, why did two-thirds
of the strike activists (as identified in the newspapers) fail to vote on this issue?
Among the strike activists who voted, four of them opposed the high school
while one supported it.

Given Katz's portrayal of sharp class antagonism in Beverly and the particular hostility of the strikers to the high school, one is surprised to learn that
some shoe manufacturers and merchants openly supported the strike and offered the shoe workers assistance. Rather than polarizing the town as in Lynn,
where the town officials mobilized the police and militia against the strikers,
the Beverly town meeting voted the strikers the use of the town hall for their
meetings, and the local newspaper expressed considerable sympathy for the
strikers. One is also amazed to discover that the Beverly strikers frequently
called upon the manufacturers and merchants to address their meetings and
applauded their statements. Indeed, Frederick Choate, a wealthy lawyer and
investor who was one of the most visible and ardent spokesmen on behalf of
the high school was called upon twice to address the strikers and cheered when
he "spoke eloquently in aid of the cause and pledged to it his full share of aid
and comfort" (100).

Interestingly, in none of the contemporary accounts of the vote on the high
school or of the shoemakers' strike in Beverly is there ever any indication of a
linkage between the two issues. Indeed, when Frederick Ober, a resident of
Beverly in 1860, wrote in the 1880s a short history of that community, his
account more closely parallels my interpretation than that of Katz:

> The High School was not established until after a conflict of several
> years, the opposition being not so much against the establishment of the
> school itself as from fear that the money devoted to its support would be
> proportionately taken from the various district schools, all of them being
> popular local institutions, and each with its special neighborhood
> attractions.
>
> The town had become large enough to be liable in law to support a
> High School, and some of its friends got so far out of patience in wait-
> ing for the town to establish it that they had it indicted. This but inten-
> sified the opposition, which was then a decided majority, and they at first
> attempted to defend the town; but eventually yielded, though the school

was at first established at the West Farms, at some distance from the center of population. (Vinovskis, 1985a: 105)

Finally, if class tensions and antagonisms were as sharp and bitter as Katz suggests, we might expect that the divisions over the high school persisted. Yet Katz left us with a misleading impression of the extent of class divisions within Beverly by not revealing that the Beverly High School was reestablished the next year under rather harmonious conditions.

I agree with Katz that much work remains to be done on analyzing working-class lives in antebellum America. But the way to proceed is to pay close attention to the local setting and not to infer that something was a class issue unless there is at least some tangible evidence for it.

Katz concludes his critique by stating that "politics cannot be divorced from scholarship, and numbers are no more neutral than words. Vinovskis is as partisan as the rest of us. I mean this as no criticism. Rather, I only wish he would make his assumptions and commitments more explicit and drop the fiction of neutrality. For history, after all, is about questions that matter."

While I find much to admire in Katz's enthusiasm and work in policy analysis, I am not sure that we share the same approach to our scholarship. Certainly I strongly agree with him that as historians we can and should be deeply involved in formulating and implementing policy. I reject the notion that scholars must distance themselves from the policy-making arena—as many of us were advised in graduate school. I also agree with Katz that history can and does inform policy making—although the connection is usually much more distant and tenuous than some of us would like. Yet as a professional historian, I see it as my responsibility to try to be as "scholarly and objective" as possible even though we are all inevitably influenced to some degree by our prior experiences and commitments. Using a social science approach does not guarantee objectivity, but it encourages us to be more explicit about our assumptions and methodology so that our colleagues, such as Katz and Stevens, can correct us if we stray too far from the evidence.

Having worked in Washington during 1978 as the deputy staff director of the U.S. House of Representatives' Select Committee on Population and from 1981 through 1985 as a consultant to the Office of Adolescent Pregnancy Programs, I was at first disturbed to see that congressmen sometimes cited scholarly studies to support their positions on domestic family planning programs in ways that differed from my own interpretation of those studies or my own political inclinations. Over time I have come to recognize that while scholarly studies can have an important impact upon the policy-making process, their usage is often shaped by the predilections of the decision makers. Yet if we as social scientists hope to convince policy makers that they should continue to consult our work, we must assure them and ourselves that we are trying to be as "scholarly and objective" in our investigations as possible—even if it means reporting findings antithetical to our own political orientation. This is not meant as a criticism of Katz, who has been exemplary as a social scientist as well as a concerned citizen, but as an explanation of why I strive to separate my own politics and values from my analyses as much as possible.

Chapter 8 / *Have We Underestimated the Extent of Antebellum High School Attendance?*

Public high schools were relatively rare in antebellum America. Given their lack, it is not surprising that many scholars have concluded that only a small percentage of children ever attended one. Indeed, Edward Krug, in his multi-volume study of high schools, observed that even by the 1880s "it was a rare thing to go to high school" (1969: 11).

It is true that most antebellum communities, especially those in states outside of New England, did not provide public high schools for their teenagers (Grizzell, 1923). But in some regions, like New England, many cities and towns had established them. The first public high school opened in Boston in 1821, but it was not until the late 1840s and 1850s that high schools became more common in Massachusetts (Vinovskis, 1985a). Did a significant proportion of adolescents in communities with public high schools attend these institutions? Most scholars seem to agree that even in towns that had high schools, only a tiny minority attended. Based on his detailed study of Massachusetts public high schools, Michael Katz (1968: 39) concluded that "high schools were minority institutions probably attended mainly by middle-class children."[1] In addition, several recent studies of urban high schools before and after the Civil War emphasize that only a small percentage of school-age children ever attended one. In nineteenth-century San Francisco, for example, no more than 4 percent of public school students enrolled in a high school (Katznelson and Weir, 1985: 230n). Similarly, in antebellum Philadelphia males in the sole public high school represented less than 1 percent of all students in the common schools (Labaree, 1988: 26–27).[2]

In contrast to the prevailing opinion that few antebellum children ever attended high school, even in those communities that had established one, in this chapter I shall analyze individual-level high school attendance data from Newburyport, Massachusetts, in the mid-nineteenth century to show a much higher level of high school attendance than heretofore believed. Almost all of the earlier studies relied on aggregate annual local high school attendance data. Therefore, it was difficult to estimate the proportion of children who ever attended high school—especially without any data on the rate of turnover among students from one year to the next. Using the results from the individual-level analysis of high school attendance in Newburyport, I have devised a procedure for estimating the proportion of those ever attending high school from the available aggregate local school statistics. I then apply this procedure to all Essex County cities and towns with high schools in 1860–61 to estimate the likelihood of children ever attending a high school. The results from this analysis provide a more accurate picture of the importance of high school education in the life course of antebellum adolescents in communities that had high schools.

High School Attendance in Newburyport, Massachusetts

This analysis of antebellum high school attendance in Newburyport, Massachusetts, is an extension of a project on death and dying in Civil War America and utilizes the extensive individual-level files gathered for that investigation (Vinovskis, 1989a).[3] No one community is ever typical or representative of all others, but Newburyport offers a reasonable setting for analyzing high school attendance because of its detailed school records and its diverse population. Newburyport was a medium-sized Massachusetts port located near the New Hampshire border. With It experienced rapid growth during the 1840s and 1850s, with the introduction of steam-powered textile mills. The population consisted mainly of Massachusetts natives plus a sizable portion of Irish immigrants (Currier, 1906–9; Smith, 1854). An earlier analysis of antebellum Newburyport by Stephan Thernstrom (1964) emphasized the lack of education received by foreign-born children and provides a useful background for this investigation.[4]

By 1860, Newburyport had a well-developed school system that included several high schools. The Brown High School provided both classical and English education for males, while the Female High School instructed females. The Putnam Free School, established from a bequest from Oliver Putnam, offered tuition-free education for both males and females from the region. In most years, nearly 60 percent of the students at the Putnam Free School were from Newburyport. The fact that Newburyport was geographically an unusually compact settlement meant that children in the community had ample opportunity to attend one of these schools.

According to local school reports, 288 different students from Newburyport attended one of the high schools in 1860 (Newburyport School Committee, 1860; *A Catalogue of the Trustees, Instructors, and Students of the Putnam Free School,* 1861). It is impossible to calculate from these aggregate enrollment figures exactly what proportion of high-school-age children ever attended one of these institutions because the reports do not provide information on the length of time students attended or the ages at which they enrolled. If the rate of turnover in high school is very large, for example, a much greater percentage of children will have attended one at some point than if the turnover is small. In addition, one cannot tell from the published reports the distribution of the ages of students in high school, and therefore it is not possible to ascertain what age-group should be used to calculate the percentage of students enrolled.

Instead of relying upon aggregate annual data for estimating high school attendance, I have used individual-level information on high school attendance and matched that information to a computerized file of the 13,439 residents of Newburyport in 1860. Altogether, 818 students enrolled in one of the three high schools from 1857 to 1863, and 699 of these could be matched to their census entry (85.5 percent). Some of the younger children in 1860 may have enrolled in high school after 1863, and some of the older ones who had attended high school may have left the community before 1860. Therefore, the estimate of the percentage of children enrolled in any of the high schools is confined to those ages eleven to sixteen in 1860.[5]

Overall, the percentage of children ages eleven to sixteen in 1860 who ever attended any high school is much higher than any of the previous estimates for the antebellum period—partly because Newburyport had such a well-developed and convenient high school system and partly because the methodology employed here permits a more accurate estimate of high school attendance than investigations based solely on more limited cross-sectional data or studies that fail to consider the population at risk of being in high school. Between 1857 and 1863, 31.9 percent of all children ages eleven to sixteen in 1860 were enrolled in one of the high schools.[6] Other studies have argued that antebellum high schools served only a very small minority of children in the community, yet in Newburyport almost one-third of the children received at least some high school education.[7]

Although a large number of Newburyport children attended one of the high schools, most of them stayed for only a short time. Overall, 30.8 percent of students who entered graduated.[8] The Newburyport School Committee recognized the high dropout rate as a serious problem and continually urged parents not to remove their children prematurely:

It is exceedingly to be regretted that parents will allow their sons to lose the great advantages of finishing the course and graduating from the School. Especially when, as it often happens, the only gain to be derived from removing a boy from school, is some slight pecuniary advantage that seems valuable only because it is present. But, after all, do such parents really make a gain? Investigations made in the city of Lawrence, by a gentleman interested in education, have shown the average annual earnings of those in that city who had received a High School education, to be several hundred dollars more than the pay received yearly by those who have not finished the prescribed course of studies.

No doubt it is absolutely necessary for some students to leave school before graduating. But parents should consider well, not merely the pecuniary motives, but the obligations they are under to furnish society with educated and well-trained minds, true and good men. (Newburyport School Committee, 1867: 8–9)

Indeed, one of the characteristics of antebellum high schools is the high dropout rate (Grizzell, 1923; Inglis, 1911).

Most secondary accounts of antebellum education have stressed that high schools were mainly for the children of the wealthy and that almost no children of working-class parents attended (Katz, 1968). In Newburyport the situation was more complex. Children whose parents were native-born, more affluent, and in the more prestigious and remunerative occupations were more likely to be enrolled in a high school and to graduate than their less fortunate counterparts. Particularly striking was the fact that girls were much more likely to graduate from high school than boys—especially those girls who attended the Female High School.[9] Yet the children of unskilled fathers were not entirely excluded from high school as earlier studies have implied. Nearly one out of every six children of unskilled fathers attended one of these institutions and about one-fifth of them graduated. As previous scholars had suggested, however, the children of foreign-born parents were much less likely to attend high school and even less likely to complete it. Thus, although children of native, upper- and middle-class parents were the main beneficiaries of the emerging high schools in Newburyport, children of unskilled fathers or of foreign-born parents were not totally excluded or ignored.[10]

High School Attendance in Essex County in 1860

It was surprising to discover that more than three out of ten children ages eleven to sixteen in 1860 attended one of the high schools in Newburyport, Massachusetts, between 1857 and 1863. How typical was this when compared to other Massachusetts communities? After all, Newburyport had three high schools and was a relatively compact settlement. In order to place the experiences of Newburyport children in a broader perspective, I examined high school attendance in all of the cities and townships in Essex County (including Newburyport) in 1860.[11]

Fourteen of the thirty-four communities in Essex County in 1860 had public high schools.[12] Although no statewide figures on high school attendance exist for Massachusetts in 1860, almost all published local school reports give the number of students attending high school. Unfortunately, these reports often do not distinguish between the total number of pupils attending high school in a particular session (such as the fall or winter term) and the total number of different students ever attending high school during that entire year. To estimate the total number of students who ever attended high school, the aggregate information provided in some of the school reports should be increased by some amount to more accurately represent the number who ever attended during the year. For high schools that do not provide information on the total number of different students attending during the year, it is necessary to estimate the amount by which the given figure should be increased. Based on data from communities that provided information on both the total number of different students and the number enrolled in a particular session, it seems appropriate to increase the highest number ever enrolled in any session during the year by 25 percent for those high schools that did not list the total number of different students.[13]

Placing the total number of different high school students in the numerator, we still need an estimate of the number of youth who might have attended in the denominator in order to calculate the percentage of children who ever attended high school. The published federal census data for 1860 provide the aggregate number of children ages ten to nineteen, but that figure needs to be reduced to reflect more precisely those of high school age. This task is even more complicated because the estimate of the percentage of children who ever attended high school is affected to some degree by the rate of student turnover from one year to the next.[14] Based on information from the detailed, individual-level study of Newburyport high schools, an estimate of 35 percent of those ages ten to nineteen in the denominator divided into the total number of different students yields a reasonably close approximation of the percentage of children ever attending a public high school.[15]

Altogether, about 1,586 students attended public high schools in Essex County communities in 1860. Using the estimating procedure developed above, approximately 14.6 percent of all children in Essex County communities ever went to high school in the mid-nineteenth century.[16] In communities that had a high school in 1860, about 19.2 percent of the children attended high school at some point.[17] Thus, a sizable minority of children in antebellum communities with high schools received at least some instruction in those institutions.[18]

Among Essex County communities with a high school in 1860, there was a great range in the percentage of children who ever attended high school. In Lawrence, a large textile center, only 8.0 percent of the children ever attended high school, while in the small community of Manchester 55.5 percent attended at some time. In part this difference reflects the fact that teenagers eager to enter the labor force probably left Manchester to seek better employment opportunities in larger and more economically developed cities like Lawrence. Nevertheless, there appears to be a pattern of higher high school attendance in smaller communities with high schools than in the larger cities (see table 8.1).

Among the cities and townships with high schools, in those with fewer than 2,500 inhabitants, 47.5 percent of the children attended high school.[19] Communities with 2,500 through 4,999 residents enrolled 25.0 percent of their children.[20] Townships with 5,000 through 9,999 inhabitants sent 22.0 percent of their children to high school.[21] Cities with 10,000 through 14,999 people had 27.4 percent of their children receiving some high school education.[22] Finally, cities with more than 15,000 residents sent 11.7 percent of their children to high school.[23] High school attendance in Newburyport (31.9 percent) was considerably higher than the estimate for the other communities with more than 10,000 inhabitants (13.0 percent).

Although the smaller communities with high schools sent a disproportionately large percentage of children to them, overall a smaller proportion of children in the rural townships went to high school because most of those areas did not have a high school (see table 8.2). Parents living in townships with fewer than 2,500 inhabitants, for example, sent only 6.8 percent of their children to high school. The highest rate of high school attendance in Essex County was found to occur in the two towns with populations of 10,000 through 14,999; one of them was Newburyport, with its unusually high rate of high school attendance.

Although the larger communities had a disproportionate number of high school attendees, the students were not as concentrated in these communities

Table 8.1 / *Percentage of Children Ever Attending High School in Essex County Communities with High Schools, by Town Size, 1860–61*

Size of Town	Percent Ever Attending
0–2,499	47.5
2,500–4,999	25.0
5,000–9,999	22.0
10,000–14,999	27.4
15,000 and above	11.7
ALL TOWNS	19.2

Table 8.2 / *Percentage of Children Ever Attending High School in All Essex County Communities, by Town Size, 1860–61*

Size of Town	Percent Ever Attending
0–2,499	6.8
2,500–4,999	12.0
5,000–9,999	18.1
10,000–14,999	27.4
15,000 and above	11.7
ALL TOWNS	14.6

as one might have imagined. Individuals living in cities with a population of more than 10,000 made up 49.9 percent of the population of Essex County, but their high school students made up only 55.4 percent of the total number of high school students in the county.

Even though many Essex County communities supported public high schools and sent substantial minority of their children to them, local educators complained about the irregularity of attendance and the low rate of graduation. The Georgetown School Committee pointed out that: "Of those, who have been admitted to our High School, quite a number have not attended but one term, and some not even that. The acquisitions of a year's study at School of youth of mature years as much exceeds those of a year in earlier childhood, as the amount of manual labor he could perform in the first named period would exceed that he could have performed in the same time in his earlier childhood" (Georgetown School Committee, 1861: 13). Similarly, the superintendent of schools in Lawrence bemoaned the unwillingness of most students to complete their high school education:

> Here, perhaps, better than in any other connection, I may call attention to a fact, in this department of our schools, which has called forth from many observations of surprise and regret—and which may or may not result from causes capable of remedy. I refer to the fact that so few of the whole number entering the High School grade complete the course of instruction and leave with the honor of Diploma. The last graduating class entered *thirty-six* in number, and *eleven* only were presented for examination, from both the Classical and English Departments. If the diploma be of any importance, or worthy of acceptance by the pupil, it must obviously be conditioned, as it has been by the Committee, on the *honorable completion of the prescribed course* of study. The small percentage of the whole thus completing the course has become matter of notoriety. (Lawrence School Committee, 1861: 11)

Thus, while a sizable minority of children received some high school education in antebellum Essex County, very few of them graduated.

There is also the question of exactly what constituted a high school education. By 1860, most public high schools in Massachusetts provided a fairly comprehensive set of courses that went well beyond those offered in the grammar schools.[24] But in some communities, especially the smaller ones, the level of instruction was not much different. Indeed, in a town such as Amesbury, which had been forced to establish a public high school by state regulations, the local school committee candidly acknowledged that "a High school, worthy of the name, is thus rendered impossible, though we often dignify our Grammar schools by this designation" (Amesbury School Committee, 1864: 9).[25]

One notes in the local school reports for Essex County in the 1860s and 1870s, however, a definite sense of progress and accomplishment as the high school curricula were enhanced and the admission requirements for entering high schools were gradually raised. Nevertheless, many of the communities in the period from 1850 through 1880 only established public high schools because of the pressure from the Massachusetts Board of Education and their allies at the local level. Complaints about the great expense of maintaining a public high school appear from time to time—often coupled with the accusation that few students graduated.[26] Yet almost all high schools survived, even when the inflationary pressures of the Civil War might have provided a convenient excuse to abandon this seemingly expensive institution.[27] By the 1870s and 1880s the public high school had become a much more established and accepted institution in the Commonwealth.[28]

Katz's Estimate of High School Attendance

Michael Katz's statements about antebellum high school attendance in Massachusetts are frequently cited, and it may be useful to reexamine his calculations to see how they compare with the results presented here. He drew a 10 percent random sample of high schools in Massachusetts in 1860 and used the published local school reports to estimate high school attendance (Katz, 1968: 39, 270). Katz investigated high school attendance in eleven communities. Although he does not identify which communities he selected, he provides the 1860 population of the city or town, so that it is possible to reconstruct the communities used in his analysis.[29]

Although Katz concluded that only a minority of children ever attended these institutions, the estimates he provides in the text actually show this minority to be quite sizable in the smaller communities: "In the smallest and most static towns (1,000–3,000), about 28 percent of the eligible attended. In the medium-sized ones (6,000–8,000), about 15 percent, and in the large, expanding cities (over 14,000), approximately 8 percent" (1968: 39). Overall, he concluded that less than one-fifth of eligible children in these cities and towns received any high school education.

A more precise estimate of high school attendance using Katz's data and assumptions can be obtained by calculating his estimate of the number of high school age students from the federal census (40 percent of those ages ten to nineteen), the number of high school students for each community based on the percentage enrolled figures presented by him, and then totaling the number of children and high school students for all eleven cities and towns. The result is that according to Katz, 11.8 percent of the eligible children in Massachusetts communities with high schools attended them—a figure much lower than my estimate of 19.2 percent of children ever attending high school in Essex County cities and towns with such institutions in 1860.[30]

Given the large difference in our estimates, it is necessary to look more closely at Katz's procedures for calculating attendance. One major difference is that Katz did not estimate the total number of different students who attended high school during the year but only "the number of children attending during the winter or third (depending on how the year was divided) session" (270)." Since the total number of different students ever enrolled in high school during the year is usually considerably larger than those enrolled in any particular session, Katz underestimates high school attendance.

Katz introduced a further downward bias by apparently using the average enrollment rather than the total enrollment for the winter or third session. This is compounded by the fact that the winter or third session does not always have the highest enrollment. In Taunton, for example, the total enrollment in winter was 96 students, whereas the total enrollment in fall was 116 (Taunton School Committee, 1861: 33).[31] Similarly, in Fall River the total winter high school enrollment was only 82, and the total summer enrollment was 109 students (Fall River School Committee, 1861: 16).[32]

Katz also underestimated high school attendance because he assumed that there was only one high school in all of the communities. There were two high schools in Chicopee in 1860–61—one in district four and one in district six (Chicopee School Committee, 1861: 31). Katz did use a fairly good estimate for the children eligible to attend high school: 40 percent of children ages ten to nineteen, which is close to the 35 percent that the detailed analysis of high school attendance in Newburyport shows is probably a better estimate.

If one recalculates the number of students ever attending high school in Katz's random sample of communities after correcting for the problems discussed above, the rate of attendance increases substantially. Instead of only 11.8 percent of children ever attending high school, the figure rises to 18.8 percent—remarkably close to the overall estimate for high school attendance in

Essex County communities that had such institutions on the eve of the Civil War.[33]

Conclusion

Contrary to the impression presented in recent studies of nineteenth-century high school attendance in large urban areas, a substantial minority of antebellum youth attended one of these institutions in many of the smaller communities that had established a high school. In Essex County, Massachusetts, in 1860, nearly one out of five children in cities and townships with high schools attended. If we included school attendance figures from such private academies as the Abbot Academy, the Bradford Academy, or the Phillips Academy, the estimate would be higher. Although we do not have complete data for private school attendance for children of Essex County parents, a partial list can be compiled from nine private school catalogs, which yield an additional 478 students taking high-school-level courses.[34] Most of these students in private schools (71.3 percent) are from communities without a public high school. As a result, if we combine the public and private attendance figures, 19.0 percent of all children in Essex County received at least some equivalent of a high school education.

Perhaps the most surprising finding was that in at least one medium-sized city—Newburyport—nearly one-third of the children received some high school education. Although high school attendance in Newburyport certainly was not typical of the other larger communities in Essex County, many of them still sent 10 to 15 percent of their children to a public high school. In addition, while public high schools have been portrayed as the exclusive preserve of middle- or upper-class children, approximately one out of six children of unskilled Newburyport laborers attended one.

Another significant finding was that in small communities with high schools, attendance was very high. Four out of ten children in Georgetown and more than one-half of those in Manchester went to high school. By focusing so heavily on high schools in the larger urban areas, historians have failed to investigate the possible importance of these institutions for the residents of smaller and more rural communities.

Even though sizable numbers of children attended high schools in some cities and towns, most of them did not stay there long. Throughout the antebellum period, educators reported that very few students who entered high school graduated, and many stayed for only one term. Why were parents so willing to send their children to a high school, often after a rigorous entrance examination, but then seemingly so indifferent to having them complete that education? What were the attitudes of adolescents toward entering and staying in high schools? Even in towns with high schools, most older children attended only grammar school. What difference did this make in terms of their academic training and their future careers? Were antebellum employers really willing to pay better wages to former high school students and even more substantial premiums to those who graduated? These and many other such questions need to be addressed before we understand the meaning and the significance of the growth of public high schools in the decades before the Civil War.

Notes

1. Katz (1968) drew a 10 percent random sample of Massachusetts communities with public high schools in 1860 and found that less than one out of every five eligible children attended. He used this estimate to argue that few children ever attended one of these institutions. The procedures he employed, however, are problematic.

2. Labaree (1988) does not attempt to estimate exactly what proportion of male or female adolescents ever enrolled in a high school, but the inference clearly is that very few of them attended; see also Perlmann (1985). Ueda (1987) also does not attempt to estimate the proportion of children who went to the Somerville High School before the Civil War, but he observes that few children from the lower classes were enrolled. His figures suggest, however, that by the late nineteenth century a substantial minority of children in Somerville were attending high school.

3. For a preliminary essay on the project on death and dying, see Vinovskis (1989a).

4. Other useful monographs on early Newburyport are Labaree (1962) and Grigg (1984).

5. For a more detailed discussion of the pattern of high school attendance, see Vinovskis (1985b). The age-specific rates for high school attendance were initially examined for all persons ages eight to twenty-four in Newburyport in 1860, but the focus on children ages eleven to sixteen was made after an inspection of those data and after an analysis of the ages at entry into the three high schools. The decision to confine the analysis to children ages eleven to sixteen was dictated in part by the fact that individual-level information on high school attendance was restricted to the period 1857–63. Some children older than sixteen in 1860, for example, were attending high school in that year, but one could

not be certain from this data set if others of that age-group had attended high school before 1857. In other words, because this individual-level analysis attempts to ascertain the percentage of children who ever went to high school at some point in their lives, it is necessary to look only at those age-groups for which we are certain that we have complete data.

6. The influx of adolescents from other communities into Newburyport in order to work undoubtedly leads to an underestimation of the percentage of native Newburyport youths receiving a high school education. If we look at children ages eleven to sixteen in 1860 living with at least one parent, 33.9 percent of them attended one of the high schools.

7. Whereas about one-third of Newburyport children ages eleven to sixteen in 1860 enrolled at some point in high school, many others attended grammar schools at those ages but never went to high school. More than three-fourths of children ages eleven to sixteen living with at least one parent were enrolled in some school in 1860, but only a fraction of these continued on to high school. For more details about those going to grammar schools, see Vinovskis (1985b).

8. A multiple classification analysis was done to see what predicted graduation from high school. The most important determinant of high school graduation was not the personal characteristics of the student or their parents, but the school attended. Whereas only 20 percent of the male students at the Brown High School and 14 percent of the male and female students at the Putnam Free School graduated, 55 percent of the female students at the Female High School graduated. Unfortunately, there is no simple explanation for this pattern. For a more detailed discussion, see Vinovskis (1985b).

9. The percentage of males and females who ever attended high school in Newburyport was almost identical (34 percent vs. 33 percent). After controlling for the effects of the other variables, males were slightly more likely to attend than females (the adjusted means in an MCA analysis were 35.1 percent vs. 32.8 percent). but it was the weakest predictor of high school attendance (Vinovskis, 1985b).

10. For details of the multiple classification analyses upon which these statements are based, see Vinovskis (1985b). Thernstrom (1964) underestimated the extent of school attendance among children whose fathers were unskilled laborers. There is growing evidence that a significant number of children from families whose fathers were in blue-collar occupations, particularly those in skilled jobs, attended public high schools (Angus, 1981a).

11. One might well ask how typical was Essex County in terms of high school attendance compared to the rest of Massachusetts. Although there is no readily available data for the state in 1860, there is information on high school attendance in 1875. At that time, high school attendance in Essex County was just slightly below that for the state as a whole. See chap. 9 for details of that analysis.

12. The communities that had a high school were determined by consulting an unpublished list compiled by the Massachusetts Board of Education in 1859–60. Each town had been asked: "Is there a High School supported by Taxation, in which the Latin and Greek languages are taught?" In addition, the published annual school reports for thirty-one of the thirty-four communities were surveyed. Finally, the list of high schools in Massachusetts provided by Inglis (1911) was used. Private academies, such as the Phillips Academy or the Bradford Academy, were not included. Furthermore, although the town of Beverly had a high school in 1859 and 1861, it did not have one during 1860 because the town meeting temporarily abolished it (Katz, 1968; Vinovskis, 1985a). Therefore, Beverly is not included among those with a high school in 1860. See also chap. 7.

13. Data on both the total number of different students and the number enrolled in a particular session are available for five Massa-

chusetts communities—Chicopee (1860), Fall River (1860), Gloucester (1874, 1875, 1876), Marblehead (1877, 1878, 1879, 1880), and Millbury (1860). In all, there is information on both items for eleven different situations (Chicopee had two high schools in 1860 and therefore provided two different cases for our purposes). From these data we can estimate how much the highest semester attendance figures would have to be increased to approximate the total number of different students enrolled during that year. For the eleven different situations, an average increase of approximately 25 percent was necessary to convert the highest semester enrollment into the total number of different students ever attending during that year; but there was some variation among the individual cases in what adjustment factor had to be employed. Therefore, although the 25 percent adjustment rate is probably a reasonable figure overall, it may introduce some small errors in estimating high school attendance for any particular community. Of the fourteen Essex County communities with high schools in 1860–61, half of them provided information on the number of different students attending during the year and therefore did not require any adjustment.

14. Using the total number of different students in high school during the year in the numerator takes into consideration the annual rate of student turnover. Because high school programs were designed for more than one year, differences in student dropout rates from one year to the next will also affect the total number of students ever attending a public high school at some point in their lives.

15. Based upon actual high school attendance data and the census information on children in 1860, we know that 31.9 percent of Newburyport children in 1860 attended high school at some point in their lives. For most communities, however, we have only the number of different students attending high school in a given year and the aggregate number of children ages ten to nineteen from the published federal census for Massachusetts. Therefore, we need a way of approximating the rate of attendance from those two figures. This can be done by placing the number of different children in a high school in the numerator and by using the detailed Newbury-

port data to calculate what adjustment needs to be made in the denominator of the number of children ages ten to nineteen to arrive at the proportion of children ever attending high school.

In Newburyport, 288 different students were enrolled in one of the three high schools in 1860, there were 2,505 children ages ten to nineteen according to the federal census, and we have estimated from the more detailed data that 31.9 percent of children attended a high school at some point. Therefore, we want to solve for x, where x is the proportion of children ages ten to nineteen that would yield an approximate estimate of the proportion of children who ever attended a high school in a particular community given information on the number of different students attending during that year:

$$288 \div 2,505x = 31.9\%$$

Solving for x, we find that it equals 36 percent or to use a more rounded number, 35 percent. Katz (1968: 270) makes a very good estimate of this correction factor without the benefit of a detailed individual-level study of high school attendance. He used an estimate of 40 percent of those ages ten to nineteen in his denominator to estimate the proportion ever attending high school (which would have yielded an estimate of 28.5 percent for New-buryport children ever attending high school).

16. We can now use our finding of 35 per-cent to estimate the proportion who ever at-tended high school in Essex County based only upon the aggregate number of different high school students in 1860 and the number of children ages ten to nineteen in that year. There were an estimated 1,586 different stu-dents who attended an Essex County public high school in 1860, and 31,011 children ages ten to nineteen. Applying our formula of mul-tiplying 31,011 by 35 percent and dividing that into the 1,586 different students attending a public high school yields an estimate of 14.6 percent who ever attended such an institution.

17. The estimating procedure assumes, of course, that the rate of turnover from one year to the next in other Essex County high schools is similar to that of Newburyport. Al-though there are no good data on turnover for those communities, it is likely that the 30 per-cent graduation rate for Newburyport is high.

Therefore, our estimating procedure probably understates the actual number of students re-ceiving some high school education in the other communities.

18. If we had not adjusted the attendance estimates upwards for those institutions that did not provide data on the total number of different students attending, the proportion of school-age children who ever attended high school in Essex County would have been 13.1 percent instead of 14.6 percent. Similarly, the percentage of those who attended in communi-ties with high schools in 1860 would have been 17.2 percent instead of 19.2 percent.

19. Georgetown had 40.9 percent attending; Manchester had 55.5 percent attending.

20. Amesbury had 22.9 percent attending; Ipswich had 26.7 percent attending; Rockport had 25.5 percent attending.

21. Danvers had 21.2 attending; Haverhill had 24.8 percent attending; Marblehead had 22.6 percent attending; South Danvers had 17.7 percent attending.

22. Gloucester had 20.5 percent attending; Newburyport had 31.9 percent attending.

23. Lawrence had 8.0 percent attending; Lynn had 11.3 percent attending; Salem had 15.1 percent attending.

24. For a very useful discussion of what courses were being offered in the Massachu-setts public high schools, see Inglis (1911).

25. Abner J. Phipps, agent for the Massa-chusetts Board of Education, observed that: "When visiting the cities and towns in which these schools [high schools] are maintained, I usually spend some time in inspecting them, as from such an inspection one can better judge of the kind of education, in its quality and extent, which the children receive in the several grades of schools through which they have passed, and what further advantages this highest grade affords them. Of a large number of these schools I can speak in terms of the highest commendation. . . . About one-third of the High Schools of Massachusetts are of this class. Another third embraces schools of much excellence, giving a very fair English ed-ucation, and a passable preparation for Col-lege. The remaining third is of a much lower order, being but little in advance of the aver-age Grammar School" (Massachusetts Board of Education, *Annual Report*, 1877: 46).

26. Although much research has focused on the abolition of the Beverly High School in 1860 (see chap. 7), little attention has been paid to complaints about the excessive cost and infrequent use of these institutions. In the school committee reports for Danvers, for example, there are frequent references to the opposition of taxpayers to the maintenance of high schools. "There are people in this town who think that the High School of but little consequence, and from what we hear sometimes we are almost led to believe that there is lurking in their busoms a wish to destroy it, and blot it out" (Danvers School Committee, 1861: 12).

In his analysis of Somerville public high schools, Ueda points out that "the unanimity of the town-meeting vote to found the Free High School was probably a consensual affirmation of the decision-making authority of the selectmen and school committeemen, rather than an expression of total support for educational innovation. If the vote reflected pervasive communal enthusiasm, it quickly waned when parents and students began to take advantage of new employment opportunities generated by Somerville's expanding economy and by its linkage through commuter travel with the job market in Boston and Cambridge. The Free High School's enrollment grew sluggishly and graduation rates were very low. In the 1850s and 1860s, popular participation in public education was achieved only at the elementary levels of schooling" (1987: 57–58).

27. During the Civil War, School committees worried that taxpayers might abandon the high schools in the name of economy. Although school committees usually reluctantly accepted reduced expenditures, they insisted that the high schools not be eliminated (Georgetown School Committee, 1862: 13; Ipswich School Committee, 1862: 9).

28. Even in the 1870s, however, there were some complaints of the high cost of public high schools. Phipps noted that "it is not to be disguised that here and there a few individuals, not in sympathy, for various reasons, with the common people in the higher education of their children in these Free High Schools, have recently endeavored to create a prejudice against them by maintaining that the education

of our Public Schools should be restricted to the most common elementary branches of study" (Massachusetts Board of Education, *Annual Report*, 1877: 46).

29. Based on the information on population in 1860, Katz's sample includes Sherborn (1,129), Bolton (1,348), Webster (2,912), Millbury (3,296), Plymouth (6,272), Chicopee (7,261), Fall River (14,026), Taunton (15,376), Lynn (19,083), and Worcester (24,960). He also lists a community of 3,333 people that is difficult to identify because no town in Massachusetts had that exact population in 1860. The town probably was either Holliston (3,339) or Uxbridge (3,133); each of them had a high school and a population close to 3,333. As the two high schools in question are similar, it does not make too much difference which one is chosen. I selected Uxbridge as the most likely candidate because of the school's general similarity to Katz's estimates of attendance.

30. Some scholars (Church, 1976: 182) have mistakenly cited Katz as saying that about 20 percent of eligible adolescents attended high schools in those communities that had such institutions. In fact, Katz states only that "in the samples as a whole under twenty percent of the estimated eligible children went to high school" (1968: 39). By not stating more precisely what percentage of eligible children in his overall sample attended high school and by mentioning the 20 percent figure, Katz may have unwittingly contributed to the confusion.

31. The same problem remains even if one uses the average attendance figures. Average attendance in winter was 92 students and in the fall was 110 students.

32. Again, the average attendance is higher in the summer than in the winter session.

33. As Katz originally observed, the smallest communities had the highest rates of enrollment. My recalculated figures show that towns with a population of less than 2,500 had a high school attendance rate of 66.7 percent; those with 2,500 through 4,999 people had 33.2 percent attending; towns with a population of 5,000 through 9,999 had 28.9 percent attending; those with a population of 10,000 through 14,999 had 10.7 percent attending; and in cities with a population of 15,000 or

more, 13.5 percent of the children received some high school education.

34. I examined the private school catalogs for Abbot Academy (Andover), Bradford Academy (Bradford), Chauney Hall School (Boston), Dummer Academy (Byfield), Lawrence Academy (Groton), Phillips Academy (Andover), Philips Exeter Academy (Exeter, New Hampshire), and the Putnam Free School (Newburyport). This certainly underestimates the total number of children of Essex County parents who attended a high-school-level private academy because the catalogs for several such institutions could not be located, and some children undoubtedly went to other private schools outside of Essex County.

In chapter 8 I explored the extent and nature of public high school attendance in Essex County, Massachusetts, in 1860. Unfortunately, I could not calculate any statewide estimates of public high school attendance because data on high school attendance were fragmentary and available only from a limited number of published local school reports. In 1875, however, the Massachusetts superintendent of education started collecting information on the number of public high school students. These data, combined with information from the state census for that year and with other government figures, enable us to examine in considerable detail the extent and determinants of public high school attendance in the townships in 1875.

Availability of Public High Schools in Massachusetts in 1875

In 1875 almost all large townships in Massachusetts, as well as many smaller ones,[1] maintained public high schools—57.8 percent of the 341 townships. Every one of the 55 townships with a population 10,000 or more had a public high school, as well as 73 of the 74 communities with a population between 2,500 and 5,000. Public high schools were becoming more common in many of the smaller communities: while only 16.4 percent of the towns with fewer than 1,250 people had a high school, 52.1 percent of the communities with a population of 1,250 to 2,500 had one.[2]

If almost six out of ten townships had a public high school, an even greater proportion of children lived in these areas because the larger communities contained a disproportionate share of the state's total population, and therefore a greater number of children. Of children ages ten through nineteen, 90.7 percent lived in townships that had a public high school in 1875.

The population size of the community is clearly the single best predictor of whether or not a town maintained a public high school in 1875. Public high schools were present in only 16.4 percent of townships with fewer than 1,250 inhabitants, but they existed in 99.2 percent of those with populations over 2,500 residents. As a result, the question of what factors predicted the existence of a public high school is statistically meaningful or interesting only for the 212 communities with fewer than 2,500 inhabitants.

To explore the determinants of the presence of a public high school in townships with a population of fewer than 2,500 residents, a multiple regression analysis was run. The presence of a public high school in 1875 was the dependent variable, and population size, valuation per capita, percent foreign-born, percent working males employed either in manufacturing or commerce, percent voting for the Republican presidential candidate in 1876, an adjusted per capita school funds, and the average length of the public school sessions were the seven independent variables (see table 9.1).

The regression analysis revealed several interesting findings. As expected, the population of the township was a strong predictor of the presence of a public high school (see table 9.2). Larger townships were more likely to have a

Table 9.1 / *Mean and Standard Deviation of Variables Used in Regression Analysis of High School Presence in Massachusetts Towns with a Population under 2,500 in 1875*

	Mean	Standard Deviation
High School present (1 = present, 0 = not present)	.325	.470
Population size	1,269.693	607.959
Valuation per capita (in dollars)	665.981	742.644
Percent foreign-born	10.844	7.482
Percent males in manufacturing and commerce	37.755	17.988
Percent Republican	66.321	13.760
Adjusted school funds per capita (in dollars)	2.057	0.682
Length of public school year (in days)	164.347	25.376
N = 212		

Table 9.2 / *Results of Regression Analysis of High School Presence in Massachusetts Towns with a Population under 2,500 in 1875 (1 = present, 0 = not present)*

	Simple R	B	Beta	Standard Error
Population size	.4884	.0003	.4239	.0001
Valuation per capita (in dollars)	.1794	.0001	.1787	.0000
Percentage foreign-born	.1480	−.0034	−.0542	.0042
Percentage males in manufacturing and commerce	.3781	.0019	.0742	.0020
Percentage Republican	.1004	.0049	.1442	.0021
Adjusted school funds per capita (in dollars)	−.0667	−.0529	−.0768	.0418
Length of public schools (in days)	.3512	.0018	.0985	.0014
	Constant = −.7190		Adjusted R^2 = .2897	

public high school. Population size was by far the single best predictor by itself, as well as after controlling for the effects of the other six independent variables.

The ability of a community to support such a relatively expensive institution as a public high school depends in part on its tax base. Communities with larger per capita valuations were more likely to have public high schools. Indeed, per capita valuation was the second best predictor of whether or not a community had a public high school after controlling for the effects of the other factors.

Previous studies have shown that first- and second-generation children were less likely to attend public high schools than children of native-born parents (Vinovskis, 1985b). Therefore, one might hypothesize that small towns with a large proportion of foreign-born might be less supportive of public high schools. Yet the results show a modest positive relation between the presence of a public high school and the proportion of the population that was foreign-born in these small communities. After controlling for the effects of the other factors, however, the relation did become negative, but the proportion of foreign-born was the weakest of the seven predictors.

The distribution of occupations in a community might affect the likelihood of a public high school in several ways. On the one hand, communities with a higher percentage of the population engaged in manufacturing or commerce might be more supportive of a public high school because the parents in those areas might be more aware of the importance of additional education for the economic well-being of their children. On the other hand, the presence of more manufacturing and commercial jobs in a town might provide attractive alternatives to continued education for the teenagers in that community. The results indicate that towns with a higher proportion of males engaged in manufacture or commerce were slightly more likely to have a public high school in 1875.[3] When the percentage of males in manufacturing by itself was substituted for the percentage of males in manufacturing and commerce, the results were almost identical.[4]

Most studies have not paid much attention to the differences in party position or party support for educational development. An analysis of the attempts to abolish the Massachusetts Board of Education in 1840, however, found strong disagreement among the legislators, with Whigs more supportive of centralized education than Democrats (Kaestle and Vinovskis, 1980). In this analysis, communities that voted more heavily for the Republican candidate for president in 1876 were more likely to have a public high school. Of the seven independent variables listed in table 9.2, this was the third best predictor after controlling for the effects of the other variables.[5]

An effort was also made to include some other measures of a town's commitment to schooling in general in the analysis. The initial assumption was that communities more supportive of education would be more likely to have a public high school. The results were not as clear-cut as had been anticipated. The amount of funds available for public schools were totaled.[6] Because a significant proportion of the total funds often included support for the local high school, it was necessary to try to subtract that amount from the overall figure.[7] The result was then divided by the population of the township and serves as the adjusted per capita public school funds for this analysis.

There was a weak negative relation between the adjusted public school funds and the likelihood of having a public high school. The explanation for this seemingly anomalous relation between one measure of commitment to education and the presence of a public high school may be that the high cost of maintaining such institutions meant that smaller communities may have been forced to reduce or limit their expenditures on the other schools. Furthermore, communities with no public high school were able to devote all of their education funds to the common schools and thereby contributed to the weak but negative relation between the adjusted per capita school funds and the presence of a public high school.[8]

A second measure of a township's commitment to education was the average number of days it maintained its public schools. Townships with longer school years were more likely to have a public high school. Nevertheless, after controlling for the effects of the other independent variables, this factor was a weak predictor.

Another seemingly plausible measure of general commitment to education is the proportion of children ages five through fifteen in school. Unfortunately, this particular index suffers from the fact that overall school attendance among this age-group was already so high that there was relatively little variation. In addition, the presence of a public high school might have affected this index by encouraging younger teenagers to stay in school longer. In any case, when the percentage of children ages five through fifteen was added as an eighth independent variable, the result was a weak but positive relation to the presence of a public high school (this was then the second weakest of the eight independent variables).

A series of other multiple regression equations were run to further explore the determinants of public high school attendance in these small communities. One of the more interesting was the addition of region to the basic seven independent variables. Massachusetts was subdivided into three regions: central (Essex, Middlesex, Suffolk, and Worcester counties), western (Berkshire, Franklin, Hampden, and Hampshire counties), and southern (Barnstable, Bristol, Dukes, Nantucket, and Norfolk counties). For communities with a population under 2,500 inhabitants, 37.7 percent of them in central, 24.5 percent in southern Massachusetts, and 10.8 percent in western Massachusetts in 1875 had a public high school. After controlling for the effects of the other variables, both central and western Massachusetts communities were more likely to have a public high school than those is southern Massachusetts.

Finally, the fact that Massachusetts townships were often quite large geographically meant that for many of them a single high school could serve only the smaller proportion of the children concentrated in the more populated area of the community. Indeed, a study (Vinovskis, 1985a) of the controversy over the Beverly High School discussed in chapter 7 suggested that considerable differences in support of that institution existed between those who lived in or near the more populated central school district and those who lived in the outlying rural areas.

We do not have a measure of the total land area of Massachusetts townships in 1875. For 1860, however, we can calculate the total number of acres in a township per capita.[9] When this factor was added as an eighth independent variable, it was a positive but extremely weak predictor of the presence of a public high school (it was the weakest of the eight independent variables in that multiple regression analysis). For these very small communities, the relative geographic size of the townships had almost no effect on whether or not a public high school was maintained.

Although there are no statewide data on Massachusetts public high school attendance before 1875, there is an estimate of the number of public high schools operating in the Commonwealth in 1860.[10] Using this, we can compare the likelihood of a community having a public high school in 1860 and 1875 (see table 9.3). The percentage of towns with public high schools rose from 33.2 percent in 1860 to 57.8 percent in 1875. Almost all of this increase occurred in communities with fewer than 5,000 inhabitants.

Table 9.4 shows the changes in the regional distribution of public high schools from 1860 to 1875. In both years, central Massachusetts communities were more likely to have a public high school than either southern or western Massachusetts towns. From 1860 to 1875, the probability of having a public high school increased significantly for each of the three regions. Interestingly, whereas there had been considerable regional differences between central Massachusetts and southern or western Massachusetts in the likelihood of having a public high school in towns with 2,500 to 10,000 inhabitants in 1860 that differential had all but disappeared by 1875.

As most large towns had a public high school in 1860, the increase in the percentage of children living in communities with such an institution was not as dramatic as the rise in the proportion of towns with a public high school. In 1860, 69.5 percent of the total population lived in communities with a public high school; in 1875 the comparable figure was 90.6 percent.[11]

Table 9.3 / *Percentage of Communities with Public High Schools in 1860 and 1875, by Town Size*

Town Size	1860	1875
0–1,249	3.0 ($N = 101$)	16.4 ($N = 116$)
1,250–2,499	11.9 ($N = 109$)	52.1 ($N = 96$)
2,500–4,999	54.7 ($N = 75$)	98.6 ($N = 74$)
5,000–9,999	90.9 ($N = 33$)	100.0 ($N = 30$)
10,000–14,999	100.0 ($N = 4$)	100.0 ($N = 9$)
15,000–49,999	100.0 ($N = 11$)	100.0 ($N = 15$)
Boston	100.0 ($N = 1$)	100.0 ($N = 1$)
TOTAL	30.8 ($N = 334$)	57.8 ($N = 341$)

Table 9.4 / *Percentage of Communities with Public High Schools in 1860 and 1875, by Region*

Region	1860	1875
Central	43.9 ($N = 148$)	70.0 ($N = 150$)
Western	15.8 ($N = 101$)	34.7 ($N = 101$)
Southern	25.9 ($N = 85$)	63.3 ($N = 90$)
TOTAL	30.8 ($N = 334$)	57.8 ($N = 341$)

Public High School Attendance in Massachusetts in 1875

Starting in 1875, information on the number of public high school students in each township was reported by the Massachusetts superintendent of education. This information, combined with state census data, can be used to estimate the number of children who ever attended a public high school in 1875.[12] Approximately 16.7 percent of Massachusetts children attended at some point a public high school. In townships with a public high school, an estimated 18.4 percent of the children received some public high school education.

The proportion of children in any community attending a public high school depends on whether or not such an institution existed in their community and if it did, on what proportion of them attended that school. There were considerable community variations in the likelihood of children ever attending a public high school (see figure 9.1). Whereas only 13.1 percent of children in townships with fewer than 1,250 inhabitants ever attended a public high school, 24.0 percent of those in communities with 2,500 to 5,000 inhabitants attended. Overall, communities with a population between 1,250 and 10,000 people had the highest rates of public high school attendance.

For communities with a public high school, the relation between attendance and township size is altered for the smaller townships. Whereas in the largest

Figure 9.1 / *Percentage of Children Ever Attending a Public High School, by Town Size*

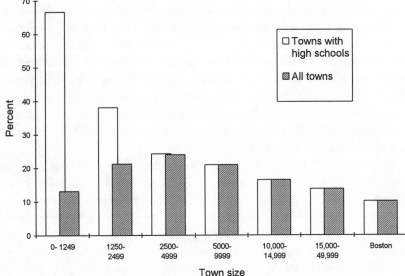

Source: Data from Massachusetts Board of Education, Annual Reports, 1875; Massachusetts Department of Labor, 1876

townships only a relatively small proportion of children ever attended a public high school, the opposite was true in the smaller communities. About 10.1 percent of Boston children and 13.8 percent of those in townships between 15,000 and 50,000 people received some public high school training; but 66.3 percent of children in townships with fewer than 1,250 inhabitants and with a public high school attended at some point. In other words, in the larger townships only a small minority of children ever attended a public high school, while in the smaller communities with such institutions a much higher proportion attended—undoubtedly in part because the small size meant that a higher proportion of children had to be encouraged to attend to justify maintaining the school.

Another useful perspective is consideration of the distribution of public high school students by the size of their township. The largest townships contributed about one-third of the total public high school students (Boston, 11.7 percent; towns 15,000 to 50,000, 22.9 percent). The smallest communities had almost one-fifth of the total (townships under 1,250, 4.3 percent; townships 1,250 to 2,500, 13.6 percent). Almost half of the total public high school students were in moderate-sized communities (townships 2,500 to 5,000, 24.4 percent; townships 5,000 to 10,000, 16.2 percent; townships 10,000 to 15,000, 6.9 percent). Thus, as I argued in chapter 8, historians of secondary education who have focused almost exclusively on larger cities have neglected the experiences of the vast majority of public high school students who attended schools in small or moderate-sized townships in the second half of the nineteenth century.

Further information about the variations in attendance can be obtained by running a multiple regression analysis of the 197 Massachusetts communities with a public high school in 1875. The dependent variable is the estimate of the percentage of children who ever attended a public high school, and the seven independent variables are population size, valuation per capita, percent foreign-born, percent working males employed in manufacturing or commerce, percent voting for the Republican presidential candidate in 1876, the amount of adjusted school funding per capita, and the average length of the public school sessions (see table 9.5).

The above discussion about the cross-tabulation analysis of the town size and public high school attendance showed an inverse relation. Similarly, the simple correlation coefficient between attendance and population size also indicates a negative relation (see table 9.6). After we control for the effects of the other six independent variables, however, population size is only the fourth best predictor of public high school attendance.

The valuation per capita is a moderately good predictor of public high school attendance after we control for the effects of the other factors. Children from more affluent towns were more likely to attend a public high school than those from less wealthy communities.

Table 9.5 / *Mean and Standard Deviation of Variables Used in Regression Analysis of Attendance in Massachusetts Towns with Public High Schools in 1875*

	Mean	Standard Deviation
Percentage attending high school	37.422	18.657
Population size	7,591.147	25,313.77
Valuation per capita (in dollars)	807.533	836.255
Percent foreign-born	18.655	9.892
Percent males in manu-facturing and commerce	59.898	17.100
Percent Republican	63.538	11.014
School funds per capita (in dollars)	2.509	0.926
Length of public schools (in days)	189.735	23.710
N = 197		

Table 9.6 / *Results of Regression Analysis of Attendance in Massachusetts Towns with Public High Schools in 1875*

	Simple R	B	Beta	Standard Error
Population size	−.2344	−.0001	−.1047	.0000
Valuation per capita (in dollars)	.0816	.0034	.1516	.0014
Percentage foreign-born	−.5059	−.7070	−.3749	.1316
Percentage males in manufacturing and commerce	−.5036	−.2935	−.2690	.0748
Percentage Republican	.3425	−.0650	−.0384	.1195
School funds per capita (in dollars)	.0673	2.0062	.0996	1.3606
Length of public schools (in days)	−.3532	−.1570	−.1995	.0556

Constant = 94.9195   Adjusted R^2 = .4048

The single best predictor of public high school attendance is the percentage of the population foreign-born. This is not particularly surprising as other studies have shown that first- and second-generation children were less likely to enroll in a public high school than children of native-born parents (Vinovskis, 1985b).

The percentage of the male population engaged in either manufacturing or commerce was the other strong negative predictor of public high school attendance. In part, townships that provided employment opportunities attracted many rural teenagers who wished to work rather than attend school. Substituting the percentage of the male population employed just in manufacturing for this variable, produced results that were basically the same, although the magnitude of this variable's relative importance was reduced.

As noted earlier in this chapter, Republican-oriented communities were more apt to have a public high school than Democratic-oriented townships. But were children in Republican-oriented areas more likely to attend public high schools? Although the simple correlation between attendance and percentage of Republican voters in 1876 was sizable, the political orientation of the community was the weakest of the seven independent variables once we controlled for the effects of the others.

As one measure of a community's commitment to education, I again used the amount of school funds per capita. After controlling for the effects of the other variables, children were slightly more likely to attend a public high school in townships that spent more money on their public schools.[13]

In contrast, the average length of public school sessions was negatively related to the percentage of children ever attending a public high school. One reason for this was that the average length of public school sessions was longer in communities with a larger population, with a higher percentage foreign-born, and with a higher proportion males employed in manufacturing and commerce. In other words, although the multiple regression analysis tries to control for the effects of these and similar factors, the type of townships that overall had fewer children attending public high schools were also the ones that kept their public schools open the longest.[14]

Region was added as an additional independent variable in another multiple regression analysis. The results indicated that after controlling for the effects of the other variables, a higher percentage of children in central Massachusetts attended a public high school at some point compared to their counterparts in either southern or western Massachusetts.

Was there an increase in public high school attendance between 1860 and 1875? Unfortunately, there is no direct answer this question because there is no statewide information on attendance before 1875. In the earlier portion of this chapter, however, we found that the number of townships with public high schools increased, and the percentage of the total population who lived in a community with such an institution rose from 69.5 percent in 1860 to 90.6 percent in 1875.

Another interesting perspective is to compare changes in the extent of public high school attendance in Essex County from 1860 to 1875. In Essex County townships with a public high school, the percentage of children who ever attended actually decreased from 19.2 percent to 17.0 percent (see table 9.7).

If one looks at the overall percentage of children in all Essex County communities who ever enrolled in a public high school, however, the results are different (see table 9.8). By 1875 nearly all Essex County children lived in communities with a public high school (95.7 percent). As a result, even though the rate of public high school attendance in communities with such institutions declined slightly over time, the overall percentage of Essex County children who ever attended rose from 14.6 percent in 1860 to 17.0 percent in 1875. Particularly dramatic were the increases in the proportion of children in the smaller communities who ever attended a public high school.

Was Essex County typical of the rest of Massachusetts in terms of its pattern of public high school attendance? Again, it is difficult to answer this question directly, but it appears that in both 1860 and 1875 a higher percentage of Essex County citizens lived in communities with public high schools (79.8 percent versus 67.9 percent in 1860 and 95.6 percent versus 89.9 percent in 1875). One should note that the differential in access to a public high school between Essex County and other Massachusetts residents had narrowed considerably by 1875.

In 1875, the overall percentage of children ever attending a public high school was 17.0 percent; the comparable figure for the rest of Massachusetts was 16.8 percent—nearly identical, even though children in Essex County were slightly more likely to live in a community with a public high school. Therefore,

Table 9.7 / *Percentage of Children Ever Attending High Schools in Essex County Communities with High Schools in 1860 and 1875, by Town Size*

	Percentage Ever Attending	
Size of Town	1860	1875
0–2,499	47.5	35.2
2,500–4,999	25.0	19.6
5,000–9,999	22.0	20.4
10,000–14,999	27.4	21.1
15,000 and above	11.7	12.0
TOTAL	19.2	17.0

Table 9.8 / *Percentage of Children Ever Attending High Schools in All Essex County Communities in 1860 and 1875, by Town Size*

	Percentage Ever Attending	
Size of Town	1860	1875
0–2,499	6.8	20.6
2,500–4,999	12.0	19.6
5,000–9,999	18.1	20.4
10,000–14,999	27.4	21.1
15,000 and above	11.7	12.0
TOTAL	14.6	17.0

it is likely that the estimate of 14.6 percent of the Essex County children attending a public high school in 1860 was somewhat higher than that of the rest of the state, but by 1875 that differential seems to have disappeared almost entirely.

Unfortunately, there are no reliable estimates of the numbers of children who received the equivalent of a public high school education in a private academy for either Essex County or Massachusetts as a whole in 1875. In 1860 almost 5 percent of Essex County children probably received some private secondary school training (see chapter 8). Therefore, the estimate of 16.7 percent of the children attending a public high school at some point in Massachusetts in 1875 undoubtedly understates by a few percentage points the actual number receiving some secondary training. As a result, one might estimate that nearly one out of five children in 1875 received at least some secondary school education.

As noted in the previous chapter, although a surprisingly large percentage of Massachusetts children received some high school training in 1875, most of them did not graduate and some of them—especially in the smaller rural communities—attended public high schools that more closely resembled a grammar school. It is not clear exactly what this educational experience meant for the students, either at that time or in their subsequent careers. But it is clear is that historians need to pay more attention to the surprisingly widespread availability of secondary education in some states in the second half of the nineteenth century, and they need to consider more carefully the wide variety of settings and institutions in which this training occurred.

Notes

1. Information on the existence of public high schools in 1875 comes from the Massachusetts Board of Education *Annual Report* (1875). Reports from 1876 and 1877 were also checked, as well as a sizable number of published local school reports for 1875. As noted in chap. 8, there was considerable variation in what was taught in Massachusetts public high schools in the nineteenth century. Particularly in the smallest communities, the public high

school was sometimes closer in nature to a grammar school. It is, however, impossible to make any such distinctions for each public high school in the Commonwealth from the existing records. Therefore, my analysis will focus on the presence or absence of a public high school in a particular community and will make no systematic effort to ascertain the nature of the education it offered.

2. These results are based on a statistical analysis of the 341 Massachusetts townships in 1875 using information from the Massachusetts Board of Education *Annual Report* of 1875, as well as other data, such as the population figures from the published state census of 1875 (Massachusetts Department of Labor, 1876).

3. The data on occupations come from the state census of 1875, which subdivided occupations into seven categories: (1) government and professional, (2) domestic and personal office, (3) trade and transportation, (4) agriculture and fisheries, (5) manufacturers and mechanical industries, (6) indefinite, nonproductive and propertied, and (7) not given. After occupations not given were excluded, the remaining six categories were totaled, and categories 3 and 5 were then used to estimate the proportion of employed males engaged in manufacturing and commerce (Massachusetts Bureau of Labor, 1876, 1:453–77).

4. A separate multiple regression analysis was run with the percentage of males in manufacturing substituted for the percentage of males in either manufacturing or commerce. In the interests of minimizing the number of tables published, the detailed statistical information on this and subsequent multiple regression analyses for such additional explorations is provided here.

5. The presidential election results are from the manuscript collections at the Massachusetts State Archives (1872–76). The votes used were from the elections of the at-large electors. Massachusetts politics underwent considerable change in the post–Civil War period. According to Dale Baum (1984), the Hayes-Tilden contest in Massachusetts in 1876 provided a reasonably accurate reflection of the Republican-Democratic split, whereas the contest four years earlier represented an unusually strong Republican vote. Another multiple regression

analysis was run with the percentage of the Republican vote for president in 1872 substituted as the political variable. The results were almost identical to those when the percentage of the Republican vote for president in 1876 had been used.

6. This included the amount raised by local taxes, contributed board for teachers, income from local school funds, and the township's share of the state school fund.

7. Information on the exact amount of public high school expenses was not available. However, data on the salary of the principal were provided and used as a crude estimate of high school expenses. Because in most of these small communities the principal was the only teacher in the high school , this estimate is a reasonable approximation of the annual expenditures on that institution.

8. If the total per capita public school funds had been used in the multiple regression analysis, the results would have been a weak positive relation with the presence of a public high school.

9. The data on the total number of acres of land in the township are based on an actual survey reported by the Massachusetts secretary of the Commonwealth (1861). Owing to several significant changes in the boundaries of Massachusetts townships between 1860 and 1875, it was impossible to use the population figures from 1875 to calculate the density. Therefore, the measure based on 1860 land and population figures is a more accurate, though somewhat dated, estimate of differential density among the townships.

10. The names of communities with a public high school were drawn from an unpublished list for 1859–60, based on responses to a question posed by the Board of Education. Each town was asked if it had "a High School supported by Taxation, in which the Latin and Greek languages are taught." In addition, some published annual local school reports were used—especially for Essex County—and the list of high schools in Massachusetts provided by Inglis (1911) was consulted.

11. For the 1860 data, I have assembled and used the total population figures rather than the number of children ages ten to nineteen. Therefore, the comparisons to 1875 are done in terms of the total population. The

percentage of children ages ten to nineteen living in communities with a public high school in 1875 was 90.7—virtually identical to the percentage of the total population living in those communities.

12. The procedures for estimating the number of children who ever attended a public high school are the same as developed and discussed in chap. 8. The average of the number of students attending a public high school in 1875, 1876, and 1877 was calculated. This was increased by 25 percent to provide an estimate of the different number of students attending. Then, to estimate the number of children who ever attended, this figure was divided by 35 percent of the children ages ten to nineteen according to the state census of 1875. It was assumed that under no circumstances should the number exceed 85 percent. Therefore, in

six cases the attendance estimates were revised downward to 85 percent. For more complete details on the rationale for developing these estimating procedures, see chap. 8.

13. In the analysis of the presence of public high schools, I used the amount of adjusted school funds per capita because I did not want to include the expenses of the high schools among the independent variables. In this situation, however, since all of the townships in the sample had a public high school, the more appropriate measure as an independent variable was the amount of school funds per capita.

14. The percentage of children ages five to fifteen in school was not used as an additional independent variable in this analysis because many of the public high school students were young teenagers.

Chapter 10 / *Historical Development of Age Stratification in Schooling*

written with David L. Angus and Jeffrey E. Mirel

Life-course analysis is exceedingly popular among social historians because it provides a flexible framework for investigating the lives of individuals. Emphasis is placed on understanding the historical background of cohorts as well as the institutional settings in which they lived. But although the role of norms and social organizations in affecting the expectations and experiences of people is stressed, it is seldom investigated. Instead, the existence of these regulatory norms and social organizations is simply assumed.

The age stratification of American society is a common theme in life-course studies. Roles and activities are frequently segregated by age. Schools, for example, are designed for the young, whereas retirement and the Social Security system are intended for the elderly. A few writers acknowledge that American society has not always been age-graded, but there has been little effort to analyze the origins of age stratification or its impact on the life course.

Schools were one of the first social organizations to stress age-grading, and they continue to play an important role in shaping the life course. An examination of the development of age-graded schooling will shed light on how age-grading has become so important. First, we shall analyze the establishment of formal schooling in colonial and nineteenth-century America and how this contributed to the demarcation of childhood as a special part of the life course. Then we shall investigate the increasing age-grading within schools in the nineteenth and twentieth centuries. Studying the emergence of youth as a period set aside mainly for formal education and analyzing the increasingly close identification of chronological age with grade in school will enable us to see how age-graded norms and institutions became an integral part of the life course in modern society.

School Attendance and the Emergence of an Age-Graded Youth

An unstated assumption today is that children are different from adults. In our age-graded society, we usually make even finer distinctions among children on the basis of age. In the past children were not as sharply distinguished from adults. Ariès (1962) claims that medieval European society regarded children as miniature adults. He argues that childhood did not emerge as a recognized separate phase in Europe until the seventeenth and eighteenth centuries.

Influenced by the work of Ariès, several family historians (Demos, 1974; Zuckerman, 1970) maintain that colonial Americans also did not differentiate between children and adults. Most scholars (Beales, 1975; Moran and Vinovskis, 1985), however, reject this interpretation because the Puritans made a distinction between adults and children. The Puritans believed young children were more capable of intellectual activity and moral responsibility than we do today. As a result, although childhood was perceived as a distinct stage, Puritans did not perceive a large intellectual or emotional gulf between older children and adults. There was no sharp or clearly defined boundary, for example, between being a youth and becoming an adult. Although early Americans also acknowledged some differences between younger and older children, the lives of children were not highly differentiated. Early Americans paid relatively little attention to the actual age of children and focused more on individual intellectual and physical differences.

New England Puritans believed that everyone should be literate enough to read the Bible.[1] A few local schools were established in the mid-seventeenth century, but most were intended only for the minority of advanced male students who planned to attend Harvard University. The primary responsibility for teaching children how to read rested with parents. The dispersed nature of settlement in the Chesapeake area, as well as the relative lack of interest in education, meant that fewer schools were established in the South (Cremin, 1970). Most children in early colonial America were taught the rudiments of reading by their parents or a neighbor rather than by a teacher in a formal public or private school.

The number of public and private schools increased greatly after the American Revolution. The Puritans had always stressed the importance of literacy from a religious perspective. The creation of the new republic necessitated an educated male electorate, and in turn stimulated education for women, who would be the mothers of the next generation of voters (Kaestle, 1983). Concerns about the social tensions caused by nineteenth-century urbanization and industrialization, as well as the necessity of bringing civilization to the frontier areas, also spurred educational expansion and reform (Katz, 1968; Vinovskis, 1985). Although regional differences in education persisted, most of this expansion in the decades before 1860 occurred in the Midwest and South as those areas initially lagged behind the Northeast in school facilities and attendance (Angus, 1980a, 1983b; Mattingly and Stevens, 1987). Throughout most of the nineteenth century gender differences in education were small, but blacks consistently received less schooling than whites (Webber, 1978).

The rapid growth of schools in the nineteenth century reflected in part the increased unwillingness of parents to educate their children at home. Although adult male and female literacy had risen dramatically, parents preferred more than ever to send their children to schools—especially if the cost of that education could be spread among all taxpayers. Some educational reformers advocated the expansion of schools to compensate for the inadequate child rearing provided by lower-class and immigrant parents, whom they regarded as incapable of providing—or unwilling to provide—a suitable education at home (Jorgenson, 1987).

The net result of all of these changes was that by the mid-nineteenth century, most children in the United States received at least some training in a school. In rural areas children of all ages frequently attended a one-room schoolhouse, while in urban areas schools were usually subdivided into several classes. Going to school in the country was a seasonal activity contingent on the need for agricultural labor at home; in urban areas schools remained open for most of the year. Consequently, there were significant differences in the amount of education available to children in rural and urban areas (Fuller, 1982; Link, 1986; Kaestle, 1973b; Troen, 1975).

At first, schools accepted children of all ages. Since colonial Americans regarded young children as capable of intellectual training at an early age, it was not unusual to see three- or four-year-olds in the same classroom as teenagers. As noted in chapter 2, the infant school movement in the 1820s emphasized the importance of early education and encouraged sending young children to schools. An estimated 40 percent of all three-year-olds in Massachusetts attended schools in 1840 (May and Vinovskis, 1977).

There was a reaction against early childhood education in the mid-1830s. Physicians like Amariah Brigham began to argue that premature intellectual stimulation of young children weakened their growing minds and eventually led to insanity. Concern over an alleged decline in the quality of American family life produced a burgeoning literature on child rearing and the responsibilities of parents, particularly mothers. School teachers and administrators joined the crusade against early education because it was difficult to educate toddlers along with the older children. As a result, schools gradually enacted regulations prohibiting young children from attending and thereby set a minimum age at which children could enter (Angus, 1981; May and Vinovskis,

1977). The introduction of kindergartens in the second half of the nineteenth century encouraged sending some younger children to schools, but at that time most parents and educators thought children should not be in school until age seven or eight.

At the same time that a minimum age for school entry was being established, educators were concerned about the presence of older boys in primary schools. Horace Mann estimated that nearly 10 percent of all rural Massachusetts schools in 1840 were terminated prematurely because the older teenagers literally threw the teacher out or wrecked the schoolhouse. Therefore, school administrators worked to lengthen the school year and increase the regularity of attendance so that children could complete their primary education earlier. With the creation of public high schools in the second third of the nineteenth century, the expected number of years of attending school was extended for some students. Since students often entered high school at age twelve or thirteen and most did not stay long enough to graduate, nineteenth-century children typically completed their formal education by their mid-teens (Angus and Mirel, 1985; Kaestle and Vinovskis, 1980).

Thus, the nineteenth century witnessed the expansion of schooling at the same time that childhood education was compressed into fewer years. The length of the school year was extended and emphasis was placed on getting everyone to attend school regularly between the ages of seven and thirteen. As a result, the life course of children of these ages was increasingly defined by their school attendance and educational experiences.

During the twentieth century, schooling in the United States has become an even more important factor in defining the life course. The proportion of the school-age population in schools has increased dramatically. In 1870 approximately one-half of the population ages five to nineteen were in school; today about nine out of ten children in that age category attend school. The large differential between black and white school attendance rates has all but disappeared (U.S. Bureau of Census, 1975: ser. H433; calculated from U.S. Bureau of Census, 1986: table 192).

Schooling is also the typical experience of younger children and of young adults. Today, more than one-third of those ages three to four are in school as are almost one-fourth of those ages twenty to twenty-four (calculated from U.S. Bureau of Census, 1986: table 192). The median number of school years completed by adults ages twenty-five to twenty-nine has risen from 10.3 years in 1940 to 12.9 years in 1985 (U.S. Bureau of Census, 1975: ser. H641; U.S. Bureau of Census, 1986: table 199).

The average length of the public elementary and secondary school year has also increased during the past one hundred years. Although school terms in cities grew shorter, from nearly year-round school in 1830s to a forty-week year by the turn of the century, rural terms expanded from as little as three months to as many as nine; thus, the average school year in the United States expanded from 132 days in 1870 to 179 days in 1970. Combined with an increase in the regularity of attendance, the average number of days attended per enrolled public school student rose from 78 in 1870 to 162 in 1970 (U.S. Bureau of Census, 1975: ser. H521–H522).

As schooling became a dominant part of the experience of American youth, full-time work lost its earlier importance. In colonial America young teenagers either worked on farms or were apprenticed to artisans and tradesmen. Child labor was normal and expected. As schools replaced home education in rural areas, older children continued to work during the summer and attended school only in the winter. In urban areas, where schools remained open most of the year, children usually either attended school or entered the labor force. Only a few children combined schooling with full-time work outside the home.

As the emphasis on education increased, child labor laws were enacted to remove young teenagers from the workplace and to put them into the classroom. Although many of these laws date from the 1870s, most observers suggest that the means for their enforcement were not in place until the 1890s. The average minimum age for leaving school increased from fourteen years five months in 1900 to sixteen years in 1930 in those states that had enacted a compulsory schooling law. The combination of more restrictions on child labor and the increase in school attendance led to a decrease in teenage labor force participation. In 1900 about 35 percent of females and 70 percent of males ages fourteen to nineteen were working whereas the comparable figures for 1950 were 25 percent and 40 percent (Mirel and Angus, 1985).[2]

The life course of children today is much more defined by the experience of schooling than ever before. Indeed, in the United States school attendance is nearly universal for children between the ages of five and seventeen, and it is being expanded for both younger and older students. In addition, the school year has become longer, and there is talk about lengthening it further to make it more comparable to the school year in other industrialized countries, such as Japan. Although the proportion of teenagers full time in the labor force has been greatly reduced in the twentieth century, the number of older students with part-time jobs has risen, so that the sharp division between schooling and work has been somewhat diminished.

Grading for Instruction in the Schools, 1840–1940

If throughout the nineteenth and twentieth century children were increasingly segregated from the activities of adults and assigned to that special institution-alization of childhood—the school—what role did age play in locating them *within* the school? The typical school at the opening of the nineteenth century enrolled pupils of widely varying age, some as old as twenty, all taught in the same room by a single teacher. Today, children enter kindergarten at five years of age and, with few exceptions, pass through the elementary and middle school grades, one year for each grade. Between the ninth and twelfth grades they either drop out of school to enter the work force or remain to graduate, again progressing one grade for each year. Thus, the internal organization of the school is fairly strictly age-graded. Children and teens spend the years from five to seventeen or eighteen within age cohorts of an extremely narrow range.[3] How, when, and why did this remarkable yet seldom remarked upon, shift occur?

Rural Schools In the one-room district schools of rural antebellum America, all children of "legal school age" were eligible to attend (Fuller, 1982; Guilliford, 1986). Legal definitions of school age were features of state school laws enacted in the 1820s and 1830s and were most often functional for the purpose of determining the amount of state financial support each district was eligible to receive annually (Tyack, James, and Benavot, 1987). This definition varied widely, from Iowa's five to twenty to Massachusetts's five to fifteen. On the low end of the scale, children sometimes went to school at three or four, but this practice declined after 1830. At the upper end of the scale, most children stopped going to school before they reached the legal maximum age.

Some modest age segregation was introduced by the common practice of dividing the school year into two terms—a summer school, attended largely by children from four to five to about ten or twelve, and a winter school, attended by those from ten to twenty. The summer school was typically taught by a local girl in her teens, and it emphasized a few rudimentary subjects (spelling, reading, ciphering) and provided much time for play and organized games. Its primary purpose seems to have been keeping the little ones out from under foot during the busy season while inculcating some school readiness skills. The winter school was more often taught by an "outsider," a man or older woman who could handle the disciplining of teenage boys and offer instruction of a more advanced nature in such subjects as history and geography, as well as the basics. Exceptions to this age-grouping were common, however, because many young children who lived near the school attended the winter sessions as well as the summer ones.

Within the school, instruction was organized according to what was called the recitation method. The school day was divided into many short periods, each devoted to a particular subject and a level of study within that subject, such as beginning spelling, intermediate reading, advanced arithmetic, and so forth. During each of these brief periods, and while the majority of students sat at their "desks" to study, the several children who were performing at the appropriate subject and level would group around the teacher's desk to "recite," reading passages, answering questions, or working problems on command. Many illustrations of these old district schools suggest that age (or at least size) had little or nothing to do with the makeup of these recitation groups. Since children differed widely with respect to when they had begun school, how many terms they had attended, how regular their attendance had been, how much time they could find at home to study, and so forth—not to mention differences in talent and motivation—age was a poor predictor of which child would be studying at which level in each subject. Teenage boys who had grown up out of the reach of a school might find themselves learning the alphabet alongside children of four or five.

Even in extracurricular activities, the reminiscences and diaries of country schoolteachers suggests only a modest amount of age segregation. The ubiquitous ball games, tag games, and hiding games were played by all but the very youngest children. The older boys had some activities of their own, sometimes as forms of rebellion against the teacher, but also sometimes in concert or even conspiracy with the teacher (Kennedy and Harlow, 1940).

Urban Schools   The situation with respect to age segregation within schools was at first little different in the cities and towns. Of course, the much greater density of population meant that a school district would contain many more children than a single room could accommodate or a single teacher could handle. But the multi-room, multi-teacher schools of the antebellum period were only roughly graded. In Detroit, for example, when the public school system was created by statute in 1842, two grades of schools were set up—primary schools, enrolling children five to twelve, and middle schools, enrolling children over those ages. Vestiges of rural influence remained. Primary teachers were female, middle teachers were male and were paid more, the recitation method of instruction predominated, and the rooms within a school building were called "schools" rather than classes or grades.

This began to change quite rapidly after 1850. In 1847, John D. Philbrick, principal of the Quincy Grammar School of Boston, worked out a system of graded instruction that went well beyond the rough division into primary, middle, or grammar schools (Cubberley, 1934: 311). As it developed and spread over the next couple of decades, the system had two features. First, the subjects to be taught were standardized with the materials arranged in an orderly sequence of increasing difficulty. A group of subjects arranged in this way was then called a *course of studies*. Second, teaching was subject to a *division of labor* in which each teacher would be responsible for teaching particular segments of material from the hierarchical arrangement of subjects. Once a school building was organized in this way, it was called a *graded school,* and the children were assigned to different teachers depending on their level of past accomplishment.

In the most advanced graded schools, the whole course of studies was divided into segments representing one year's work on the part of the average child. There might be eight or nine such segments. The ideal was that a child would enter school at five or six, progress through the required work at the rate of one segment, or grade, per year, completing the course at fourteen or fifteen, passing into the high school by examination or leaving school at that time. Passage into each level was based on attaining a particular score on an examination or maintaining a particular average on all subjects throughout the year. In actual fact, this orderly progress seldom occurred.

It is important to emphasize that it was the *curriculum* and the work of the teacher that was graded, not the children. They were *classified,* that is, placed into classes based on what they had learned. Age was irrelevant. In fact, public school leaders in Detroit, describing their new graded system to parents and taxpayers, explained, "On the Union plan several hundred scholars in different departments are placed under the general superintendence of a principal teacher, and *subject to his classification.* This classification is based upon the *degree of attainment* in studies, regardless of age or condition in life" (Detroit Board of Education, 1853: 7). It is wrong then to assume, as a number of writers have, that the graded school was either intentionally or actually organized according to chronological age. There was only a loose relation between children's ages and their grade placement in the urban graded school of the nineteenth century.

The graded school was immensely popular. As one commentator later put it: "By 1860 the schools of most of the cities and large towns were graded. By 1870 the pendulum had swung from no system to nothing but system" (Shearer, 1899: 21). There were a number of advantages to this form of school organization. In grouping children according to their level of accomplishment, the teacher could work with larger groups instead of with two or three at a time, as in the district school. Eventually, a system of "class" instruction emerged, much like the "chalk and talk" system that dominates today. Under this instructional arrangement, discipline became easier to maintain, and because of grade-level specialization, teachers could be effective with less training. This in turn allowed city school boards to hire more female teachers, which they could do at little more than half the salary of a male teacher. With the children seated at fixed desks in neat rows, the number of children per classroom could be quite large, and school buildings were built to contain eight or ten rooms, instead of the four rooms more common in the 1830s.

These features of schools would hardly be thought of as advantages today, and indeed they have been heavily criticized as elements of the process of bureaucratization that are said to have made urban schools such sterile and oppressive places for children (Katz, 1971). When understood against the background of the demographic conditions of the time, however, they were highly advantageous—even essential. As Angus (1988) has observed elsewhere, the most important urban educational problem of the nineteenth century was over-crowded schools. Caught between exploding numbers of school-age children on the one hand and miserly common councils on the other, urban school boards were desperate simply to provide a place in school for every eligible child. Any organizational scheme that could stretch scarce dollars, and at the same time give some semblance of order and progression, was seen as a blessing.

Attacks on the "Lockstep" in Education

Criticism of the graded school began to be heard as early as 1872. W. T. Harris, superintendent of schools in St. Louis, in his annual reports for 1872, 1873, and 1874 and in an 1874 speech to the National Education Association, attacked two features of the system (St. Louis Board of Education, 1872: 80–87; 1873: 24–29; 1874: 121–48). He argued that annual promotions held back students who might be moving through the curriculum at a more rapid pace, and that many students, failing to be promoted a second time, withdrew and were permanently lost to the school. He proposed a more flexible grading scheme with each grade divided into several levels under the same teacher and with the brighter pupils promoted into the next level every ten weeks. The plan produced considerable debate among superintendents, and though it was not generally adopted, it started a trend toward half-yearly or quarterly promotions rather than the more traditional practice of annual promotions. More important, school leaders all over the country began to think about and work on alternative forms of instructional organization.[4]

One was William J. Shearer, who as superintendent in New Castle, Pennsylvania, and Elizabeth, New Jersey, perfected a plan of frequent promotions based on subject mastery flexible enough to allow each student to be at different grade levels in different subjects. Throughout the 1890s, the plan was touted in the press and adopted in a few other cities. In 1899, Shearer described his plan in a book entitled *The Grading of Schools, Including a Full Explanation of a Rational Plan of Grading*, "the first book written upon this important phase of school organization." Shearer defined the graded school as one in which "a definite course of study" is taught and in which "the pupils are roughly classified according to their supposed ability to do the work of a given year: and each class is placed in charge of a teacher, who is expected to give the same lesson to all members." Although he accepted the idea that the graded school was superior to the ungraded school of earlier times, it had numerous defects, chief among which was the fact that it did "not properly provide for the individual differences of the pupils" (Shearer, 1899: 8).

> No one dares deny that the children of every grade differ widely in age, in acquirements, in aptitude, in physical endurance, in power of attention, in home advantages, in the rate of mental development, in the time of entering school, in regularity of attendance, and in many other ways affecting their progress. . . . Because of the manner of grading and promoting, the graded school of today keeps all the children of each grade in intellectual lock step, not only month after month, but year after year, for their whole school lives. . . . Is not individuality of more importance than evenness of grading? (Shearer, 1899: 24–25)

Apparently not, for the idea that was to dominate the attention of Progressive educators in the next two decades was not the individuality of the child, but the inefficiency of school systems in which thousands of children failed each year, some time after time, leaving the schools in their early teens having completed only a few elementary grades. Rather than educational lock-step, it was these two features of urban schools—called *retardation* and *elimination*—that would become the focus of reform efforts.

The Age-Grade Standard of School Efficiency

Early elimination from school, what today is called the dropout problem, had received some attention in the nineteenth century (Woodward, 1896, 1902). The problem of retardation, defined as the number of children overage for their grade, and its relation to elimination was first brought to attention in the 1904 report of the superintendent of schools in New York City, William H. Maxwell. Maxwell gathered and reported data on the ages of the pupils in each grade of the New York schools and found that 39 percent of all elementary pupils were "retarded" (that is, overage) for their grade. The finding caused a stir among big city superintendents, and several of them, notably those of Philadelphia, Chicago, St. Louis, and Detroit, followed Maxwell's lead in collecting and commenting on similar data. A number of academics also became interested in the question. Edward Thorndike began collecting age-grade data from as many cities as possible; the Russell Sage Foundation agreed to fund a "backward child" study of urban schools; George Strayer designed a set of forms to carry out a nationwide survey; and Lightner Witmer, the founder of "America's first psychological clinic" and of the journal *The Psychological Clinic*, began to devote space to articles on the problem (Napoli, 1981).

The school-efficiency movement based on age-grade statistics began in earnest with the publication of Thorndike's *The Elimination of Pupils from School* in 1908. Analyzing the statistics he had gathered with great care, Thorndike concluded in part:

> At least 25 out of 100 children of the white population of our country who enter school stay only long enough to learn to read simple English, write such words as they commonly use, and perform the four operations for integers without serious errors. A fifth of the children (white) entering city schools stay only to the fifth grade. . . . Of the children entering public schools of our more favored cities over half probably never have a man teacher. Less than 1 in 10 graduate from the high school. Only about a third graduate from an elementary school of seven grades or more. . . . One main cause of elimination is incapacity for and lack of interest in the sort of intellectual work demanded by present courses of study. (9–10)

When this study appeared, it was greeted by widespread newspaper comment with numerous editorials chiding schools for the "shocking degree of inefficiency" disclosed by the data, and a storm of defensive criticism on the part of superintendents who denied the accuracy of Thorndike's findings.

An even bigger stir was created by the publication a year later of Leonard P. Ayres's *Laggards in Our Schools: A Study of Retardation and Elimination in City School Systems.* Ayres had been general superintendent of schools for Puerto Rico and chief of the division of statistics of the Insular Department of Education before becoming chief investigator in the Russell Sage "backward children" investigation. The book not only stamped Ayres as the chief apostle of the school-efficiency movement, it raised the ante on the level of statistical sophistication a well-informed educator would need to follow the new developments.

Ayres reported his findings under three headings: the condition, the causes, and the remedies. With respect to the amount of retardation and elimination in the schools, Ayres found that "the general tendency of American cities is to carry all of their children through the fifth grade, to take one half of them to the eighth grade and one in ten through the high school," though there was enormous variability between cities. Since the number of overage children in the grades exceeded those who were under age by a wide margin, Ayres concluded that *"our courses of study as at present constituted are fitted not to the slow child or to the average child but to the unusually bright child."* He analyzed an array of causes—late entrance, irregular attendance, illness, physical defects, the nationality of the child, the sex of the child—but none was shown to be a preponderant cause. As remedies, Ayres called for better compulsory attendance laws, better medical inspection, courses of study better fitted to the average child, more flexible grading, and above all, better collection of school statistics (Ayres, 1909a: 3–7).

Ayres's book created a greater storm than Thorndike's book had. Over the next decade, lucky was the superintendent who was not challenged by the local press to report the numbers of students who were overage for grade and to begin to show progress on this important new measure of school efficiency.[5] The age-grade table, displaying the numbers of children of each age with each grade, rapidly became a routine aspect of the annual report of many districts.[6] Calculations were made of the "money cost of the repeater," though this concept was hotly debated (Ayres, 1909b; Falkner, 1908a). A study of random selection of one hundred city school reports from 1905 to 1912 showed that three-quarters of them made some mention of the concept of retardation and that half presented adequate statistics on the problem (Volkner and Noble, 1914).

Raymond Callahan (1962) has developed an interpretation of the school-efficiency movement that gives primacy to such factors as the vulnerability of city administrators to the pressures of the business community. Callahan's account downplays the search for legitimacy and confidence on the part of the newly emerging, university-based field of educational psychology and the developments in educational measurement and statistics. The importance of these elements can be illustrated, first, with the case of Lightner Witmer and, second, with some of the debates that occurred between proponents of the efficiency movement.

In 1910, in an article in *The Psychological Clinic,* Witmer described his involvement in the age-grade question. After tracing the origin of his interest in the education of the retarded to Itard's work with the wild boy of Aveyron, through the work of Itard's pupil Edward Seguin, to the development of special institutions for children of various degrees of retardation in the United States, Witmer argued that:

> Seguin's message to the teacher of normal children has been neglected and "retardation" has come to be regarded as synonymous with an incurable mental defect. Feeblemindedness, imbecility, and idiocy are but classes or grades of retardation. In these severe forms of retardation the mental defect usually rests upon some incurable brain defect. In milder forms of retardation the child may be backward because of no organic defect but because of functional nervous disease, of inadequate or improper nutrition, of defects of sight or hearing, or perhaps merely because he has not been sent regularly to school or may not have been subjected to satisfactory home discipline. Many of these cases of retardation are curable under appropriate physical and educational treatment, that is to say, the child can be restored to the mental and physical status of the normal child of his age. (124)

To Witmer, the age-grade statistic held out the best chance to measure the extent of "backwardness," or "pedagogical retardation," in the general school-age population and to explore its causes and treatment. To this end, he encouraged superintendents in Philadelphia and Camden to collect age-grade data and devoted considerable space in his journal to the debate between Thorndike, Ayres, Roland Falkner, Oliver Cornman, and others.

When Thorndike gathered data from city school reports for his 1908 elimination study, the best available statistics were tables of enrollment by grade and the numbers of children in the schools at each whole year of age. To answer such questions as the degree of overageness, the rate of progress through the grades, the typical age and grade of elimination, and so forth, he was forced to make certain estimates based on assumptions, particularly concerning the number of children entering a system in a given year. Ayres's study was based on better age-grade data for New York City, but he had no better data than Thorndike had for other cities. Nevertheless, Thorndike's assumptions, and thus his estimate of the extent of retardation, were sharply attacked. Over the next few years, the argument was joined by others, on Thorndike's side by his graduate students and on Ayres's by his colleague in Puerto Rico, Roland Falkner (Ayres, 1908; Blan, 1911; Cornman, 1907; Falkner, 1908a, 1908b; Keyes, 1911; Thorndike, 1909). As better statistics became available, the arguments shifted. Should educators be concerned with overageness for grade or only with failure to make normal progress regardless of age? What are the prime causes of retardation and elimination? What is an adequate system of "child accounting" (Ayres, 1915; Falkner, 1910; Moehlman, 1924; U.S. Bureau of Education, 1913)? What is the best age for a child to begin school?

If those in the newly emerging profession of psychology saw in the concept of age-grading a measurement tool that could lend scientific legitimacy to their work, the same can also be said of the emergent field of scientific school administration. Administrators in the Progressive era were enthralled by statistics and numbers. During these years, many fervently believed that the truths contained in tables and graphs could transform education from a jumble of well-worn clichés and practices into a full-fledged science grounded in objectivity and research (Tyack and Hanscot, 1982). Few numbers proved to be more important than those detailed in age-grade tables. Arthur Moehlman, a leading advocate of this scientific administration and of child accounting, described the utility of age-grade tables:

> The gross determination of curricular fit is made through semester or annual promotions and failure reports, age-grade placement, and age-grade progress studies. The grades organization is based on the assumption of orderly progress, one grade per year, through school. When the theoretical rate of progress is exceeded, the result is acceleration, and where the theoretical rate is not attained the result is retardation. The relationship of children to progress, regardless of other factors, is se-

cured from a study of failure to make grades in terms of the total possibility. A study of conditions within a building or a total school district may be made from a chart showing a two-way distribution of age in relation to grade. The age-grade study shows the condition and indicates the point of attack. [These charts provide] a quick picture of conditions prevailing at any time. (1940: 328)

But if the age-grade table provided a "quick picture" of a school's quality, what standard of age-grade "fit" should schools attempt to attain and how should it be measured? Here, too, numbers formed the language of the assessment of educational quality. In the early work, both Thorndike and Ayres had used a two-year age range from each grade as normal. For example, children who were six or seven and in the first grade were considered at grade level. This was made necessary, in part, because school districts collected their statistics at different times of the year. As child accounting became more standardized, administrators realized the value of an early fall data collection because this greatly reduced the percentage of overage students, and some districts shifted to a one-year or one-and-a-half-year standard. This shift in the standard makes cross-time comparisons more difficult. Some educational leaders, such as Ellwood P. Cubberley of Stanford University, declared that a normal rate of progress would result in about 70 percent of all students being at grade level with about 15 percent being accelerated and 15 percent being retarded (Cubberley, 1916: 370–71). This is only about 10 percent better than New York City reported in 1904, but at that time, the two-year interval standard was being used, and the ages of the students were collected in June.

However measured, these proved to be tough standards. Applied to George Strayer's national survey of 1911, few cities and towns would have met them. Over the next decade, as cities continued to publish age-grade tables and strive for higher efficiency, few were able to show progress, even using a fairly broad definition of the proper age for each grade. New York, for example, which had led the nation in identifying and attacking the problem of overaged pupils with its report of 39 percent overage in 1904, reported an overage rate of 31 percent in 1922, and Superintendent Ettinger referred to "the promiscuous distribution of children of all ages or of children of a given age through the grades" (Ettinger, 1922: 507; Tyack, 1974).

As such results became publicized, it began to appear that school leaders were unable to meet the standards they had set. Adding to administrators' problems was the fact that business leaders, key allies in the campaign for efficient school systems, frequently complained about the obvious inefficiency of schools that forced students to take eight or nine years to complete six years of elementary education (Tyack, 1974). As David Tyack notes, "In an age that worshipped efficiency, over-aged students and school leavers were signs of malfunctions that required analysis and correction" (1974:199).

By the early 1920s, educators were employing a variety of means to extricate themselves from this age-grading trap. For example, some readily shifted the blame for skewed age-grade distributions onto students. They claimed that the enormous increase in urban school enrollments was responsible for the high rates of failure and overageness, particularly because of the large numbers of foreign-born or rural children whose previous education was inadequate (Detroit Public Schools, 1922: 3). A subtle means for actually improving age-grade distributions was for school administrators to change the way that systems determined whether a student was at grade level. As one critic later noted: "In most school systems a high rate of non-promotion was considered an admission of educational inefficiency. Therefore, school authorities tended to decrease the number of non-promotions by their accounting practices" (Saunders, 1941: 8). School systems, for example, began passing large numbers of children with conditional promotions. Administrators recorded these students as promoted and at grade level, even if the students were later demoted. Administrators also changed the listing of students who were demoted but who subsequently left school from "nonpromoted" to "dropped." Finally, new students who were placed below grade level were listed as "transfers" rather than overage (Saunders, 1941: 7–8).

Although these changes in child accounting did improve the age-grade distributions of many school systems, other changes that school reformers introduced during this era proved to have an greater impact on normalizing age-groupings. They included the expanded use of ungraded classes, special education programs, IQ testing, tracking, ability grouping, and substantial curriculum reform designed it easier for larger numbers of students to achieve success in school. As William Ettinger, superintendent of schools in New York City, asserted, "I believe that the rapid advance in the technique of measuring mental ability and accomplishments means that we stand on the threshold of a new era in which we will increasingly group our pupils on the basis of both intelligence and accomplishment quotients and of necessity, provide differentiated curricula, varied modes of instruction, and flexible promotion schemes to meet the crying needs of our children" (1922: 512). The age-grade movement was a catalyst for the widespread adoption of all of these educational practices.

Age-Grading and Reform in Detroit   In 1907, the Detroit public school system conducted its first age-grade survey. The number of students at grade level in 1907, in 1914, and again in 1917 was nowhere near Cubberley's norm of 70 percent. For example, 49 percent of sixth graders in 1917 were overage for grade (Detroit Board of Education, 1907–8, 1916, 1917–18). Such figures forced the system toward a major reassessment of its educational program (Detroit Board of Education, 1907–8; Moehlman, 1925). School leaders moved to correct the problem: they ordered studies on the causes of retardation and overageness, created a department of special education to absorb handicapped students, and introduced "a differentiated course of study to meet the different abilities within a grade" (Detroit Public Schools, 1922: 3). By 1922, Detroit officials were estimating that about 3 percent of the system's students should be in special education or ungraded classes (Moehlman, 1925: 230).[7]

A central feature of this effort was mental testing and ability grouping. In September 1920, Detroit began testing all entering first graders and developed an elaborate system of programs and tracks to meet the needs of the various ability groups (Tyack, 1974; Williams, 1986). In addition to these efforts, school leaders sought to reorganize both the structure and the content of elementary education. As one Detroit official put it: "The appalling situation with respect to retardation and elimination in many of the larger centers of population had been pointed out by scholars some years before. The plain inference was established that a discipline which so great a percentage of pupils were unable to master were not a suitable discipline for the majority of children" (Detroit Public School Staff, 1943: 238–39). Thus, in the early 1920s, Detroit adopted a version of the Gary Plan for its elementary program. Known as platoon schools, this program combined the teaching of traditional elementary subjects, such as reading and arithmetic, with enrichment courses, such as music and art, while also providing classes in physical education, dramatics, and so forth (Detroit Public School Staff, 1943; Moehlman, 1925; Spain, 1924). These changes were, in part, intended to improve the progress of students through the grades. In addition to restructuring elementary education, Detroit's school leaders transformed secondary education, shifting to a 6–3–3 pattern of organization for the system and adding vocational and practical courses in junior high schools (called intermediate schools) as a means of reducing overage students in grades seven and eight (Detroit Public School Staff, 1943).

By 1922, in a spirit of self-congratulation for these efforts, Detroit boasted that 74 percent of its elementary students were either at or above grade level (Detroit Public Schools, 1922: 8, 11). This may have represented considerable progress for Detroit, although it is not clear whether this calculation was based on the one-year or two-year interval for the proper age in each grade.

Age-Grade Developments Elsewhere   Although Detroit reported some success in achieving high rates of at-grade-level students, the nationwide trend was quite uneven. In states outside the industrial Northeast and Midwest, schools usually lagged behind in implementing age-grading and in reaching normal age-grade distributions. During the 1930s, many of these states reported very high rates of failure and consequently high levels of overageness among elementary pupils. In West Virginia, for example, the failure rate in some counties ran as high as 75 percent in the 1934–35 school year. In 1938, Maryland teachers failed 22.4 percent of white first-grade boys and 14.4 percent of white first-grade girls. Figures were higher for black children. That same year in Tennessee about 16 percent of the state's black children and 12 percent of its white children were required to repeat a grade (Saunders, 1941). Rural schools, even in the Northeast and Midwest, were also slow in reaching normal rates of students at grade level. A 1935 study of students in 292 one-room rural schools in Michigan found an average of 59 percent of the students at grade level and an average of 19 percent overage, with the percent of overage students rising in every grade (Smith, 1937).

Even in major urban school systems, the rates of nonpromotion and the numbers of overage students remained high into the 1930s. In New York City, for example, retardation rates for elementary children within the fifty-four subdistricts of the school system ranged from a low of 16.2 percent to a high of 40.8 percent in the 1934–35 school year. School officials in Chicago reported nonpromotion rates for first graders in 1936 running between 10 and 20 percent. In 1939, in St. Louis 30 percent of the city's first graders were not promoted, an increase of 11 percent from 1930 (Elsbree, 1947; Saunders, 1941: 10–13).

Despite the persistence of large numbers of overage students, and notwithstanding the difficulties of cross-time comparisons, there does appear to have been a significant movement toward higher rates of students at grade level during the 1930s. One study of the Virginia public schools, for example, analyzed state level data from 1924 to 1937 and found that "the median [age] and distribution of ages in the individual grades have dropped—a phenomena [*sic*] which suggests improved grading and promotion practices. Presumably, there is less retardation of older children, and children in the same grade are more nearly of the same age" (Harvey, 1939: 754). Similarly, a study of changes in retardation rates in seven major American cities showed a definite decline in the percentage of nonpromotions and, we can assume, a higher percentage of at-grade-level students between the early 1920s and 1938–39 (Saunders, 1941).

It is important to note that throughout the three decades in which the age-grade movement became a powerful catalyst for a broad range of Progressive reforms, educators never abandoned the notion that children's grade placement should have something to do with what they had learned. While they were prepared to experiment with a host of devices to improve age-grade fit, and thus the efficiency of the systems, they did not take the simple expedient of placing children in grades based on their chronological age alone. This step remained to be taken by more advanced Progressive thinkers.

Social Promotion and the Attainment of Age-Graded Schools

The movement to get the majority of students at grade level received a final, and ultimately triumphant, push in the 1940s. These years witnessed a shift in conventional educational wisdom as important as the one associated with the introduction of age-grading itself. Much as age-grading changed the definition of a quality school system from one with high rates of failure to one with high rates of promotion, so in the 1940s, educators began to adopt the idea that automatic promotion, or as it would later be called "social promotion," of virtually all students was the sign of true educational quality.

The Concept of Automatic Promotion   As early as 1931, a committee of school administrators in New York City urged that "grade standards be abolished and that pupils in the elementary and junior high schools be promoted on the basis of school attendance and chronological age" (*Elementary School Journal*, 1935: 241). The essence of the administrators' plan was to "virtually do away with non-promotion and put the city school system on a 100 percent promotion schedule" (242). Although New York did not adopt the plan at that time, by the late 1930s the concept of automatic promotion was gaining legitimacy in educational circles. In 1937, for example, A. C. Krey predicted that "universal school enrollment up to the age of sixteen, if not also beyond this point possibly even to the age of twenty, will continue and that this will be accompanied with an administrative policy approaching automatic promotion" (1937: 457).[8]

As in the earlier campaigns to make more frequent promotions (1870s to 1890s) and to adjust age-grading norms to account for individual differences (1920s), advocates of this policy focused their attacks on traditional, inflexible promotion practices. Willard Elsbree, a leading advocate of flexible promotions, railed that "in most communities, it is still taken for granted that each grade has established achievement norms; that the curriculum should be geared to these standards; and that pupils should master in orderly sequence the subject matter and skills prescribed in the elementary program. Failing the mastery of subject matter and skills, the pupil should repeat the year's work" (1947: 430). In place of these practices, educators sought "a plan of education that emphasizes the development of social human beings rather than the performance of certain routines which may over the course of years happen to give some factual information which will be retained in after life and may incidentally develop the characters of children so they will be able to meet the world" (*Elementary School Journal*, 1935: 242).

In many ways, the call for automatic promotion was the logical culmination of a number of elements of Progressive educational thought, which stressed the need to (1) accommodate individual differences within the classroom, (2) educate the whole child, particularly with regard to the psychological health of children, and (3) educate all American youth. Relying on what they claimed was the best educational research, social promotion advocates argued, first, that failing children was a clear indication that a school was not motivating children properly. If children failed the fault lay not in the children but in the outmoded organization and practices of the school. Furthermore, students who failed a grade generally did not improve in achievement. Failure, and the threat of failure, simply did not prove to be a good motivator.

A second line of argument was that students who failed were psychologically damaged by the experience and that this had profound, negative educational consequences. Studies showed that children who failed had greater self-doubts (which later researchers would call lower self-esteem) and a strong sense of inferiority and disgrace. Once branded a failure, these students evidenced increased feelings of antagonism and bitterness toward the schools and teachers, often leading to discipline problems in the classroom.

Finally, students who failed frequently became high school dropouts; they saw an early exit from school as the best solution to their ongoing educational and behavioral problems. Advocates of social promotion thus perceived the policy of failing student to be a manifestation of the undemocratic character of traditional educational practices that forced students to abandon their education and denyied them equal educational opportunity (Aretz, 1940; Brechbill, 1944; Elsbree, 1947; Goodlad, 1952; Saunders, 1941).

Many educators, especially those in leading urban systems, eagerly accepted these ideas. As early as 1938, a National Education Association survey of twenty-three cities found that most superintendents favored some form of social promotion (Saunders, 1941: 45–55). By the early 1940s, such major school systems as Minneapolis and New York City put social promotion policies into place (Elliott, 1944, 1948). In a 1955 study, Roger Lennon and Blythe Mitchell compiled data from five national reports that contained information on age-grading. They concluded that "policy with respect to promotion of elementary school pupils has undergone considerable modification in the past 30 years or so, moving unmistakably in the direction of so-called 'social' or chronological-age-based promotion and away from promotion premised on attainment of any fixed level of achievement" (Lennon and Mitchell, 1955: 123).[9] The introduction, development, and consequences of social promotion in urban schools can be illustrated by the experiences of Philadelphia and New York City.

Social Promotion in Philadelphia Philadelphia had played a key role in the earliest debates on age-grading and had adopted a modified form of social promotion earlier than most major districts. In the late 1930s, Philadelphia administrators introduced a policy of "continuous pupil progress." This policy set in motion a major reorganization of elementary education in which "emphasis has been placed on group work and different ways of classifying pupils. Courses of study and time allotments are viewed as guides. . . . Diagnostic and remedial teaching is resulting in development of all kinds of self-teaching, self-directing, and self-checking arrangements. Individualization of instruction is recognized as the basis of a program of continuous pupil progress. Informality in classroom procedure is becoming more prevalent. The entire administrative setup is more flexible" (Artez, 1940: 680–81). The most important aspect of this program was that "grade, for all practical purposes, has become synonymous with school age" (680).

The policy, however, generated intense opposition. By the late 1940s, Philadelphia school officials were forced to defend social promotion from charges that it had contributed to a loss of standards, rigor, and accountability (on the part of both teachers and students). One group of critics claimed that as a consequence of this policy, "some pupils who should still be in grade school are in high school and many high-school pupils graduate without fundamentals" (*Elementary School Journal*, 1948: 532). In 1947, the city's board of superintendents issued a statement denying that the school system had ever adopted a policy of 100-percent promotion. At the same time, the board staunchly defended the practice of continuous pupil progress. The statement by the board specifically denounced past practices that provided educational opportunities only for students strong enough to survive a system of "rigid, predetermined requirements." The board argued that the only way to encourage all children to reach their full potential, to truly provide "equality of educational opportunity," was to drastically decrease the number of failures and allow children to progress at their own rate. Given these goals, the board concluded "that chronological age is the most satisfactory basis for general class grouping" (*Elementary School Journal*, 1947: 62–64).[10]

Promotion Practices and Age-Grading in New York City   Events in New York City demonstrate that the adoption of automatic, or continuous, promotion was not of itself sufficient to create the high degree of age stratification that characterizes contemporary schools. Between 1942 and 1946, New York replaced a decades-old system of twice-yearly admissions and promotions with a policy of continuous promotion. Students would be admitted only in September, promoted only in June; a clear assumption was that nonpromotion would be extremely rare. In fact, by 1948, the promotion rate for the elementary schools, which had reached a citywide average of 90 percent early in the century, moved to 99 percent (New York Board of Education, 1949: 125).

In spite of this, the administration continued to express concern about age-grade relations. Tables and text on age of pupils, age-grade status of pupils, and rate of progress of pupils continued to appear in the annual reports well into the 1960s. Over the years, as a result of the reforms discussed earlier, the percentage of overage students had steadily declined, but the district now faced a new problem. "Since 1923 when attention was concentrated on the problems of overageness and retardation the proportion of overage pupils had been reduced from 29.9 percent to 5.3 percent in 1948. . . . While the problem of 'overageness' has been brought under control there are indications in the data . . . of a new problem, that of 'underageness'" (New York Board of Education, 1949: 152, 155). How could this have happened?

As a school district's rate of pupil promotion approaches 100 percent, the only factor that can affect the age range of the pupils in each grade is age of entry. In 1948, the New York State school code entitled anyone between the ages of five and twenty-one to attend school. The state's compulsory attendance law required everyone from seven to sixteen to be enrolled. Theoretically, then, children might enter the first grade as young as five and as old as six years, eleven months, assuming no one violated the law. In actual fact, the policy of the New York City Board was to admit children as young as four to kindergartens and to admit no one under five years, four months to the first grade. Also, a few parents must have held children out of school past the seven-year limit.[11] Given a September data collection and a two-year standard for normal (in other words, six or seven for the first grade), it is easy to see why few pupils would be classified as overage and many as underage. The problem was further compounded by the postwar baby boom and, possibly, by an increased interest in early child education. Between 1942 and 1948, the number of enrolled four-year-olds increased by 163 percent and the number of five-year-olds by 78 percent (New York Board of Education, 1949: 142). Reflecting on this state of affairs, the superintendent's remarks were a powerful echo of the early days of the age-grade movement. "The outstanding characteristic of the data . . . is the variability, as to age, of pupils in the same grade. In the fourth grade, for instance, the ages of pupils range from seven to fourteen years inclusive. The standard age for fourth grade is nine years. Similarly for each of the other grades" (New York Board of Education, 1949: 145).[12]

This is not to suggest that all the efforts expended over the years in New York and other places had no appreciable effect on the degree to which schools were stratified by age. Quite the opposite. There can be no doubt that the distribution of children's ages in the grades had been narrowed and that they clustered more strongly around the mean. The key factors in approaching the current level of age stratification in school were the adoption of social promotion and a decrease in the range of age at entry. Nationally aggregated data suggest that as more and more of the nation's school districts adopted such policies after 1940, schools became more age-stratified. From 1940 to 1960, there continued to be incremental movement in this direction; however, a comparison of age-grade relations in the period 1964–66 with those in 1983 show little further change.[13]

Conclusion

Age segregation in American educational history has two aspects. The first is the simple segregation of children from adults that occurred largely because of the expansion of public schooling in the nineteenth and early twentieth centuries. The second, and for our purposes more significant, is the fact that there has been increasing stratification of children by age within schools because of the practice of age-grading.

The most startling aspect of age stratification in schooling is the relatively recent date of its widespread implementation. Leading urban school systems did not succeeded in getting most children at grade level until the 1920s and 1930s, and they did this by an assortment of devices that included special classes, ability grouping within classes, and a host of child-accounting tricks. Rural school systems lagged considerably behind urban ones in approaching normal rates of at-grade-level students. Today's taken-for-granted level of age-grade homogeneity was not approximated in many schools before the 1940s and probably not in most schools until the 1950s.

Equally important is the way in which age-grading served as a catalyst for a variety of Progressive educational practices including such efficiency-oriented practices as child accounting, intelligence testing, ability grouping, and tracking. Of these practices, social promotion remains one of the most controversial.

After age-grade relations became a measure of school efficiency in the early twentieth century, educational leaders worked diligently to improve their schools on this measure. Their intention was not to age-stratify the young, but to discover more effective ways of grouping children for maximum learning. With the introduction of the idea of social promotion in the late Progressive period, age stratification itself became the institutional goal. This shift of intention may be the aspect of age stratification that has had the most serious consequences for the nation's schools.

Whether to hold students back or to keep them with their classmates remains a volatile issue. Should the grade placement of children be based, at least in part, on whether they have learned or failed to learn the expected material? Is automatic promotion an example of the schools' alleged lack of interest in excellence? Or does it stem from a deep regard for the psychological well-being of the child and does it reflect an abiding commitment to equal opportunity? These issues will divide the educational community for some time to come, but it is important to see both how perennial the debate over grouping children for instruction has been and how recent the social promotion solution is.

Notes

This chapter appeared in an earlier form in *Teachers College Record*, 90, no. 2 (winter 1988): 211–36. Reprinted by permission of *Teachers College Record*.

1. For a discussion of literacy in colonial America and the Puritan emphasis on being able to read the Bible, see chap. 1.

2. The most significant post–World War II development is the emergence of part-time student work. In 1947 approximately 27 percent of school-going boys ages sixteen or seventeen were working; in 1980 that figure had increased to 44 percent. Among school-going girls of that same age, the percentage working increased even more dramatically, from 17 percent to 41 percent (Greenberg and Steinberg, 1986).

3. In Robert Dreeben's (1968) study of how the structure of the school contributes to the socialization of the child, the strict age-graded character of the school is recognized as playing a vital role.

4. Emmet Giltner (1907) discusses a host of plans for "conserving the individual": the Pueblo plan, the Denver plan, the Seattle plan, the Batavia plan, Stratton Brooks's plan, and schemes worked out in Chicago, St. Louis, Cambridge, Massachusetts, Elizabeth, New Jersey, and Providence.

5. The rates that were most often cited from Ayres's book were those of Medford, Massachusetts, with 7 percent retardation, and the "colored children" of Memphis, with 75 percent.

6. The earliest true age-grade table I have found was in the annual report for 1874–75 of the Dayton, Ohio, public schools, although such tables were still found, on rare occasions, at the turn of the century.

7. For an excellent discussion of the development of special education in Detroit, see Tropea (1987).

8. By the early 1940s, automatic promotion had become so established a part of the pro-motion literature that the phrase appeared as a heading in the 1941–44 volume of *The Education Index*.

9. Although the data from each report were quite disparate, one covering only urban schools, another including schools in all forty-eight states, the studies did have very large samples, including over 116,000 in the 1926 study, 250,000 in the 1940 survey, 400,000 in the 1946 and 1952 studies, and over 1,000,000 in the 1918 study.

10. After continued opposition to the policy, the board released a new policy directive on promotions in 1948, stating that teachers were not required to either promote or not promote a "particular percentage of the pupils." Although conciliatory in tone, the new directive left the power to decide these matters in the hands of the teacher and "within the discretion of school authorities," in effect, it appears, it left the original policy intact (Editor, 1948: 534). For additional criticism of social promotion, see Elliott (1948), Foley (1944), and Reed (1949).

11. The age distribution for the first grade in 1948 included 927 seven-year-olds, 97 eight-year-olds, 12 nine-year-olds, and 5 ten-year-olds—too many overaged children to be accounted for by nonpromotion (New York Board of Education, 1949: 144).

12. In New York City, promotion rates remained at near 100 percent until the mid-fifties, when both nonpromotion and the percent of overage students began to rise. The schools of New York City were somewhat less age-graded in 1965 than they were in 1948 (New York Board of Education, 1965: 74, 84–86).

13. Although comparison with earlier studies based on different conceptions and measurements is potentially misleading, a grasp of the post–World War II conditions can be gleaned from U.S. Bureau of Census (1967–87), *Current Population Reports*, ser. P-20; the federal censuses for 1940, 1950, and 1960 also include tables on age-grade relations.

Chapter 11 / *A Historical Perspective on Support for Schooling by Different Age Cohorts*

The strain on government resources during the 1970s and 1980s has raised concern about direct or indirect competition for assistance among subgroups of the population. In particular, there is a widespread and growing belief that the elderly have benefited from government assistance at the expense of children. Figures showing the decrease in poverty among the elderly and an increase in poverty among children frequently are cited as evidence of this trend. Critics often accuse the elderly of using their political power to maintain their relative advantages over groups such as children that cannot personally participate in the political process (Bengston, 1989; Preston, 1984; Torres-Gil, 1989).

One of the largest public expenditures on children is support of education—most of it funded by state or local governments. Since much of local funding of public education depends on passage of school millages and bond issues, voters frequently are called on to express their views in this area. An analysis of support of and opposition to public school expenditures by different age cohorts can provide an interesting and useful opportunity to examine the nature and extent, if any, of the so-called generational conflict.

Most of the discussion about the conflict between age cohorts regarding support for social services focuses almost exclusively on the present. Many studies look at only one issue, such as support for education or Social Security, rather than comparing several different areas simultaneously. Furthermore, some analysts look only at the factor of age without taking into consideration other possible influences that may affect an individual's views. As a result, many studies of this conflict are ahistorical, narrowly defined, or focused exclusively on the impact of age.

To understand the origins and development of our complex system of organizing and financing public education, first I shall examine changing attitudes toward the responsibility of parents and governments for the education of children in colonial and nineteenth-century America. Next I shall analyze changes in education in twentieth-century America, with particular attention to the growth of secondary and higher education and to the increasing role of the state and federal governments in financing public education. Finally I shall look specifically at the role of the elderly in supporting or opposing public education in the post–World War II era and try to ascertain, based upon an analysis of survey data from 1988, whether there is a real and serious difference between age cohorts. Although some analysts believe that there are important differences by age in regard to support for additional educational funding, others argue that there are few, if any, differences between younger and older people on this issue—especially after accounting for the impact of other characteristics of the voters.

Education in Colonial and Nineteenth-Century America

In seventeenth-century America, education was primarily intended to teach individuals how to read and interpret the Bible. The responsibility for education rested with the household rather than with schools or the government (Axtell, 1974). The father, as the head of household, had the primary responsibility of educating the other members of the household, although the mother often assisted him. The community intervened only when the household failed to carry out its duties (Moran and Vinovskis, 1986).[1]

Some schools were established in early America—particularly in New England. But most of these were grammar schools intended to educate future clergymen, rather than elementary schools designed to teach children the basics of reading and writing (Bailyn, 1960). By the end of the eighteenth century in the Northeast, private schools began to supplement or replace the educational training in the home. The nineteenth century witnessed the rapid expansion of schooling in the North (Soltow and Stevens, 1981).

In the early nineteenth century, there was not a clear separation between public and private financing of education. Local governments funded education, but parents of students were often expected to contribute as well. Over time, however, private and family contributions to elementary schooling declined as public support for common schools increased (Benson and O'Halloran, 1987; Cremin, 1980). At the same time, public school reformers like Horace Mann succeeded in eliminating any public assistance to private academies, and many of these institutions were replaced by public schools (Jorgenson, 1987). By the time of the Civil War, common school education was mainly under local control and was financed almost entirely by the public.

Although school reformers tried to increase state expenditures and control of education, local resistance to centralization was intense. Drawing on the Revolutionary ideology of fear of centralized power, most Americans insisted that their public common schools be financed and controlled by voters in the small school districts where they were located (Kaestle and Vinovskis, 1980).

Most nineteenth-century Americans had relatively large families with school-age children present in most homes, and so opposition to local school taxes came mainly from those who felt too much was being spent on schools, from wealthier families that sent their children to private academies, and from those who opposed public education for religious reasons (Glen, 1988; Kaestle, 1983; Katz, 1968; Vinovskis, 1985). There is little evidence of concern among nineteenth-century educational reformers that elderly voters in particular opposed higher local school taxes.

There are a few tentative suggestions that older voters may sometimes have been less supportive of some of the educational innovations, such as centralization and the establishment of public high schools, but there is no definitive, direct evidence of differences in public support of schools by age. Several studies provide some intriguing indirect evidence on the role of age in support of public schools in nineteenth-century America. An individual-level study of schooling in eight communities in Essex County, Massachusetts, in 1860 and 1880 did not find the age of the parents to be a strong predictor of their children's school attendance. Moreover, after controlling for the effects of other variables, parents ages sixty and older in 1860, but not in 1880, were more likely than the rest of the population to send their children to school (Kaestle and Vinovskis, 1980: 87–89). A study of the Massachusetts House of Representatives in 1840 on the vote to abolish the state Board of Education, however, found that older legislators were considerably more likely to oppose the board. This probably reflects the concerns of older legislators about recent efforts to centralize control of education rather than their opposition to public education in general (Kaestle and Vinovskis, 1980: 222–23).

An analysis of the recorded public meeting vote to abolish the Beverly Public High School in Massachusetts in 1860 found that those ages sixty and older were the most likely to oppose that institution. The meaning of this vote was very complicated because it involved compliance with a state law (the town had been sued for noncompliance) rather than just whether or not someone favored a high school (see chapter 7; Vinovskis, 1985: 86–88). There are some hints in these fragmentary data that older voters may have been less supportive of some of the newer and more centralized aspects of public school reform efforts, but they do not necessarily indicate opposition to public schooling in general. Moreover, when there were serious disputes over education in nineteenth-century America, the divisions do not seem to have been strongly age related.

One intriguing recent development in the study of aging in the past is the argument that parents invested in their children's education with the expectation that they would be repaid with old age assistance. Thus, there would have been an explicit or implicit contract between the young and their parents in nineteenth-century America. Unfortunately, there is little or no evidence for such an interpretation at this time. As one reads through the extensive published literature promoting schooling in nineteenth-century America, one is struck by the lack of references to such a contract or to future benefits for parents who educated their children. Moreover, historians have not found evidence of such thinking in the private letters or diaries of the period. Although the idea of a contract between parents and children is appealing and seemingly plausible, there is little reason to believe it existed for most nineteenth-century Americans.

Twentieth-Century Changes in Education

In colonial and nineteenth-century America, most households contained some children under age eighteen and therefore helped to foster support for schooling. The long-term decline in fertility, as well as the increasing likelihood of individuals living by themselves, meant that fewer twentieth-century households included school-age children (Vinovskis, 1987b). In 1940 slightly less than half of the households (47.2 percent) included children under age eighteen (Sweet and Bumpass, 1987: 340). By 1980 that figure had declined to 38.4 percent, and in 1988 the number of households with children under eighteen had dropped to 35.1 percent (U.S. Bureau of Census, 1990: no. 61). In other words, today almost two-thirds of households do not have any school-age children, and therefore they may be less willing to support educational expenditures—perhaps also in part because many of those of school age are minority children.

If the proportion of households with children has decreased, the amount of education each child receives has increased dramatically. Few students graduated from high school in 1900, but 38.1 percent of the population ages twenty-five through twenty-nine in 1940 had completed high school; by 1988 the comparable rate was 86.1 percent (U.S. Bureau of Census, 1990: no. 215). Similarly, whereas college education in the early twentieth century was limited to few individuals, by 1940 the percentage of the population ages twenty-five through twenty-nine who had completed at least four years of college was 5.9 percent, and in 1988 it was 22.7 percent (U.S. Bureau of Census, 1990: no. 215).

Along with the increase in the length of schooling, the costs of education have risen. In constant 1987–88 dollars, the total expenditure (per pupil in average daily attendance) for public elementary and secondary schools skyrocketed from $389 in 1919–20 to $4,724 in 1988–89 (National Center for Education

Statistics, 1989: table 145). Furthermore, the sources of that funding have changed dramatically. In 1919–20, most of the revenue for public elementary and secondary schools came from local sources (83.2 percent), with only a small amount from either the state (16.5 percent) or the federal government (0.3 percent). By 1986–87 the situation had changed considerably, with almost equal amounts coming from local governments (43.9 percent) and the state government (49.8 percent). Federal funding of public elementary and secondary education reached 6.4 percent (National Center for Education Statistics, 1989: table 138; Garms, Guthrie, and Pierce, 1978; Salmon, 1987).

If one looks at total expenditures for education (including public and private elementary, secondary, and higher education), there has been a significant increase during the past three decades—particularly in the area of higher education. As a percentage of the gross national product, the cost of all educational institutions rose from 4.8 percent in 1959 to 5.9 percent in 1987, with most of that increase due to the expansion of higher education. It is interesting to observe, however, that educational expenditures as a percentage of gross national product peaked in the mid-1970s and have decreased slightly since then (National Center for Education Statistics, 1989: table 25). Moreover, educational expenditures relative to Social Security and Medicare costs have declined considerably from 1960 to 1987.

Voter Reactions to Increased Educational Spending

The funding of education, especially at the local level, is very diverse and complicated. In the mid-nineteenth century, most of the funding for public schools came from allocations at either the township or county levels, with only a very small proportion of expenditures from state funds (Kaestle and Vinovskis, 1980). During the 1870s and 1880s, however, as part of conservative efforts to curb excessive municipal spending, most states set limits on the amount of property taxes or borrowing that could be undertaken without a referendum by the local voters. One of the unanticipated consequences was the difficulty of raising funds for public schools and thus a growing reliance on state funding. Another consequence was the necessity of holding frequent local school-tax and bond elections, which gave voters more opportunities to participate in the financial affairs of their schools (Hamilton and Cohen, 1974).

There is considerable variation in the frequency of school referenda. According to a comprehensive survey of school referenda in the early 1970s, there were about seven thousand annual tax levies and budget elections throughout the United States, with eight states accounting for more than five thousand of these referenda. Factors such as the size of school districts; the proportion of operating revenues based on local sources; the minimum school tax mandated by state statute; the duration of voted levies; the possibility of school boards calling repeat elections; and the number of defeats (which necessitates another campaign) all affected the frequency of school-tax levy and bond elections. In a few states fewer than a dozen school referenda were held each year, while at the other extreme eighteen hundred such elections were held in Oklahoma alone (Hamilton and Cohen, 1974).

Although public school expenditures per pupil rose during the 1960s and early 1970s, there was growing resistance among taxpayers. One index of this discontent was the an increase in the disapproval of school bond issues. In the early 1960s, approximately 72 percent of school bonds passed, but in 1967 that figure declined to 67 percent and then leveled off at approximately 50 percent in the 1970s. Furthermore, in constant dollars, the amount of school bonds passed dropped by about one-half from the early 1960s to the late 1970s (calculated from Piele and Hall, 1973: 3; U.S. Bureau of Census, 1981: no. 254). In other words, concerns about public schooling and high taxes persuaded many voters in the late 1960s and 1970s to reconsider the extent of their financial commitment to education.

As school levies and bond issues faced increasing public resistance, scholars initiated a series of studies to ascertain the characteristics of the small minority who voted in these local elections and to differentiate between those who supported and those who opposed increases in school funding. In general, these studies found that the most likely participants were more affluent, better educated, parents of school-age children, homeowners, whites, and highly interested in schools. Among the voters, those who supported the bond issues were likely to be better educated, more affluent, parents of school-age children, African-American and to have a high interest in their schools and community. Conversely, those who opposed increased taxes for education were less educated, less affluent, without school-age children, white, and more alienated from the community and the schools (Hamilton and Cohen, 1974; Piele and Hall, 1973).

In regard to age, almost all of the studies found that older voters were less supportive of educational expansion than younger ones. Even after controlling for the effects of other factors, such as socioeconomic status and parenthood, most of these analyses found elderly voters less supportive of increases in educational expenditures. A few did find, however, that the effects of age became relatively unimportant once other personal and family characteristics were controlled for (Button and Rosenbaum, 1973; Hamilton and Cohen, 1974; Piele and Hall, 1973).

The Phi Delta Kappa–Gallup Polls of Public Attitudes toward the Public Schools can be used to determine if there have been any recent national changes in public support for education. Starting in 1969, the survey included the question: "Suppose the local public schools said they needed much more money. As you feel at this time, would you vote to raise taxes for this purpose, or would you vote against raising taxes for this purpose" (Elam, 1989: 17). This question was repeated intermittently for several years and provides us with information on changes in public support for education.

In 1969, 45 percent those surveyed replied that they would vote for additional school taxes, but this support declined to 37 percent the next year and remained at approximately that level for the next three years (see figure 11.1). By 1981 support for additional school taxes dropped to 30 percent, but it recovered quickly in 1983 with the publicity surrounding the publication of *A Nation at Risk* (1983). (The education survey was conducted two weeks after the release of that report.) For the next three years, support for additional school taxes remained at about the same level (Elam, 1989).

Overall, it appears that public willingness to support schooling through additional local taxes decreased from 1969 to 1970, then briefly stabilized before dropping to a new low in 1981; it recovered after 1983 to a level comparable to the early 1970s. Throughout most of the 1970s and 1980s, approximately four out of ten Americans favored additional local taxes to support the public schools. Those without school children and those with children in parochial schools generally were less supportive of local school tax increases than those with children in the public schools. Furthermore, for the one year (1969) for which we have age breakdowns, 56 percent of those ages twenty-one through twenty-nine, 47 percent of those ages thirty through forty-nine, and 39 percent of those ages fifty and older supported additional local taxes for education.

Roughly comparable changes in support for additional educational expenditures are found in the General Social Surveys for 1973 and 1986. These

Figure 11.1 / *Percentage Supporting Local School Tax Increase, 1969–86*

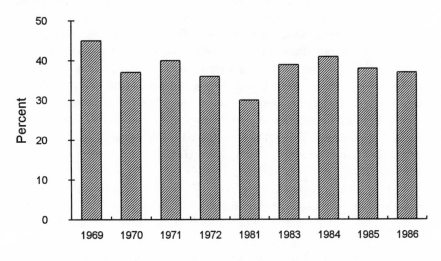

Source: Data from Elam, 1989

Figure 11.2 / *Percentage Supporting Increase in Spending for Education, by Age-Group*

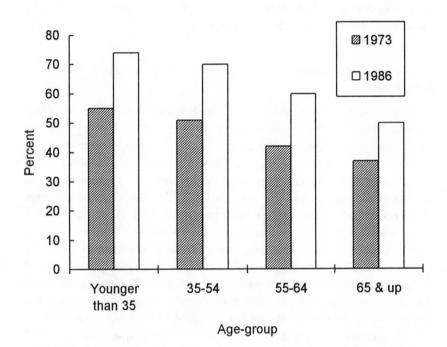

Source: Data from Ponza et al., 1988

surveys inquired about the willingness of the public to support certain programs: "We are faced with many problems in this country, none of which can be solved easily or inexpensively. I'm going to name some of the problems, and for each one I'd like you to tell me whether you think we're spending too much money on it, too little money, or about the right amount. First, space exploration [education, Social Security, welfare]: are we spending too much, too little, or about the right amount on (item)" (quoted in Ponza et al., 1988: 444).

According to a recent analysis of these data, public support for increased spending on education rose from 49 percent in 1973 to 67 percent in 1986 (Ponza et al., 1988). In addition, older age-groups were consistently less likely to support increased educational expenditures than younger groups (see figure 11.2). The authors, however, point out that older respondents, along with every other age-group, increased their support for educational funding from 1973 to 1986; moreover, the older age-groups were also less supportive of increases in Social Security payments than other age-groups. Noting that these particular questions about spending are so broad, the authors caution against concluding that the elderly acted in their own, narrow self-interest in deciding on which social programs to endorse. Unfortunately, this otherwise interesting and useful study does not attempt to examine in more detail the pattern of responses by age to these different domestic social programs.

Age Differences in Support for Increased Federal Spending for Public Schools in 1988

The American National Election Survey for 1988, which interviewed a representative sample of 2,040 United States citizens of voting age living in the forty-eight coterminous states, can be used to explore the importance of age in determining support for education.[2] Unlike most of the studies of school bond issues or analyses of the Gallup poll results, this survey focused specifically on the role of the federal government in providing assistance to public education or to college students as well as to other programs.

The survey prefaced its questions about federal expenditures with this statement: "If you had a say in making up the federal budget this year, for which of the following programs would you like to see spending increased and for which would you like to see spending decreased?" The interviewer would then ask about a series of programs. For example, the question on public education specifically asked: "Should federal spending on public schools be increased, decreased, or kept about the same?" Comparable questions were asked about federal spending for aid to college students, for improving and protecting the environment, for assistance to the unemployed, for space and scientific research, for assistance to African-Americans, for child care, for care of the elderly, for the homeless, for the war on drugs, for Social Security, for food stamps, for aid to the Contras, for Star Wars, and for fighting AIDS. Questions were asked about federal spending for fifteen different activities, as well as the standard inquiries about the demographic, socioeconomic, and political characteristics of the respondents.

There was considerable variation in the willingness of the public to increase federal spending for these programs. At one extreme, only a very small minority of Americans favored increased spending for aid to the Contras (10.9 percent) or for the development of the Star Wars program (15.7 percent). At the other extreme, most citizens favored more federal expenditures for fighting drugs (73.8 percent) or helping the elderly (75.2 percent). In terms of education, 63.9 percent favored additional federal spending for public schools, and 44.8 percent supported more federal assistance for college students.

We can study the age variation by subdividing the sample into six age-groups: eighteen through twenty-nine, thirty through thirty-nine, forty through forty-nine, fifty through fifty-nine, sixty through sixty-nine, and seventy and older. Coefficients of variation by age-group were calculated for each of the fifteen issues. For some items (such as more aid for the Contras, for the war on drugs, for help for the homeless, and for Social Security) there was relatively little variation by age. Support for additional federal spending on Star Wars had the most overall variation by age. Interestingly, approval of increased spending for public schools or for college students had the next highest amount of variation by age.

In general, individuals ages fifty through fifty-nine, sixty through sixty-nine, and seventy and older were less supportive of increased federal spending for almost all of these issues than the population as a whole. In addition, in most situations, support for increased federal aid tended to diminish for these three age-groups as one moved from the youngest age-group to the next older group and then to seventy and older. The only clear exception to this pattern was the question about the war on drugs, where those ages fifty through fifty-nine and sixty through sixty-nine were slightly more supportive than those in all of the other age-groups.

We can look in more detail at the age pattern of support comparing the responses to the questions about education with those about the elderly or the unemployed (see figure 11.3). For additional federal assistance for the unemployed, there is much less overall support than for public schools, but there is also less variation by age. For more federal aid to the elderly, there is more overall support than for the public schools, but again there is less variation by age. For all three issues—but especially for more federal funding of public schools—there is a general decrease in support with age.

Support for additional federal assistance for public schools drops rather dramatically from 77.1 percent among those ages eighteen through twenty-nine to 46.9 percent among those ages seventy and older. At the same time, support for additional public school spending by those in their fifties and sixties is nearly identical, and about one-half of those age sixty and older still endorse increased federal aid for public education. Therefore, any discussions of older respondents as a homogeneous group are incorrect and misleading.

We can take another look at the issue of age and support for increased federal expenditures for public schools and comparing those with and without children under eighteen in their households (only for those under age sixty because very few older individuals had children in their households). In each age-group, those with children under eighteen in the household are more supportive of increased federal assistance for public schools than those without. Nevertheless, even those under age fifty without children in their household are more supportive of increased federal funding of public schools than those age sixty and above—perhaps in part because the childless individuals in the younger cohorts may expect to have children who will eventually use the public schools.

Figure 11.3 / *Percentage Favoring More Federal Spending for Public Schools, the Elderly, and the Unemployed, by Age-Group*

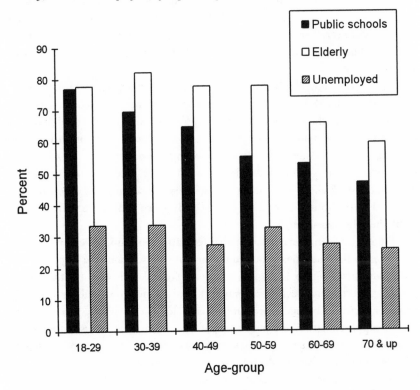

Source: Data from W. Miller, 1989

One might argue, as some have, that the age differences in support for increased funding of public education are only the result of the impact of other factors, such as educational level or family income, which may be highly correlated with age. Therefore, to ascertain the relative impact of age compared to other characteristics in accounting for differences in support of more public school funding, a multiple classification analysis was run, with support for or opposition to increased federal spending as the dependent variable (1 = support, 0 = opposition). The nine independent variables were age, sex, race, education, family income, liberal-conservative index, party identity, population size of the community, and the region where the individual lived.

After controlling for the effects of the other variables, age is the best predictor of whether or not someone supports additional federal funding for public schools (see table 11.1). Whether one looks at the beta weights or the changes in the adjusted R^2 when age is removed from the analysis, it is the single best predictor. Moreover, the tendency of older individuals to oppose additional

Table 11.1 / *Support for Increasing Federal Aid to Public Schools in 1988*

Variable	Eta^2	Beta	Changes in R^2 if Variable Removed
Age	.0395	.1691	−.0227
Sex	.0027	.0412	−.0011
Race	.0277	.0666	−.0019
Education	.0062	.0366	+.0029
Income	.0096	.0569	−.0006
Liberal–conservative index	.0391	.1098	−.0062
Party identity	.0452	.1469	−.0122
Population of residence	.0160	.0682	−.0018
Census region	.0102	.0664	−.0027
Adjusted R^2 = .1019			

federal funding for public schools remains almost the same after adjusting for the impact of the other variables (see table 11.2).

The sex of the respondent was not an important predictor of support for or opposition to increased federal spending for public schools (see table 11.1). Women were more likely than men to support additional funding (see table 11.2).

Several studies have suggested that African Americans are more apt to support increased educational expenditures than whites. This study found that African Americans and others were more supportive of federal funding for public schools than whites (see table 11.2), but the variable of race was only the fifth best predictor (see table 11.1).

It had been anticipated that education would be a strong predictor of support for increased federal school funding, but it was the weakest of the nine independent variables (see table 11.1). In addition, the pattern of support by educational level was not consistent. Those who had an advanced degree were the most supportive of more federal funding for education (after controlling for the effects of the other factors), but those who had some college education or had received their bachelor's degree were less supportive than those with some high school education or those who had graduated from high school (see table 11.2).

Family income was not a particularly strong predictor of support for increased federal funding for public schools (see table 11.1). Interestingly, the most wealthy Americans were the least supportive of further federal expenditures for public schools—perhaps either because they could afford to send their children to private schools or because they felt they would bear the cost of the increases through additional taxes.

Whether individuals identify themselves as liberal or conservative was the third best predictor (see table 11.1). Not surprisingly, those who identified

Table 11.2 / *Support for Increasing Federal Aid to Public Schools in 1988*
(0 = do not increase aid, 1 = increase aid)

	Class Mean	Adjusted Mean	Net Deviation	Number of Cases
Age				
18–29	78.0	75.6	+10.2	410
30–39	70.0	69.4	+ 4.0	466
40–49	66.0	67.1	+ 1.7	313
50–59	55.0	55.2	−10.2	238
60–69	55.0	57.1	− 8.3	219
70 and above	51.0	53.5	−11.9	204
Sex				
male	63.0	63.1	− 2.3	795
female	67.0	67.1	+ 1.7	1,055
Race				
white	62.0	64.0	− 1.4	1,561
African-American	84.0	72.7	+ 7.3	231
other	83.0	72.6	+ 7.2	58
Education				
8 grades or less	55.0	61.4	− 4.0	155
9–11 grades	69.0	67.3	+ 1.9	210
high school graduate	67.0	66.3	+ 0.9	665
some college	66.0	64.4	− 1.0	436
BA, no advanced degree	61.0	64.0	− 1.4	275
advanced degree	69.0	68.1	+ 2.7	109
Income (in dollars)				
0–9,999	69.0	65.7	+ 0.3	301
10,000–19,999	68.0	68.1	+ 2.7	380
20,000–29,999	69.0	67.1	+ 1.7	319
30,000–39,999	67.0	66.0	+ 0.6	263
40,000 and above	61.0	63.6	− 1.8	449
not ascertained	53.0	57.6	− 7.8	138

themselves as liberals were more supportive of increased federal expenditures than those who identified themselves as conservatives (see table 11.2).

Party identification was the second best predictor (see table 11.1). Democrats were more favorable to additional federal money for public schools, and Republicans were more opposed (see table 11.2).

The population size of the communities in which respondents lived was moderately important in predicting their position (see table 11.1). Individuals in rural areas or small towns were generally less favorable to further federal financing of public schools than those who lived in the larger cities (see table 11.2).

Finally, the region of the country in which respondents lived had a moderate impact on support or opposition to increased federal funding for the public

Table 11.2 / *(continued)*

	Class Mean	Adjusted Mean	Net Deviation	Number of Cases
Liberal-Conservative index				
extremely liberal	82.0	72.5	+ 7.1	33
liberal	81.0	74.2	+ 8.8	108
slightly liberal	78.0	72.5	+ 7.1	178
moderate	69.0	67.9	+ 2.5	423
slightly conservative	62.0	65.1	− 0.3	298
conservative	50.0	58.2	− 7.2	260
extremely conservative	43.0	49.6	−15.8	58
haven't thought much about it	66.0	64.0	− 1.4	492
Party Identity				
strong Democrat	77.0	74.5	+ 9.1	325
weak Democrat	74.0	71.9	+ 6.5	331
Independent-Democrat	74.0	68.4	+ 3.0	217
Independent-Independent	66.0	65.2	− 0.2	196
Independent-Republican	59.0	60.4	− 5.0	256
weak Republican	57.0	58.8	− 6.6	261
strong Republican	48.0	54.8	−10.6	264
Population of Residence				
0–2,499	61.0	63.4	− 2.0	617
2,500–10,499	59.0	63.0	− 2.4	234
10,500–50,499	64.0	63.5	− 1.9	481
50,500–350,499	70.0	69.9	+ 4.5	311
350,500 and above	79.0	71.5	+ 6.1	207
Census Region				
Northeast	62.0	61.2	− 4.2	332
North Central	59.0	62.6	− 2.8	526
South	70.0	67.7	+ 4.5	636
West	70.0	69.2	+ 6.1	356
TOTAL	65.4			1,850

schools (see table 11.1). Whereas those in the Northeast and the North Central states were the least likely to support additional federal funds, those in the South and West were the most likely to favor additional expenditures (see table 11.2).

Overall, the ability of these nine independent variables to predict support of federal funding of public schools was relatively modest. The adjusted R^2 for the multiple classification analysis was .1019.

Several other analyses were done to explore further the importance of age in predicting support for additional federal funding of public schools. To see if the presence or absence of children under eighteen years old in the household made any difference, this variable was added in another MCA run. Presence of children was the fifth best predictor among the ten independent variables; after controlling for the other variables, 62.7 percent of those from households without children under eighteen years old supported more federal funding, while 69.1 percent of those from households with children under eighteen supported such additional assistance. Interestingly, the inclusion of the presence of children under eighteen years old in the household did not increase the overall adjusted R^2 very much (+.0020), but it appears to have reduced the overall explanatory power of the age variable (beta = .1407) slightly, so that it was now just below that of the political identity variable in importance (beta = .1405). After controlling for the effects of the other variables, including the presence or absence of children under eighteen years old, the gap between younger and older individuals in support for additional federal spending for public schools decreased very slightly.

One of the potential problems in the addition of the presence-of-child variable is the overlap between that variable and the age variable. Individuals who were ages sixty through sixty-nine or seventy and older were very unlikely to be living in households with children under eighteen. To cope with this potential problem, a new variable was created to replace the two dealing with age and children. The same age categories were used, but individuals below the age of fifty were subdivided by whether or not a child under eighteen was in their household. For those sixty through sixty-nine, and seventy and older, no subdivision was made.

Another MCA was run using the new age-child variable in place of the age and presence-of-child variables (the other independent variables remained the same). Compared to the previous MCA, in which the presence or absence of a child under eighteen in the household had been added, there was almost no change in the adjusted R^2, but the age-child variable now was the single best predictor of support for or opposition to increased federal funding for public schools. After controlling for the effects of the other independent variables, individuals living in households with children under eighteen were more likely to support additional federal funding, but the differences at the younger ages (eighteen through twenty-nine and thirty through thirty-nine) were quite small.

Support for federal aid to education varies considerably by whether one is asking about assisting public schools or college students. Some Americans believe that parents are responsible for their children's higher education, and they therefore oppose federal aid to college students. Whereas 65.4 percent of the public supports increased federal aid for public elementary or secondary schools, only 45.3 percent support increased federal assistance for college students. Again, a multiple classification analysis was run with support for or opposition to increased federal spending for college students as the dependent variable (1 = support, 0 = opposition) and age, sex, race, education, family income, liberal-conservative index, party identity, population size of the community, and the region in which the individual lives as the nine independent variables.

The results of this multiple classification analysis were similar to those of the earlier analysis. The adjusted R^2s were almost the same, and most of the independent variables were roughly similar in their relative predictive power. (Race became a stronger predictor because support for more federal spending for college students was particularly pronounced among African Americans.) Without controlling for any of the other factors, age was a weaker predictor, but after controlling for the effects of the other variables, age continued to be the single best predictor.

We have found that age is the best overall predictor of support for increased federal funding either of public schools or of college students, and that the older population is much less supportive of these increases than the younger population. But what about other issues? Does age continue to play such an important role in predicting support for increased federal funding of other domestic social programs?

Two comparable multiple classification analyses were run to determine the support for or opposition to increased federal expenditures for the elderly or for the unemployed. Although in both instances older individuals were less supportive of additional federal funding than younger ones, age by itself was a less powerful predictor of support for more aid to the unemployed than of support for more assistance to the elderly. Moreover, age by itself was a weaker predictor in both of these situations than in explaining differences in support for more federal aid either for public schools or for college students. Controlling for the effects of the other variables, age continued to be the best overall predictor of more federal support for the elderly, but only the fifth best predictor of more federal money for the unemployed.

A more detailed examination of the 1988 data on the willingness of the public to support increased federal funding for certain programs suggests that the impact of age vary from one issue to another. Usually, but not always, older age-groups are less supportive of increased funding than younger age-groups; but the age-group differences vary depending on which issue is being considered. Particularly in the cases of increased federal aid for public education and for college students, age differences were quite strong and age was the single best predictor of support after taking into consideration the impact of the other eight independent variables . Whereas some scholars have tried to minimize the role of age in affecting support for educational expenditures, this analysis suggests that age is indeed a very important factor—even after taking into consideration the impact of the other characteristics of the respondents.

Conclusion

Americans have usually made education a high priority, but the organization and financing of schooling has changed dramatically over time. The continually evolving mixture of parental, local, state, and federal responsibility for schooling makes the governance and delivery of educational services very complex and difficult today. Moreover, the shifting coalitions of support for educational expansion and reforms are equally diverse, and they defy any simplistic explanations, whether based on social control by capitalists or the so-called conflict between generations. At the same time, basic demographic and ideological changes in our society and economy suggest that the current concern about age-cohort differences in support of education may continue and may be exacerbated in the future.

Since the mid-nineteenth century, most Americans have accepted the notion that every child is entitled to a free public education, but there is considerable disagreement over how much education is needed, how it should be paid for, and who should control the schools. Although there are some hints that age differences may have played some role in the nineteenth-century decisions about schooling, they were not perceived by contemporaries to be particularly important or threatening. Nor is there any evidence in the past of an explicit or implicit contract between the young and their parents about investing in the children's education so that parents could be repaid in their old age. Today there is growing concern and some evidence that age may be a primary factor— among several others—in determining one's position and behavior on educational issues.

Nevertheless, given the variety of school systems and the complex and multiple mechanisms for financing them, there is little reason to suspect many, if any, direct and explicit trade-offs between support for education and support for programs to help the elderly. Indeed, the diverse and specialized institutions of the American political structure at all levels usually make it more difficult— if not impossible—for voters and policy makers to make such trade-offs between programs. Moreover, much of the future expenditures on schooling and other social programs depend on such basic changes as the rate of economic growth and our willingness to tax ourselves for further government services, rather than on taking money from one program and transferring it to another. If there is a period of relative stagnation in overall public expenditures in the near future, demands for additional educational spending may clash with demands for other important societal goals, such as increased welfare support, more funding for the war on drugs, and additional assistance for the elderly.

If we were relatively content with the levels of educational spending as well as with the quality of our existing schools, it might not be too difficult to maintain the present system. There are strong indications, however, that people are not satisfied with the status quo. Growing recognition of the importance of education for enhancing the economic productivity of our workers and of the need to maintain our international competitiveness have led to calls for major educational reforms. As the proportion of minority students in our schools increases, many of them from economically disadvantaged households, there will be a need for additional educational expenditures. Efforts to provide equal access to quality education in local elementary and secondary public schools will necessitate increased state and federal aid to compensate for the inadequate local financial resources in many school districts. At the same time, the growing demand for equal access for everyone to higher education may lead to efforts to increase federal aid for college students.

All of these efforts to increase public funding of education will be complicated by continued differences over the locus of control for schooling; over the relative role of local, state, and federal financial assistance; and over the responsibility of parents for providing for the higher education of their children. The future battles for additional educational funding will be as complex and difficult as ever because they will be based in large part on the many different and often contradictory principles and values that are part of our historical heritage.

Given the increasingly small proportion of households with school-age children and the reluctance of some voters to provide for much more than a minimal level of education for other people's children, it is likely that the issue of equity between different age cohorts will be raised in the future. As supporters of increased school funding are frustrated by the difficult and never-ending task of convincing voters and policy makers that more funds are needed, it is inevitable that some will raise questions about the relatively privileged status of entitlement programs like Social Security and Medicare. There will be the temptation to reduce the complex set of factors that account for past and present educational expenditures under the rubric of a generational conflict—especially since there is considerable empirical evidence that older voters are less supportive of more educational funding than younger ones.

Rather than being diverted from the real and serious problems facing education by focusing on age differences in voter support for educational spending, we should concentrate on convincing everyone of the importance of improving the education of our children in our homes and in the schools. It would also be particularly unfortunate if we confuse educational quality only with increased spending and then single out the elderly as a monolithic group opposed to educational improvements when, in fact, many of them have supported such reforms. The genius of nineteenth-century school reformers like Horace Mann was that they were able to build diverse coalitions for improved schooling and to develop a broad public consensus on the value of education for everyone, and that they did not try to pit one segment of the population against another in the name of school reform.[3] We should tackle the complex problems of providing quality education for all children in this spirit, rather than look for simple-minded and misleading excuses for our educational difficulties and deficiencies.

Notes

Reprinted with permission from *The Changing Contract across Generations*, ed. Vern L. Bengtson and W. Andrew Achenbaum (New York: Aldine de Gruyter, 1993). Copyright © 1993 Walter de Gruyter, Inc., New York.

1. For an overview of these developments, see chap. 1.

2. The data utilized in this chapter were made available by the Inter-University Consor-tium for Political and Social Research. The data for *American National Study, 1988: Pre- and Post-Election Survey* (Miller, 1989) were originally collected by Warren E. Miller and the National Election Studies. Neither the collector of the original data nor the consortium bears any responsibility for the analyses or interpretations presented here.

3. Mann's multiple rationales for support of school reform are discussed in chap. 5.

References

Abrashkin, William H., and Ernest Winsor. 1989. *Freedom of Information in Massachusetts: A Practical Guide Including Fair Information Practices, Criminal Records, Open Meetings, and Comparison with Other States.* Dover, Mass.: Auburn House.

A Catalogue of the Trustees, Instructors and Students of the Putnam Free School. 1861. Newburyport, Mass.

Alcott, Amos B. 1830. *Observations on the Principles and Methods of Infant Education.* Boston: Cater and Hendee.

Allen, David Grayson. 1981. *In English Ways: The Movement of Societies and the Transferral of English Local Law and Custom to Massachusetts Bay in the Seventeenth Century.* Chapel Hill: University of North Carolina Press.

American Annals of Education. 1830.

American Journal of Education. 1826–29.

Amesbury School Committee. 1864. *School Report of the Town of Amesbury for the Year 1863–64.* Amesbury, Mass.: W. H. B. Currier.

Andrews, Frank M., et al. 1973. *Multiple Classification Analysis: A Report on a Computer Program for Multiple Regression Using Categorical Predictors.* Ann Arbor, Mich.: Institute for Social Research.

Angus, David I. 1980a. "Detroit's Great School Wars: Religion and Politics in a Frontier City, 1842–1853." *Michigan Academician* 12: 261–80.

———. 1980b. "Families against the System: Fifty Years of Survival, 1880–1930." *Educational Considerations* 7:9–14.

———. 1981a. "A Note on the Occupational Backgrounds of Public High Schools Prior to 1940." *Journal of the Midwest History of Education Society* 9:158–83.

———. 1981b. "Precursors of the American Family Crisis." In *For Children: Their Education and Development,* ed. Jane Schwertfeger and Terrence Tice, 23–30. Ann Arbor, Mich.: University of Michigan School of Education.

———. 1983a. "The Empirical Mode: Quantitative History." In *Historical Inquiry in Education: A Research Agenda,* ed. John Hardin Best, 75–93. Washington, D.C.: American Educational Research Association.

———. 1983b. "Common School Politics in a Frontier City: Detroit, 1836–1842." In *Schools in Cities: Consensus and Conflict in American Educational History,* ed. Ronald Goodenow and Diane Ravitch, 183–222. New York: Holmes and Meier.

———. 1988. "Conflict, Class, and the Nineteenth Century Public High School in the Cities of the Midwest, 1840–1900." *Curriculum Inquiry* 18:7–31.

Angus, David I., and Jeffrey E. Mirel. 1985. "From Spellers to Spindles: Work-Force Entry by the Children of Textile Workers, 1888–1890." *Social Science History* 9:123–43.

Aretz, Carl. 1940. "Administration of a Program of Continuous Pupil Progress." *Elementary School Journal* 40:679–87.

Ariès, Philippe. 1962. *Centuries of Childhood: A Social History of Family Life*, trans. Robert Baldick. New York: Vintage.

Arnold, Marybeth H. 1989. "'The Life of a Citizen in the Hands of a Woman': Sexual Assault in New York City, 1790–1820." In *Passion and Power: Sexuality in History*, ed. Kathy Peiss and Christina Simmons, 35–56. Philadelphia: Temple University Press.

Auwers, Linda. 1980. "Reading the Marks of the Past: Exploring Female Literacy in Colonial Windsor, Connecticut." *Historical Methods* 4:204–14.

Axtell, James. 1974. *The School upon a Hill: Education and Society in Colonial New England*. New Haven: Yale University Press.

Ayres, Leonard P. 1908. "Some Factors Affecting Grade Distribution." *Psychological Clinic* 2:121–33.

———. 1909a. *Laggards in Our Schools: A Study of Retardation and Elimination in City School Systems*. New York: Charities Publication Committee.

———. 1909b. "The Money Cost of the Repeater." *Psychological Clinic* 3:49–57.

———. 1915. *Child Accounting in the Public Schools*. Cleveland Educational Survey. Cleveland: Survey Committee of the Cleveland Foundation.

Bailyn, Bernard. 1960. *Education in the Forming of American Society*. Chapel Hill: University of North Carolina Press.

Balmer, Randall H. 1989. *A Perfect Babel of Confusion: Dutch Religion and English Culture in the Middle Colonies*. New York: Oxford University Press.

Barlow, Thomas A. 1977. *Pestalozzi and American Education*. Boulder, Colo.: Este Es Press.

Barnett, Redmond. 1973. "From Philanthropy to Reform: Poverty, Drunkenness, and the Social Order in Massachusetts, 1780–1825." Ph.D. diss., Harvard University.

Barton, Joseph J. 1975. *Peasants and Strangers: Italians, Rumanians and Slovaks in an Amer-ican City, 1890–1950*. Cambridge: Harvard University Press.

Baylor, Ruth M. 1965. *Elizabeth Palmer Peabody: Kindergarten Pioneer*. Philadelphia: University of Pennsylvania Press.

Beales, Ross W., Jr. 1975. "In Search of the Historical Child: Miniature Adulthood and Youth in Colonial America." *American Quarterly* 27:379–98.

———. 1978. "Studying Literacy at the Community Level: A Research Note." *Journal of Interdisciplinary History* 9:93–102.

———. 1985. "The Child in Seventeenth-Century America." In *American Childhood: A Research Guide and Historical Handbook*, ed. Joseph M. Hawes and N. Ray Hiner, 3–56. Westport, Conn.: Greenwood Press.

Bean, Frank D., and Marta Tienda. 1987. *The Hispanic Population of the United States*. New York: Russell Sage Foundation.

Becker, Gary S. 1960. "Underinvestment in College Education?" *American Economic Review* 50:346–54.

———. 1964. *Human Capital: A Theoretical and Empirical Analysis, with Special Reference to Education*. New York: Columbia University Press.

Bengtson, Vern L. 1989. "The Problem of Generations: Age Group Contrasts, Continuities, and Social Change." In *The Course of Later Life: Research and Reflections*, ed. Vern L. Bengtson and K. Warner Schaie, 25–54. New York: Springer.

Bennett, William J. 1988. *Our Children and Our Country*. New York: Simon and Schuster.

Benson, Charles S., and Kevin O'Halloran. 1987. "The Economic History of School Finance in the United States." *Journal of Education Finance* 12:495–515.

Berkner, Lutz. 1972. "The Stem Family and the Developmental Cycle of the Peasant Household: An Eighteenth-Century Austrian Example." *American Historical Review* 77:398–418.

Bernard, Richard M., and Maris A. Vinovskis. 1977. "The Female School Teacher in Antebellum America." *Journal of Social History* 3:332–45.

Blan, Louis B. 1941. *A Special Study of the Increase of Retardation*. Contributions to Education, no. 40. New York: Bureau of

Publications, Teachers College, Columbia University.

Blaug, Mark. 1986. *Economic History and the History of Economics*. New York: New York University Press.

Bloom, Benjamin S., Allison Davis, and Robert Hess. 1965. *Compensatory Education for Cultural Deprivation*. New York: Holt, Rinehart, and Winston.

Boles, John B. 1983. *Black Southerners, 1619–1869*. Lexington: University Press of Kentucky.

Boston Chief of Police. (1857). *Annual Report*. Boston.

Boston City Marshall. 1851–60. *Annual Report*. Boston.

Boston Daily Advertiser. 1856–57.

Boston Daily Bee. 1856–57.

Boston Daily Evening Transcript. 1856–57.

Boston Daily Journal. 1856–57.

Boston Investigator. 1856–57.

Boston Journal. 1856–57.

Boston Pilot. 1856–57.

Boston Post. 1856–57.

Boston Recorder and Religious Telegraph. 1828.

Boston Recorder and Scriptual Transcript. 1827–29.

Boston School Committee. 1848–65. *Annual Examination Subcommittee*. Boston.

Boston School Committee. 1848–65. *Annual Reports*. Boston.

Boston School Committee. 1856–57. Minutes.

Boston Society for the Religious and Moral Instruction of the Poor. 1817–31. *Annual Reports*. Boston.

Boutwell, George S. 1902. *Reminiscences of Sixty Years in Public Affairs*. 2 vols. Boston: McClure & Phillips.

Bowles, Samuel, and Herbert Gintis. 1976. *Schooling in Capitalist America: Educational Reform and the Contradictions of Economic Life*. New York: Basic Books.

Bowman, Mary J. 1966. "The Human Investment Revolution in Economic Thought." *Sociology of Education* 39:111–37.

Boyer, Paul. 1978. *Urban Masses and Moral Order in America, 1820–1920*. Cambridge: Harvard University Press.

Boylan, Anne M. 1979. "The Role of Conversion in Nineteenth-Century Sunday Schools." *American Studies* 20:35–48.

———. 1985. "Growing Up Female in Young America, 1800–1860." In *American Childhood: A Research Guide and Historical Handbook*, ed. Joseph M. Hawes and N. Ray Hiner, 153–84. Westport, Conn.: Greenwood Press.

———. 1986. "Timid Girls, Venerable Widows and Dignified Matrons: Life Cycle Patterns among Organized Women in New York and Boston, 1797–1840." *American Quarterly* 38: 779–97.

———. 1988. *Sunday School: The Formation of an American Institution, 1790–1880*. New Haven: Yale University Press.

Brace, Charles Loring. 1872. *The Dangerous Classes of New York, and Twenty Years' Work among Them*. New York: Wynkoop & Hallenbeck.

Brechbill, Henry. 1944. "'Passing All Pupils': Another Comment." *School and Society* 60: 425–26.

Brenzel, Barbara. 1983. *Daughters of the State: A Social Portrait of the First Reform School for Girls in North America, 1856–1905*. Cambridge: MIT Press.

Brigham, Amariah. 1833. *Remarks on the Influence of Mental Cultivation and Mental Excitement upon Health*. 2d ed. Boston: Marsh, Capen and Lyon.

Brown, Richard D. 1989. *Knowledge is Power: The Diffusion of Information in Early America, 1700–1865*. New York: Oxford University Press.

Burns, Rex. 1976. *Success in America: The Yeoman Dream and the Industrial Revolution*. Amherst, Mass.: University of Massachusetts Press.

Burton, Orville B. 1985. *In My Father's House Are Many Mansions: Family and Community in Edgefield, South Carolina*. Chapel Hill: University of North Carolina Press.

Button, James W., and Walter A. Rosenbaum. 1989. "Seeing Gray: School Bond Issues and the Aging in Florida." *Research on Aging* 11: 158–73.

Callahan, Raymond E. 1962. *Education and the Cult of Efficiency*. Chicago: University of Chicago Press.

Caplan, Nathan, John K. Whitmore, and Marcella H. Choy. 1989. *The Boat People and Achievement in America: A Study of Family*

Life, Hard Work, and Cultural Values. Ann Arbor: University of Michigan Press.

Carlton, Frank Tracy. 1908. *Economic Influences upon Educational Progress in the United States, 1820–1850.* Madison: University of Wisconsin Press.

Carr, Lois Green, and Lorena S. Walsh. 1977. "The Planter's Wife: The Experience of White Women in Seventeenth Century Maryland." *William and Mary Quarterly,* 3d ser. 34:542–71.

Cawelti, John G. 1965. *Apostles of the Self-Made Man.* Chicago: University of Chicago Press.

Chicopee School Committee. 1861. *Report of the School Committee of Chicopee for the Year Ending March 1st, 1861.* Springfield, Mass.: Samuel Bowles.

Chubb, John E. 1988. "Why the Current Wave of School Reform Will Fail." *Public Interest* 90:28–49.

Church, Robert L. 1976. *Education in the United States: An Interpretative History.* New York: Free Press.

Clark, Anna. 1987. *Women's Silence, Men's Violence: Sexual Assault in England, 1770–1845.* London: Pandora Press.

Clubb, Jerome M., Erik W. Austin, and Gordon W. Kirk, Jr. 1989. *The Process of Historical Inquiry: Everyday Lives of Working Americans.* New York: Columbia University Press.

Cohen, Sheldon S. 1974. *A History of Colonial Education, 1607–1776.* New York: Wiley.

Cohen, Sol, ed. 1974. *Education in the United States: A Documentary History.* 2 vols. New York: Random House.

Coleman, James S., Thomas Hoffer, and Sally Kilgore. 1982. *High School Achievement: Public, Catholic, and Private Schools Compared.* New York: Basic Books.

Coontz, Stephanie. 1988. *The Social Origins of Private Life: A History of American Families, 1600–1900.* London: Verso.

Cornman, Oliver P. 1907. "The Retardation of Pupils of Five City School Systems." *Psychological Clinic* 1:245–57.

Cott, Nancy F. 1977. *The Bonds of Womanhood: "Women's Sphere" in New England, 1780–1835.* New Haven: Yale University Press.

Cranston, Maurice. 1983. *Jean-Jacques: The Early Life and Work of Jean-Jacques Rousseau, 1712–1754.* New York: Norton.

———. 1991. *The Noble Savage: Jean-Jacques Rosseau, 1754–1762.* New York: Penguin.

Cremin, Lawrence A. 1970. *American Education: The Colonial Experience, 1607–1783.* New York: Harper and Row.

———. 1976. *Traditions of American Education.* New York: Basic Books.

———. 1978. "Family-Community Linkages in American Education: Some Comments on the Recent Historiography." *Teachers College Record* 79:683–704.

———. 1980. *American Education: The National Experience, 1783–1786.* New York: Harper and Row.

———. 1988. *American Education: The Metropolitan Experience, 1876–1980.* New York: Harper and Row.

Cubberley, Ellwood P. 1916. *Public Education in the United States.* Boston: Houghton Mifflin.

———. 1934. *Public Education in the United States.* Rev. ed. Boston: Houghton Mifflin.

Culver, Raymond B. 1929. *Horace Mann and Religion in the Massachusetts Public Schools.* New Haven: Yale University Press.

Cunningham, Hugh. 1991. *The Children of the Poor: Representations of Childhood since the Seventeenth Century.* Oxford: Blackwell.

Currier, John J. 1906–9. *The History of Newburyport, 1764–1905.* 2 vols. Newburyport, Mass.: John J. Currier.

Curti, Merle. 1965. *The Social Ideas of American Educators.* Patterson, N.J.: Littlefield and Adams.

Daniels, Bruce C. 1979. *The Connecticut Town: Growth and Development, 1635–1790.* Middletown, Conn.: Wesleyan University Press.

Danvers School Committee. 1861. *Annual Report of the School Committee of the Town of Danvers for the Year Ending April 1861.* Danvers, Mass.: Charles D. Howard.

Darling, Arthur B. 1925. *Political Changes in Massachusetts, 1824–1848: A Study of Liberal Movements in Politics.* New Haven: Yale University Press.

Degler, Carl N. 1980. "Women and the Family." In *The Past before Us: Contemporary Historical Writings,* ed. Michael Kammerman, 308–26. Ithaca: Cornell University Press.

Demos, John. 1970. *A Little Commonwealth: Family Life in Plymouth Colony.* New York: Oxford University Press.

———. 1974. "The American Family in Past Time." *American Scholar* 43:422–46.

———. 1982. "The Changing Faces of Fatherhood: A New Exploration of American Family History." In *Father and Child: Developmental and Clinical Perspectives*, ed. Stanley H. Cath, Alan R. Gurwitt, and John Munder Ross, 425–45. Boston: Little, Brown.

Detroit Board of Education. 1853, 1907–8, 1916, 1917–18. *Annual Reports*. Detroit.

Detroit Public School Staff. 1943. *Frank Cody: A Realist in Education*. New York: Macmillan.

Detroit Public Schools, Bureau of Statistics and Reference. 1922. *Age-Grade and Nationality Survey*. The Detroit Educational Bulletin, no. 7.

Dinnerstein, Leonard. 1982. "Education and the Advancement of American Jews." In *American Education and the European Immigrant, 1840–1940*, ed. Bernard J. Weiss, 44–60. Urbana: University of Illinois Press.

Dorfman, Joseph. 1946. *The Economic Mind in American Civilization, 1606–1865*. 2 vols. New York: Viking Press.

———. 1967. "Economic Thought." In *The Growth of the Seaport Cities, 1790–1825*, ed. David T. Gilchrist, 151–77. Charlottesville: University of Virginia Press.

Dreeben, Robert. 1968. *On What Is Learned in School*. Reading, Mass.: Addison-Wesley.

Dunn, Mary Maples. 1980. "Saints and Sinners: Congregational and Quaker Women in the Early Colonial Period." In *Women in American Religion*, ed. Janet Wilson James, 27–46. Philadelphia: University of Pennsylvania Press.

Dunn, William K. 1958. *What Happened to Religious Education? The Decline of Religious Teaching in the Public Elementary School, 1776–1861*. Baltimore: Johns Hopkins University Press.

Dunstan, L. 1966. *A Light to the City: 150 Years of the City Missionary Society of Boston, 1816–1966*. Boston: Beacon Press.

Earle, Carville V. 1979. "Environment, Disease, and Mortality in Early Virginia." In *The Chesapeake in the Seventeenth Century: Essays on Anglo-American Society and Politics*, ed. Thad W. Tate and David I. Ammerman, 96–125. New York: Norton.

Elam, Stanley M. 1989. *The Gallup/Phi Delta Kappa Polls of Attitudes toward the Public Schools, 1969–88*. Bloomington, Ind.: Phi Delta Kappa.

Elbaum, Bernard. 1989. "Why Apprenticeship Persisted in Britain but Not in the United States." *Journal of Economic History* 49: 337–49.

Elementary School Journal. 1935. "Shall Grade Standards Be Abolished?" 36:241–46.

———. 1947. "Philadelphia." 48:62–64.

———. 1948. "Philadelphia Schools Solve the Promotion Problem." 48:531–32.

Elliott, Lloyd (1944. "New York City Schools Base Promotion on 'Social Maturity.'" *School and Society* 60:67–68.

———. 1948. "Promote All—in the Public Schools?" *Educational Forum* 13:69–72.

Elsbree, Willard. 1947. "Promotion Policies in the Elementary School: The Case for Normal Progress." *Teachers College Record* 48: 429–34.

Essex County Mercury. 1856–57.

Ettinger, William L. 1922. "Facing the Facts." *School and Society* 16:505–12.

Falkner, Roland P. 1908a. "Some Further Considerations upon the Retardation of the Pupils of Five City School Systems." *Psychological Clinic* 2:57–74.

———. 1908b. "Elimination of Pupils from School: A Review of Recent Investigations." *Psychological Clinic* 2:255–75.

———. 1910. "What Can and Do School Reports Show?" *Psychological Clinic* 4:1–18.

Fall River School Committee. 1861. *Report of the School Committee of the City of Fall River for the Year 1860–61*. Fall River, Mass.

Farley, Reynolds, and Walter R. Allen. 1987. *The Color Line and the Quality of Life in America*. New York: Russell Sage Foundation.

Featherman, David L., and Robert M. Hauser. 1978. *Opportunity and Change*. New York: Academic Press.

Fenner, Ball. 1856. *Raising the Veil; Or, Scenes in the Courts*. Boston: James French.

Ferdinand, Theodore N. 1967. "The Criminal Pattern of Boston since 1849." *American Journal of Sociology* 73:84–99.

———. 1992. *Boston's Lower Criminal Courts, 1814–1850*. Newark: University of Delaware Press.

Field, Alexander. 1974. "Educational Reform and Manufacturing Development in Mid-

Nineteenth-Century Massachusetts." Ph.D. diss., University of California, Berkeley.

Finkelstein, Barbara. 1979. "Reading, Writing, and the Acquisition of Identity in the United States: 1790–1860." In *Regulated Children, Liberated Children: Education in Psycho-historical Perspective,* ed. Barbara Finkel-stein, 114–39. New York: Psychohistory Press.

———. 1985. "Casting Networks of Good Influence: The Reconstruction of Childhood in the United States, 1790–1870." In *American Childhood: A Research Guide and Historical Handbook,* ed. Joseph M. Hawes and N. Ray Hiner, 111–52. Westport, Conn.: Greenwood Press.

———. 1989. *Governing the Young: Teacher Behavior in Popular Primary Schools in Nineteenth-Century United States.* London: Falmer Press.

Fishlow, Albert. 1966. "The American Common School Revival: Fact or Fancy?" In *Industrialization in Two Systems: Essays in Honor of Alexander Gershenkron,* ed. Henry Rosovsky, 40–67. New York: Wiley.

Fitts, Deborah. 1979. "Una and the Lion: The Feminization of District School-Teaching and Its Effects on the Roles of Students and Teachers in Nineteenth-Century Massachusetts." In *Regulated Children, Liberated Children: Education on Psychohistorical Perspective,* ed. Barbara Finkelstein, 140–57. New York: Psychohistory Press.

Foley, Louis. 1944. "Passing All the Pupils—and the Buck." *School and Society* 59:353–56.

Foster, Stephen. 1984. "English Puritanism and the Progress of New England Institutions, 1630–1660." In *Saints and Revolutionaries: Essays on Early American History,* ed. David Hall, John M. Murrin, and Thad N. Tate, 3–37. New York: Norton.

Fuller, Wayne E. 1982. *The Old Country School.* Chicago: University of Chicago Press.

Garms, W. I., Guthrie, J. W., and L. C. Pierce. 1978. *School Finance: The Economics and Politics of Public Education.* Englewood Cliffs, N.J.: Prentice-Hall.

Georgetown School Committee. 1861–62. *Annual Reports.* Georgetown, Mass.: Salem Observer.

Getis, Victoria L., and Maris A. Vinovskis. 1992. "History of Child Care in the United States to 1950." In *Child Care in Context: Cross-Cultural Perspectives* ed. Michael E. Lamb, Kathleen J. Sternberg, Carl-Philip Hwang, and Anders G. Broberg, 185–206. Hillsdale, N.J.: Lawrence Erlbaum.

Gilmore, William J. 1982. "Elementary Literacy on the Eve of the Industrial Revolution: Trends in Rural New England, 1760–1830." *Proceedings of the American Antiquarian Society* 92:87–177.

———. 1989. *Reading Becomes a Necessity of Life: Material and Cultural Life in Rural New England, 1780–1835.* Knoxville: University of Tennessee Press.

Giltner, Emmet E. 1907. "Graduation and Promotion." Master's thesis, Teachers College, Columbia University.

Glazer, Nathan. 1981. "Ethnicity and Education: Some Hard Questions." *Phi Delta Kappan* 62:386–89.

———. 1988. "Education for American Citizenship in the 21st Century." *Education and Society.*

Glenn, Charles L., Jr. 1988. *The Myth of the Common School.* Amherst, Mass.:University of Massachusetts Press.

Goodland, John I. 1952. "Research and Theory Regarding Promotion and Nonpromotion." *Elementary School Journal* 53:150–55.

Gordon, Michael. 1978. *The American Family: Past, Present, and Future.* New York: Random House.

Gould, Stephen Jay. 1981. *The Mismeasure of Man.* New York: Norton.

Graff, Harvey J. 1977. "The 'New Math': Quantification, the 'New' History, and the History of Education." *Urban Education* 11: 403–40.

———. 1979. *The Literacy Myth: Literacy and Social Structure in the Nineteenth-Century City.* New York: Academic Press.

Gray, Horace, Jr. 1858. *Reports of Cases Argued and Determined in the Supreme Judicial Court of Massachusetts,* vol. 4. Boston: Little, Brown.

Greenberg, Ellen, and Laurence Steinberg. 1986. *When Teenagers Work: The Psychological and Social Costs of Adolescent Employment.* New York: Basic Books.

Greer, Colin. 1972. *The Great School Legend: A Revisionist Interpretation of American Public Education.* New York: Basic Books.

Greven, Philip J. Jr. 1970. *Four Generations: Population, Land, and Family in Colonial Andover, Massachusetts.* Ithaca: Cornell University Press.

Grigg, Susan. 1984. *The Dependent Poor of Newburyport: Studies in Social History, 1800–1830.* Ann Arbor, Mich.: UMI Research Press.

Grizzell, Emit D. 1923. *Origin and Development of the High School in New England before 1865.* New York: Macmillan.

Guilliford, Andrew. 1986. *America's Country Schools.* Washington, D.C.: Preservation Press.

Gutek, Gerald L. 1968. *Pestalozzi and Education.* New York: Random House.

Habakkuk, H. J. 1962. *American and British Technology in the Nineteenth Century: The Search for Labour-Saving Inventions.* Cambridge: Cambridge University Press.

Hakuta, Kenji, and Eugene E. Garcia. 1989. "Bilingualism and Education." *American Psychologist* 44:374–79.

Hall, David D., ed. 1968. *The Antinomian Controversy, 1636–1638: A Documentary History.* Middletown, Conn.: Wesleyan University Press.

———. 1972. *The Faithful Shepherd: A History of the New England Ministry in the Seventeenth Century.* Chapel Hill: University of North Carolina Press.

———. 1989. *Worlds of Wonder, Days of Judgment: Popular Religious Beliefs in Early New England.* New York: Alfred A. Knopf.

Hamilton, Howard D., and Sylvan H. Cohen. 1974. *Policy Making by Plebiscite: School Referenda.* Lexington, Mass.: Lexington Books.

Handlin, Oscar. 1951. *The Uprooted: The Epic Story of the Great Migrations that Made the American People.* New York: Grosset and Dunlap.

———. 1968. *Boston's Immigrants: A Study in Acculturation.* Rev. ed. New York: Atheneum.

Handlin, Oscar, and Mary F. Handlin, eds. 1966. *The Popular Sources of Political Authority: Documents on the Massachusetts Constitution of 1780.* Cambridge: Harvard University Press.

Hansen, W. Lee. 1963. "Total and Private Rates of Return to Investments in Schooling." *Journal of Political Economy* 71:128–41.

Harvey, O. L. 1939. "Use of Age-Grade and Promotion Tables in the Study of Enrollment Trends." *Elementary School Journal* 39: 751–59.

Hawes, Joseph M. 1971. *Children in Urban Society: Juvenile Delinquency in Nineteenth-Century America.* New York: Oxford University Press.

Higham, John. 1955. *Strangers in the Land: Patterns of American Nativism, 1860–1925.* New Brunswick, N.J.: Rutgers University Press.

Hindus, Michael S. 1980. *Prison and Plantation: Crime, Justice, and Authority in Massachusetts and South Carolina, 1767–1878.* Chapel Hill: University of North Carolina Press.

Hiner, N. Ray. 1973. "The Cry of Sodom Enquired Into: Educational Analysis in Seventeenth-Century New England." *History of Education Quarterly* 13:3–22.

———. 1989. "'Look into Families': The New History of Children and the Family and Its Implications for Educational Research." In *Education and the American Family: A Research Synthesis,* ed. William J. Weston, 4–31. New York: New York University.

Hinsdale, Burke A. 1898. *Horace Mann and the Common School Revival in the United States.* New York: Charles Scribner's Sons.

Hobson, Barbara M. 1987. *Uneasy Virtue: The Politics of Prostitution and the American Reform Tradition.* New York: Basic Books.

Hoffman, Nancy. 1981. *Woman's "True" Profession: Voices from the History of Teaching.* New York: Feminist Press.

Hogan, David J. 1985. *Class and Reform: School and Society in Chicago, 1880–1930.* Philadelphia: University of Pennsylvania Press.

Holloran, Peter C. 1989. *Boston's Wayward Children: Social Services for Homeless Children, 1830–1930.* Rutherford, N.J.: Fairleigh Dickinson University Press.

Horton, James O., and Lois E. Horton. 1979. *Black Bostonians: Family Life and Community Struggle in the Antebellum North.* New York: Holmes and Meier.

Hosmer, William. 1851. *The Young Lady's Book; Or, Principles of Female Education.* Auburn, N.Y.: Derby and Miller.

Houlbrooke, Ralph A. 1984. *The English Family, 1450–1700.* London: Longman.

Hovey, Alvah. 1902. *Barnas Sears: A Christian Educator, His Making and Work.* New York: Silver and Burdett.

Howe, Daniel Walker. 1970. *The Unitarian Conscience: Harvard Moral Philosophy, 1805–1861.* Cambridge: Harvard University Press.

Hsia, Jayjia. 1988. *Asian Americans in Higher Education and at Work.* Hillsdale, N.J.: Lawrence Erlbaum.

Huse, Charles Phillips. 1916. *The Financial History of Boston from May 1, 1822, to January 31, 1909.* Cambridge: Harvard University Press.

Infant School and Children's Home Association. 1870. *First Annual Report.* Boston: Arthur W. Locke.

Infant School Society of the City of Boston. 1829–35. *Annual Reports.* Boston: T. R. Marvin.

Inglis, Alexander J. 1911. *The Rise of the High School in Massachusetts.* New York: Teachers College, Columbia University.

Ipswich School Committee. 1862. *Report of the School Committee of the Town of Ipswich for the Year Ending March, 1862.* Salem, Mass.: Salem Observer.

Jencks, Christopher. 1972. *Inequality: A Reassessment of the Effect of Family and Schooling in America.* New York: Basic Books.

———. 1979. *Who Gets Ahead? The Determinants of Economic Success in America.* New York: Basic Books.

Jenkins, John W. 1978. "The Infant Schools and the Development of Public Primary Schools in Selected Cities before the Civil War." Ph.D. diss., University of Wisconsin.

Jensen, Arthur R. 1969. "How Much Can We Boost I.Q. and Scholastic Achievement?" *Harvard Educational Review* 39:1–123.

Johnson, E. A. J. 1964. "The Place of Learning, Science, Vocational Training, and 'Art' in Pre-Smithian Economic Thought." *Journal of Economic History* 24: 129–44.

Jones, Jacqueline. 1980. *Soldiers of Light and Love: Northern Teachers and Georgia Blacks, 1865–1873.* Chapel Hill: University of North Carolina Press.

Jones, Maldwyn A. 1960. *American Immigration.* Chicago: University of Chicago Press.

Jorgenson, Lloyd P. 1987. *The State and the Non-Public School, 1825–1925.* Columbia: University of Missouri Press.

Kaeble, Harmut. 1985. *Social Mobility in the Nineteenth and Twentieth Centuries: Europe and America in Comparative Perspective.* Lea-

mington Spa, Eng.: Berg Publishers.

Kaestle, Carl F. 1973a. *The Evolution of an Urban School System: New York City, 1750–1850.* Cambridge: Harvard University Press.

———. 1976. "Between the Scylla of Brutal Ignorance and the Charybdis of a Literary Education: Elite Attitudes toward Mass Schooling in Early Industrial England and America." In *Schooling and Society: Studies in the History of Education,* ed. Lawrence Stone, 177–91. Baltimore: Johns Hopkins University Press.

———. 1978. "Social Change, Discipline, and the Common School in Early Nineteenth-Century America." *Journal of Interdisciplinary History* 9:1–17.

———. 1983. *Pillars of the Republic: Common Schools and American Society, 1780–1860.* New York: Hill and Wang.

Kaestle, Carl F., ed. 1973b. *Joseph Lancaster and the Monitorial School Movement: A Documentary History.* New York: Teachers College Press.

Kaestle, Carl F., and Maris A. Vinovskis. 1978. "From Apron Strings to ABCs: Parents, Children, and Schooling in Nineteenth-Century Massachusetts." In *Turning Points: Historical and Sociological Essays on the Family,* ed. John Demos and Sarene S. Boocock, 39–80. Chicago: University of Chicago Press.

———. 1980. *Education and Social Change in Nineteenth-Century Massachusetts.* Cambridge: Cambridge University Press.

Kaestle, Carl F., Helen Damon-Moore, Lawrence C. Stedman, Katherine Tinsley, and William Vance Trollinger, Jr. 1991. *Literacy in the United States: Readers and Reading since 1880.* New Haven: Yale University Press.

Katz, Michael B. 1968. *The Irony of Early School Reform: Educational Innovation in Mid-Nineteenth-Century Massachusetts.* Cambridge: Harvard University Press.

———. 1971. *Class, Bureaucracy, and Schools.* New York: Praeger.

———. 1975a. *The People of Hamilton, Canada West: Family and Class in a Mid-Nineteenth Century City.* Cambridge: Harvard University Press.

———. 1975b. *Class, Bureaucracy and Schools: The Illusion of Educational Change in America.* Expanded ed. New York: Praeger.

———. 1976. "The Origins of Public Education: A Reassessment." *History of Education Quarterly* 16:381–407.

———. 1980. "Hardcore Educational Historiography." *Reviews in American History* 8: 504–10.

———. 1982. "School Attendance in Philadelphia, 1850–1900." Working paper, Organization of School, Work and Family Life in Philadelphia, 1838–1920 Project, University of Pennsylvania.

———. 1987. *Reconstructing American Education.* Cambridge: Harvard University Press.

Katz, Michael B., and Ian E. Davey. 1978. "School Attendance and Early Industrialization in a Canadian City: A Multivariate Analysis." *History of Education Quarterly* 18: 271–93.

Katz, Michael B., Michael J. Doucet, and Mark J. Stern. 1982. *The Social Organization of Early Industrial Capitalism.* Cambridge: Harvard University Press.

Katznelson, Ira, and Margaret Weir. 1985. *Schooling for All: Class, Race, and the Decline of the Democratic Ideal.* New York: Basic Books.

Kendall, Kathleen E. 1968. "Education as 'the Balance Wheel of Social Machinery': Horace Mann's Arguments and Proof." *Quarterly Journal of Speech and Education* 54:13–21.

Kennedy, Millard F., and Alvin F. Harlow. 1940. *Schoolmaster of Yesterday.* New York: McGraw Hill.

Kertzer, David I. 1982. "Generation and Age in Cross-Cultural Perspective. In *Aging from Birth to Death: Sociotemporal Perspectives,* ed. Matilda W. Riley, Ronald P. Abeles, and Michael S. Teitelbaum, 27–50. Boulder, Colo.: Westview.

Kerber, Linda K. 1980. *Women of the Republic: Intellect and Ideology in Revolutionary America.* Chapel Hill: University of North Carolina Press.

Kett, Joseph F. 1985. "Women and the Progressive Impulse in Southern Education." In *The Web of Southern Social Relations: Women, Family, and Education,* ed. Walter J. Fraser, Jr., R. Frank Sanders, Jr., and Jon I. Wakelyn, 166–80. Athens: University of Georgia Press.

Keyes, Charles H. 1911. *Progress through the Grades of City Schools: A Study of Acceleration and Arrest.* Contributions to Education,

no. 42. New York: Bureau of Publications, Teachers College, Columbia University.

Kiker, B. F. 1966. "The Historical Roots of the Concept of Human Capital." *Journal of Political Economy* 74:481–500.

Knights, Peter R. 1971. *The Plain People of Boston, 1830–1860: A Study in City Growth.* New York: Oxford University Press.

Koehler, Lyle. 1980. *A Search for Power: The "Weaker Sex" in Seventeenth-Century New England.* Urbana: University of Illinois Press.

Korzenik, Diana. 1985. *Drawn to Art: A Nineteenth-Century American Dream.* Hanover, N.H.: University Press of New England.

Krey, A. C. 1937. "Implications of Universal Education for Grade Placement." In *Readings in Curriculum Development,* ed. Hollis Caswell and Doak Campbell, 457. New York: American Book Company.

Krug, Edward A. 1969. *The Shaping of the American High School, 1880–1920.* Madison: University of Wisconsin Press.

Kuhn, Ann I. 1947. *The Mother's Role in Childhood Education.* New Haven: Yale University Press.

Kusmer, Kenneth L. 1976. *A Ghetto Takes Shape: Black Cleveland, 1870–1930.* Urbana: University of Illinois Press.

Labaree, Benjamin W. 1962. *Patriots and Partisans: The Merchants of Newburyport, 1764–1815.* Cambridge: Harvard University Press.

Labaree, David F. 1988. *The Making of an American High School: The Credential Market and the Central High School in Philadelphia, 1838–1939.* New Haven: Yale University Press.

Ladies' Magazine. 1828–36.

LaGumina, Salvatore J. 1982. "American Education and the Italian Immigrant Response." In *American Education and the European Immigrant, 1840–1940,* ed. Bernard J. Weiss, 61–77. Urbana: University of Illinois Press.

Lane, Roger. 1968. "Crime and Criminal Statistics in Nineteenth Century Massachusetts." *Journal of Social History* 2:157–63.

———. 1971. *Policing the City: Boston, 1822–1885.* New York: Atheneum.

———. 1986. *Roots of Violence in Black Philadelphia, 1860–1900.* Cambridge: Harvard University Press.

Laqueur, Thomas W. 1976. *Religion and Respectability: Sunday Schools and Working Class*

Culture, 1780–1850. New Haven: Yale University Press.

Laslett, Peter. 1965. *The World We Have Lost: England before the Industrial Age.* New York: Charles Scribner's Sons.

———. 1969. "Size and Structure of the Household in England over Three Centuries." *Population Studies* 23:199–223.

———. 1972. *Household and Family in Past Time.* Cambridge: Cambridge University Press.

———. 1977. *Family Life and Illicit Love in Earlier Generations: Essays in Historical Sociology.* Cambridge: Cambridge University Press.

Lawrence School Committee. 1861. *Lawrence School Committee, Fifteenth Annual Report of the School Committee of the City of Lawrence Embracing Reports of Superintendent and Sub-Committees, 1861.* Lawrence, Mass.: George S. Merrill.

Lazerson, Marvin. 1971. *Origins of the Urban School: Public Education in Massachusetts, 1870–1915.* Cambridge: Harvard University Press.

Lebergott, Stanley. 1964. *Manpower in Economic Growth: The American Record Since 1800.* New York: McGraw-Hill.

Leibenstein, Harvey. 1965. "Shortages and Surpluses in Education in Underdeveloped Countries: A Theoretical Foray." In *Education and Economic Development,* ed. C. Arnold Anderson and Mary J. Bowman, 51–62. Chicago: Aldine.

Lennon, Roger, and Blythe Mitchell. 1955. "Trends in Age-Grade Relationships: A 35-Year Review." *School and Society* 81: 123–25.

Lieberson, Stanley. 1980. *A Piece of the Pie: Blacks and White Immigrants since 1880.* Berkeley: University of California Press.

Lieberson, Stanley, and Mary C. Waters. 1988. *From Many Strands: Ethnic and Racial Groups in Contemporary America.* New York: Russell Sage Foundation.

Link, William A. 1986. *A Hard Country and a Lonely Place: Schooling, Society, and Reform in Rural Virginia, 1870–1920.* Chapel Hill: University of North Carolina Press.

Lindemann, Barbara S. 1984. "'To Ravish and Carnally Know': Rape in Eighteenth-Century Massachusetts." *Signs* 10:63–82.

Lockerbie, Brad, and Stephen A. Borrelli. 1990. "Question Wording and Public Support for Contra Aid, 1983–1986." *Public Opinion Quarterly* 54:195–208.

Lockridge, Kenneth A. 1970. *A New England Town: The First Hundred Years: Dedham, Massachusetts, 1636–1736.* New York: Norton.

———. 1974. *Literacy in Colonial New England: An Enquiry into the Social Context of Literacy in the Early Modern West.* New York: Norton.

Luther, Seth. 1832. *An Address to the Working-Men of New England, on the State of Education, and on the Condition of the Producing Classes in Europe and America.* Boston: Seth Luther.

McCall, Laura, and Maris A. Vinovskis. 1991. "Changing Approaches to the Study of Family Life." In *American Families: A Research Guide and Historical Handbook,* ed. Joseph M. Hawes and Elizabeth I. Nybakken, 15–32. Westport, Conn.: Greenwood Press.

McCann, Philip, and Francis A. Young. 1982. *Samuel Wilderspin and the Infant School Movement.* London: Croon Helm.

McCaughey, Robert A. 1970. "Josiah Quincy, 1772–1864: The Last of the Boston Federalists." Ph.D. diss., Harvard University.

McClymer, John F. 1982. "The Americanization Movement and the Education of the Foreign-Born Adult, 1914–25." In *American Education and the European Immigrant, 1840–1940,* ed. Bernard J. Weiss, 96–116. Urbana: University of Illinois Press.

McCuskey, Dorothy. 1940. *Bronson Alcott, Teacher.* New York: Macmillan.

McGrane, Reginald C. 1924. *The Panic of 1837: Some Financial Problems of the Jacksonian Era.* Chicago: University of Chicago Press.

McLanahan, Sara S., and Larry Bumpus. 1988. "Comment: A Note on the Effect of Family Structure on School Enrollment." In *Divided Opportunities,* ed. G. D. Dandeur and M. Tienda, 195–201. New York: Plenum.

Main, Gloria L. 1991. "An Inquiry into When and Why Women Learned to Write in Colonial New England." *Journal of Social History* 24:579–89.

Mann, Horace. 1834. *Remarks upon the Comparative Profits of Grocers and Retailers as Derived from Temperate and Intemperate Customers.* Boston.

————. 1838–41. Journal. Horace Mann Papers. Massachusetts Historical Society, Boston.

————. 1845. Letter to, from Thirty-four Bostonians. Jan. 13. Horace Mann Papers. Massachusetts Historical Society, Boston.

Mann, Mary, and George C. Mann, eds. 1891. *Life and Works of Horace Mann*. 2 vols. Boston: Lee and Shepard.

Mason, Karen, Maris A. Vinovskis, and Tamara K. Hareven. 1978. "Women's Work and the Life Course in Essex County, Massachusetts, 1880." In *Transitions: The Family and the Life Course in Historical Perspective*, ed. Tamara K. Hareven, 187–216. New York: Academic Press.

Massachusetts Board of Education. 1850–60. *Abstracts*. Boston.

Massachusetts Board of Education. 1837–80. *Annual Reports*. Boston.

Massachusetts. House of Representatives. 1840–43. *Documents of the House of Representatives of the Commonwealth*. Boston.

Massachusetts Teacher. 1855–65.

Mattingly, Paul H., and Edward W. Stevens, Jr., eds. 1987. *"Schools and the Means of Education Shall Forever Be Encouraged": A History of Education in the Old Northwest, 1787–1880*. Athens: Ohio University Libraries.

May, Dean, and Maris A. Vinovskis. 1977. "A Ray of Millennial Light: Early Education and Social Reform in the Infant School Movement in Massachusetts, 1826–1840." In *Family and Kin in American Urban Communities, 1800–1940*, ed. Tamara K. Hareven, 62–99. New York: Watts.

Menand, Catherine S. 1987. *A Research Guide to the Massachusetts Courts and Their Preservation*. Boston: Massachusetts Supreme Judicial Court.

Mennel, Robert M. 1973. *Thorns and Thistles: Juvenile Delinquents in the United States, 1825–1940*. Hanover, N.H.: University Press of New England.

Messerli, Jonathan C. 1963. "Horace Mann: The Early Years, 1796–1837." Ph.D. diss., Harvard University.

————. 1965. "Localism and State Control in Horace Mann's Reform of the Common Schools." *American Quarterly* 17:104–18.

Metcalf, Theron, et al. 1854. *General Laws of the Commonwealth of Massachusetts Passed Subsequently to the Revised Statutes*. Vol. 1, *Containing the Statutes from 1836 to 1853 Inclusive*. Boston: Dutton and Wentworth.

Miller, Perry. 1953. *The New England Mind: From Colony to Province*. Cambridge: Harvard University Press.

Miller, Warren E., and the National Election Studies. 1989. *American National Election Study, 1988: Pre- and Post-Election Survey*. Ann Arbor, Mich.: Inter-University Consortium for Political and Social Research.

Mintz, Steven, and Susan Kellogg. 1988. *Domestic Revolutions: A Social History of American Family Life*. New York: Free Press.

Mirel, Jeffrey. 1981. "The Matter of Means: The Campaign and Election for the New York Free Academy, 1846–1847." *Journal of Midwest History* 9:134–55.

Mirel, Jeffrey E., and David L. Angus. 1985. "Youth, Work and Schooling in the Great Depression." *Journal of Early Adolescence* 5: 489–504.

Moehlman, Arthur B. 1924. *Child Accounting*. Detroit: Courtis Standard Tests.

————. 1925. *Public Education in Detroit*. Bloomington, Ind.: Public School Publishing Company.

————. 1940. *School Administration*. Boston: Houghton Mifflin.

Mohl, Raymond. 1971. *Poverty in New York, 1783–1825*. New York: Oxford University Press.

————. 1981. "Cultural Assimilation versus Cultural Pluralism." *The Educational Forum* 45:323–32.

Monkkonen, Eric H. 1975. *The Dangerous Class: Crime and Poverty in Columbus, Ohio, 1860–1885*. Cambridge: Harvard University Press.

Monroes, Will S. 1907. *History of the Pestalozzian Movement in the United States*. Syracuse, N.Y.: Bardeen.

Morain, Thomas. 1980. "The Departure of Males from the Teaching Profession in Nineteenth-Century Iowa." *Civil War History* 26: 161–70.

Moran, Gerald F. 1979. "Religious Renewal, Puritan Tribalism, and the Family in Seventeenth-Century Milford, Connecticut." *William and Mary Quarterly*, 3d ser. 36: 236–54.

————. 1980. "'Sisters' in Christ: Women and the Church in Seventeenth-Century New

England." In *Women in American Religion*, ed. Janet Wilson James, 47–65. Philadelphia: University of Pennsylvania Press.

Moran, Gerald F., and Maris A. Vinovskis. 1982. "The Puritan Family and Religion: A Critical Reappraisal." *William and Mary Quarterly*, 3d ser. 39:29–63.

———. 1985. "The Great Care of Godly Parents: Early Childhood in Puritan New England." In *History and Research in Child Development*, ed. Alice B. Smuts and John W. Hagen, Monographs of the Society for Research in Child Development 50:24–37.

———. 1992. *Religion, Family, and the Life Course: Explorations in the Social History of Early America*. Ann Arbor: University of Michigan Press.

Morgan, Edmund S. 1966. *The Puritan Family: Religion and Domestic Relations in Seventeenth-Century New England*. New York: Harper and Row.

Mott, Frank L. 1957. *A History of American Magazines, 1741–1850*. Cambridge: Harvard University Press.

Murphy, Joanne Geraldine. 1960. "Massachusetts Bay Colony: The Role of Government in Education." Ph.D. diss., Harvard University.

Napoli, Donald S. 1981. *Architects of Adjustment: The History of the Psychological Profession in the United States*. Port Washington, N.Y.: Kennikat Press.

National Center for Education Statistics. 1989. *Digest of Education Statistics: 1989*. Washington, D.C.: U.S. Government Printing Office.

Nelson, William. 1975. *The Americanization of the Common Law*. Cambridge: Harvard University Press.

Newburyport Herald. 1856–57.

Newburyport School Committee. 1850–80. *Annual Reports*. Newburyport, Mass.

New York Board of Education. 1949, 1965. *Annual Report of the Superintendent of Schools*. New York.

North, Douglas C. 1961. *The Economic Growth of the United States, 1790–1860*. New York: Prentice-Hall.

Norton, Mary Beth. 1980. *Liberty's Daughters: The Revolutionary Experience of American Women, 1750–1800*. Boston: Little, Brown.

O'Day, Rosemary. 1982. *Education and Society, 1500–1800: The Social Foundations of Education in Early Modern Britain*. London: Longman.

Ogbu, John U. 1978. *Minority Education and Caste: The American System in Cross-Cultural Perspective*. New York: Academic Press.

———. 1986. "The Consequences of the American Caste System." In *The School Achievement of Minority Children: New Perspectives*, ed. Ulric Neisser, 19–56. Hillsdale, N.J.: Lawrence Erlbaum.

Olneck, Michael R. 1989. "Americanization and Education of Immigrants, 1900–1925: An Analysis of Symbolic Action." *American Journal of Education* 97:398–423.

Olneck, Michael R., and Ki-Seok Kim. 1975. "The Relationship between Education and Income among American Men: Some Revisions and Extensions." Unpub. paper, Wisconsin Center for Education Research. University of Wisconsin.

Olneck, Michael, and Marvin Lazerson. 1974. "The School Achievement of Immigrant Children, 1900–1930." *History of Education Quarterly* 14:453–82.

———. 1980. "Education." In *Harvard Encyclopedia of American Ethnic Groups*, ed. Stephan Thernstrom, Ann Orlov, and Oscar Handlin, 303–19. Cambridge: Harvard University Press.

Owen, Robert. 1920. *The Life of Robert Owen by Himself*. New York: Alfred A. Knopf.

Page, David P. 1859. *Theory and Practice of Teaching: Or, The Motives and Methods of Good School-Keeping*. 25th ed. New York: A. S. Barnes and Burr.

Papke, David R. 1987. *Framing the Criminal: Crime, Cultural Work, and the Loss of Critical Perspective, 1830–1900*. Hamden, Conn.: Archon Books.

Perlmann, Joel. 1985a. "Curriculum and Tracking in the Transformation of the American High School: Providence, R.I., 1880–1930." *Journal of Social History* 19: 29–55.

———. 1985b. "Who Stayed in School?" Social Structure and Academic Achievement in the Determination of Enrollment Patterns, Providence, Rhode Island, 1880–1925." *Journal of American History* 72:588–614.

———. 1988. *Ethnic Differences: Schooling and Social Structure among the Irish, Italians, Jews, and Blacks in the American City, 1880–1935*. Cambridge: Cambridge University Press.

Peterson, Paul E. 1985. *The Politics of School Reform, 1870–1940.* Chicago: University of Chicago Press.

Phillips, Willard. 1828. *A Manual of Political Economy with Particular Reference to the Institutions, Resources, and Condition of the United States.* Boston: Hilliard, Gray, Little and Wilkins.

Pickett, Robert S. 1969. *House of Refuge: Origins of Juvenile Reform in New York State, 1815–1857.* Syracuse, N.Y.: Syracuse University Press.

Piele, Philip. 1973. *Budget, Bonds, and Ballots.* Lexington, Mass.: Lexington Books.

Platt, Anthony M. 1977. *The Child Savers: The Invention of Delinquency.* 2d ed. Chicago: University of Chicago Press.

Pollard, Hugh M. 1957. *Pioneers of Popular Education, 1760–1850.* Cambridge: Harvard University Press.

Ponza, Michael, Greg J. Duncan, Mary Corcoran, and Fred Groskind. 1988. "The Guns of Autumn? Age Differences in Support for Income Transfers to the Young and Old." *Public Opinion Quarterly* 52:492–512.

Pope, Robert G. 1969. *The Half-Way Covenant: Church Membership in Puritan New England.* Princeton: Princeton University Press.

Powell, Sumner Chilton. 1963. *Puritan Village: The Formation of a New England Town.* Middletown, Conn.: Wesleyan University Press.

Prest, W. R. 1976. "Stability and Change in Old and New England: Clayworth and Dedham." *Journal of Interdisciplinary History* 6:359–574.

Preston, S. H. 1984. "Children and the Elderly: Divergent Paths for America's Dependents." *Demography* 21:435–57.

Rasinski, Kenneth A. 1989. "The Effect of Question Wording on Public Support for Government Spending." *Public Opinion Quarterly* 53:388–94.

Ravitch, Diane. 1974. *The Great School Wars: New York City, 1805–1973.* New York: Basic Books.

———. 1978. *The Revisionists Revised: A Critique of the Radical Attack on the Schools.* New York: Basic Books.

———. 1983. *The Troubled Crusade: American Education, 1945–1980.* New York: Basic Books.

Reed, Conner. 1949. "All the Children of All the People: Mawkish Nonsense!" *Clearing House* 24:224–25.

Rice, Edwin W. 1917. *The Sunday-School Movement, 1780–1917, and the American Sunday School Union, 1817–1917.* Philadelphia: American Sunday-School Union.

Rorabaugh, W. J. 1986. *The Craft Apprentice: From Franklin to the Machine Age in America.* New York: Oxford University Press.

Rousseau, Jean Jacques. 1979. *Emile or Education,* ed. Allan Bloom. New York: Basic Books.

Russell, William. 1829. *Address on Infant Schools.* Boston: Tupper.

———. 1831. *The Introductory Discourse and Lectures Delivered in Boston before the Convention of Teachers, and Other Friends of Education to Form the American Institute of Instruction, August, 1830.* Boston: Hilliard, Gray, Little and Wilkins.

Rutman, Darrett B., and Anita H. Rutman. 1979. "'Now-Wives and Sons-in-Law': Parental Death in a Seventeenth-Century Virginia County." In *The Chesapeake in the Seventeenth Century: Essays on Anglo-American Society and Politics,* ed. Thad W. Tate and David Ammerman, 153–82. New York: Norton.

———. 1984. *A Place in Time: Middlesex County, Virginia, 1650–1750.* New York: Norton.

Ryan, Mary P. 1981. *Cradle of the Middle Class: The Family in Oneida County, New York, 1790–1865.* Cambridge: Cambridge University Press.

———. 1982. "The Explosion of Family History," *Reviews in American History* 10:181–95.

St. Louis Board of Education. 1872–74. Annual Reports. St. Louis.

Salem Gazette. 1856–57.

Salem Observer. 1856–57.

Salem Register. 1856–57.

Salmon, David, and Winifred Hindshaw. 1904. *Infant Schools: Their History and Theory.* London: Longmans and Green.

Salmon, Richard G. 1987. "State/Local Fiscal Support of Public Elementary and Secondary Education: A Look Backward and Prospects for the Future." *Journal of Education Finance* 12:549–60.

Sanders, James W. 1976. *The Education of an Urban Minority: Catholics in Chicago, 1833–1965.* New York: Oxford University Press.

Saunders, Carleton M. 1941. *Promotion or Failure for the Elementary Pupil?* New York: Bureau of Publications, Teachers College, Columbia University.

Savage, Edward H. 1865. *A Chronological History of the Boston Watch and Police from 1631 to 1865; Together with the Recollections of a Boston Police Officer, or Boston by Daylight and Gaslight.* 2d ed. Boston: J. E. Farwell.

Schlossman, Steven I. 1977. *Love and the American Delinquent: The Theory and Practice of Progressive Juvenile Justice, 1825–1920.* Chicago: University of Chicago Press.

Schneider, Eric C. 1992. *In the Web of Class: Delinquents and Reformers in Boston, 1810s–1930s.* New York: New York University Press.

Schultz, Stanley K. 1973. *The Culture Factory: Boston Public Schools, 1789–1860.* New York: Oxford University Press.

Schultz, Theodore W. 1961a. "Investment in Human Capital." *American Economic Review* 51:1–17.

———. 1961b. "Education and Economic Growth." In *Social Forces Influencing American Education,* ed. H. G. Rochey, 48–88. Chicago: University of Chicago Press.

Shearer, William J. 1899. *The Grading of Schools.* 3d ed. New York: H. P. Smith.

Shepherd, Odell. 1937. *Pedlar's Progress: The Life of Bronson Alcott.* Boston: Little, Brown.

Silber, Kate. 1960. *Pestalozzi: The Man and His Works.* London: Routledge and Kegan Paul.

Silver, Harold. 1965. *The Concept of Popular Education: A Study of Ideas and Social Movements in the Early Nineteenth Century.* London: MacGibbon and Kee.

Silver, Harold, ed. 1969. *Robert Owen on Education.* Cambridge: Cambridge University Press.

Simpson, Stephen. 1831. *The Working Man's Manual: A New Theory of Political Economy, on the Principle of Production the Source of Wealth.* Philadelphia: Thomas L. Bonsal.

Smith, Adam. 1937. *An Inquiry into the Nature and Causes of the Wealth of Nations.* New York: Modern Library.

Smith, Daniel B. 1980. *Inside the Great House: Planter Family Life in Eighteenth-Century Chesapeake Society.* Ithaca: Cornell University Press.

Smith, E. Vale. 1854. *History of Newburyport from the Earliest Settlement of the Country to the Present Time.* Boston: Damrell and Morre.

Smith, Maude W., Fern E. Bickford, Deland A. Davis, and Henry J. Otto. 1937. "Age-Grade and Grade-Progress Data from Children in One-Room Rural Schools." *Elementary School Journal* 37:336–43.

Smith, Sherman M. 1926. *The Relation of the State to Religious Education in Massachusetts.* Syracuse, N.Y.: Syracuse University Book Store.

Smith-Rosenberg, Carroll. 1971. *Religion and the Rise of the American City: The New York City Mission Movement, 1812–1870.* Ithaca: Cornell University Press.

———. 1985. *Disorderly Conduct: Visions of Gender in Victorian America.* New York: Alfred A. Knopf.

Solomon, Lewis C. 1969. "Capital Formation Expenditures on Formal Education, 1880 and 1890." Ph.D. diss., Purdue University.

Soltow, Lee, and Edward Stevens. 1981. *The Rise of Literacy and the Common School in the United States: A Socio-Economic Analysis to 1870.* Chicago: University of Chicago Press.

Spain, Charles. 1924. *The Platoon School.* New York: Macmillan.

Spener, David. 1988. "Transitional Bilingual Education and the Socialization of Immigrants." *Harvard Educational Review* 58:133–53.

Spring, Joel H. 1972. *Education and the Rise of the Corporate State.* Boston: Beacon Press.

Stansell, Christine. 1986. *City of Women: Sex and Class in New York, 1789–1860.* New York: Alfred A. Knopf.

Stern, Mark J. 1987. *Society and Family Strategy: Erie County, New York, 1850–1920.* Albany: State University of New York Press.

Stolarik, M. Mark. 1977. "Immigration, Education, and the Social Mobility of Slovaks, 1870–1930." In *Immigrants and Religion in Urban America,* ed. Randall M. Miller and Thomas D. Marzik, 103–16. Philadelphia: Temple University Press.

Stone, Lawrence. 1964. "The Educational Revolution in England, 1560–1640." *Past and Present* 28:41–80.

Stowe, Steven M. 1985. "The Not-So-Cloistered Academy: Elite Women's Education and Family Feeling in the Old South." In *The Web of Southern Social Relations: Women, Family, and Education*, Walter J. Fraser, Jr., R. Frank Saunders, Jr., and Jon L. Wakelyn, 90–106. Athens: University of Georgia Press.

Suarez-Orozco, Marcello M. 1987. "Hispanic Americans: Comparative Considerations and Educational Problems of Children." *International Migration* 25:141–63.

———. 1989. *Central American Refugees and U.S. High Schools: A Psychosocial Study of Motivation and Achievement*. Stanford: Stanford University Press.

Sweet, J. A., and L. L. Bumpass. 1987. *American Families and Households*. New York: Russell Sage Foundation.

Tank, Robert M. 1980. "Young Children, Families, and Society in America Since the 1820s: The Evolution of Health, Education and Child Care Programs for Preschool Children." Ph.D. diss., University of Michigan.

Taunton School Committee. 1861. *Report of the School Committee of the Town of Taunton*. Taunton, Mass.: C. A. Hack.

Taylor, Philip. 1971. *The Distant Magnet: European Emigration to the U.S.A.* New York: Harper and Row.

Teaford, Jon. 1970. "The Transformation of Massachusetts Education, 1670–1780." *History of Education Quarterly* 10:287–307.

Thernstrom, Stephan. 1964. *Poverty and Progress: Social Mobility in a Nineteenth-Century City*. Cambridge: Harvard University Press.

———. 1973. *The Other Bostonians: Poverty and Progress in the American Metropolis, 1880–1970*. Cambridge: Harvard University Press.

Thomas, John L. 1965. "Romantic Reform in America, 1815–1865." *American Quarterly* 17:656–81.

Thorndike, Edward L. 1908. *The Elimination of Pupils from School*. Bureau of Education Bulletin 1907, no. 4. Washington, D.C.: U.S. Government Printing Office.

———. 1909. "Promotion, Retardation, and Elimination. *Psychological Clinic* 3:232–43, 255–65.

Torres-Gil, Fernando. 1989. "The Politics of Catastrophic and Long-Term Care Coverage." *Journal of Aging and Social Policy* 1: 61–86.

Troen, Selwyn K. 1975. *The Public and the Schools: Shaping the St. Louis System, 1838–1920*. Columbia: University of Missouri Press.

Tropea, Joseph. 1987. "Bureaucratic Order and Special Children: Urban Schools, 1950s–1960s." *History of Education* 27:339–61.

Tucker, Barbara. 1984. *Samuel Slater and the Origins of the American Textile Industry*. Ithaca: Cornell University Press.

Turner, James. 1985. *Without God, Without Creed: The Origins of Unbelief in America*. Baltimore: Johns Hopkins University Press.

Tyack, David. 1974. *The One Best System*. Cambridge: Harvard University Press.

Tyack, David, and Elisabeth Hansot. 1982. *Managers of Virtue*. New York: Basic Books.

———. 1990. *Learning Together: A History of Coeducation in American Public Schools*. New Haven: Yale University Press.

Tyack, David, Thomas James, and Aaron Benavot. 1987. *Law and the Shaping of Public Education*. Madison: University of Wisconsin Press.

Ueda, Reed. 1987. *Avenues to Adulthood: The Origins of the High School and Social Mobility in an American Suburb*. Cambridge: Cambridge University Press.

Ulrich, Laurel Thatcher. 1980. "Vertuous Women Found: New England Ministerial Literature, 1668–1735." In *Women in American Religion*, Janet Wilson James, 67–87. Philadelphia: University of Pennsylvania Press.

———. 1982. *Good Wives: Images and Reality in the Lives of Women in Northern New England, 1650–1750*. New York: Alfred A. Knopf.

U.S. Bureau of Census. 1967–87. *Current Population Reports*. Washington, D.C.: U.S. Government Printing Office.

———. 1975. *Historical Statistics of the United States, Colonial Times to 1970, Bicentennial Edition*. 2 pts. Washington, D.C.: U.S. Government Printing Office.

———. 1981. *Statistical Abstract of the United States: 1981*. 102d ed. Washington, D.C.: U.S. Government Printing Office.

———. 1986. *Statistical Abstract of the United States: 1987*. 107th ed. Washington, D.C.: U.S. Government Printing Office.

———. 1989. *Statistical Abstract of the United States: 1989*. 109th ed. Washington, D.C.: U.S. Government Printing Office.

———. 1990. *Statistical Abstract of the United States: 1990*. 110th ed. Washington, D.C.: U.S. Government Printing Office.

U.S. Bureau of Education. 1913. *Report of the Committee on Uniform Records and Reports*. Bulletin 1912, no. 3. Washington, D.C.: U.S. Government Printing Office.

Vaizey, John. 1962. *The Economics of Education*. London: Farber and Farber.

Vinovskis, Maris A. 1970. "Horace Mann on the Economic Productivity of Education." *New England Quarterly* 43:550–71.

———. 1971. "American Historical Demography: A Review Essay." *Historical Methods Newsletter* 4:141–48.

———. 1972a. "Mortality Trends in Massachusetts Before 1860." *Journal of Economic History* 32:184–213.

———. 1972b. "Trends in Massachusetts Education, 1826–1860." *History of Education Quarterly* 12:501–29.

———. 1981. *Fertility in Massachusetts from the Revolution to the Civil War*. New York: Academic Press.

———. 1983a. "Community Studies in Urban Educational History: Some Methodological and Conceptual Observations." In *Schools in Cities: Consensus and Conflict in American Educational History*, ed. Ronald W. Goodenow and Diane Ravitch, 287–304. New York: Holmes and Krier.

———. 1983b. "Quantification and the Analysis of Ante-Bellum Education." *Journal of Interdisciplinary History* 13:761–86.

———. 1985a. *The Origins of Public High Schools: A Reexamination of the Beverly High School Controversy*. Madison: University of Wisconsin Press.

———. 1985b. "Patterns of High School Attendance in Newburyport, Massachusetts in 1860." Paper presented at the American Historical Association Annual Meeting, New York City.

———. 1986. "Young Fathers and Their Children: Some Historical and Policy Perspectives." In *Adolescent Fatherhood*, ed. Arthur B. Elster and Michael E. Lamb. 171–92. Hillsdale, N.J.: Lawrence Erlbaum.

———. 1987a. "Family and Schooling in Colonial and Nineteenth-Century America." *Journal of Family History* 12:19–37.

———. 1987b. "The Unraveling of the Family Wage Since World War II: Some Demographic, Economic, and Cultural Considerations." In *The Family Wage: Work, Gender, and Children in the Modern Economy*, ed. Bryce J. Christensen, 33–58. Rockford, Ill.: Rockford Institute.

———. 1988a. "The Historian and the Life Course: Reflections on Recent Approaches to the Study of American Family Life in the Past." In *Life-Span Development and Behavior*, ed. Paul B. Baltes, David L. Featherman, and Richard M. Lerner, vol. 8, pp. 33–59. Hillsdale, N.J.: Lawrence Erlbaum.

———. 1988b. "Have We Underestimated the Extent of Antebellum High School Attendance?" *History of Education Quarterly* 28: 551–67.

———. 1988c. *An "Epidemic" of Adolescent Pregnancy? Some Historical and Policy Considerations*. New York: Oxford University Press.

———. 1989. "Have Social Historians Lost the Civil War? Some Preliminary Demographic Speculations." *Journal of American History* 76:34–58.

———. 1994. "Education and the Economic Transformation of Nineteenth-Century America." In *Age and Structural Lag*, ed. Matilda White Riley, Robert L. Kahn, and Anne Foner, 171–96. New York: John Wiley.

Vinovskis, Maris A., and Richard M. Bernard. 1978. "Beyond Catherine Beecher: Female Education in the Antebellum Period." *Signs* 3:856–69.

Volkmer, Hilda, and Isabel Noble. 1914. "Retardation as Indicated by One Hundred City School Reports." *Psychological Clinic* 8:74–81.

Wall, Helena M. 1990. *Fierce Communion: Family and Community in Early America*. Cambridge: Harvard University Press.

Ware, Caroline F. 1966. *Early New England Cotton Manufacture: A Study in Industrial Beginnings*. New York: Russell and Russell.

Ware, Norman. 1924. *The Industrial Worker, 1840–1860: The Reaction of American Industrial Society to the Advance of the Industrial Revolution*. Boston: Houghton Mifflin.

Warner, Oliver. 1867. *Abstract of the Census of Massachusetts, 1865: With Remarks on the Same and Supplementary Tables.* Boston: Wright and Potter.

Wayland, Francis. 1843. *The Elements of Political Economy.* 4th ed. Boston: Gould, Kendall and Lincoln.

Webber, Thomas L. 1978. *Deep Like the Rivers: Education in the Slave Quarter Community, 1831–1865.* New York: Norton.

Weisbrod, B. A. 1962. "Education and Investment in Human Capital." *Journal of Political Economy* 70:106–23.

West, E. G. 1964. "Private versus Public Education: A Classical Economic Dispute." *Journal of Political Economy* 72:465–75.

Whitbread, Nanette. 1972. *The Evolution of the Nursery-Infant School: A History of Infant and Nursery Education in Britain, 1800–1970.* London: Routledge and Kegan.

Wightman, Joseph M. 1860. *Annals of the Boston Primary School Committee From Its First Establishment in 1818 to Its Dissolution in 1855.* Boston: Geo. C. Rand and Avery.

Wilderspin, Samuel. 1825. *Infant Education; or Remarks on the Importance of Educating the Infant Poor, from the Age of Eighteen Months to Seven Years.* 3d ed. London: J. S. Hodson.

Williams, Edward I. F. 1937. *Horace Mann: Educational Statesman.* New York: MacMillan.

Williams, Stephen S. 1986. "From Polemics to Practice: IQ Testing and Tracking in the Detroit Public Schools and Their Relationship to the National Debate." Ph.D. diss., University of Michigan.

Williamson, Jeffrey G. 1965. "Ante-Bellum Urbanization in the American Northeast." *Journal of Economic History* 25:592–608.

Winterer, Caroline. 1992. "Avoiding a 'Hothouse System of Education': Nineteenth-Century Early Childhood Education from the Infant Schools to the Kindergarten." *History of Education Quarterly* 32:289–314.

Wirkkala, John C. 1973. "Juvenile Delinquency and Reform in Nineteenth-Century Massachusetts: The Formative Era in State Care, 1846–1879." Ph.D. diss., Clark University.

Witmer, Lightner. 1910. "What is Meant by Retardation." *Psychological Clinic* 4:121–31.

Woodward, Calvin M. 1896. "At What Age Do Pupils Withdraw from the Public Schools?" In U.S. Commissioner of Education, *Annual Report for 1894–1895,* vol. 2, pp. 1161–70. Washington, D.C.: U.S. Government Printing Office.

———. 1902. "When and Why Pupils Leave School—How to Promote Attendance in the Higher Grades." In U.S. Commissioner of Education, *Annual Report for 1899–1900,* vol. 2, pp. 1364–74. Washington, D.C.: U.S. Government Printing Office.

Wright, Carroll D. 1876. *The Census of Massachusetts, 1875,* vol. 1. Boston: Albert J. Wright.

Wright, Conrad E. 1992. *The Transformation of Charity in Postrevolutionary New England.* Boston: Northeastern University Press.

Wyatt-Brown, Bertram. 1985. "Black Schooling during Reconstruction." In *The Web of Southern Social Relations: Women, Family, and Education,* ed. Walter J. Fraser, Jr., R. Frank Saunders, Jr., and Jon L. Wakelyn, 146–65. Athens: University of Georgia Press.

Wyllie, Irwin G. 1954. *The Self-Made Man in America: The Myth of Rags to Riches.* New Brunswick, N.J.: Rutgers University Press.

Zuckerman, Michael. 1970. *Peaceable Kingdoms: New England Towns in the Eighteenth-Century.* New York: Alfred A. Knopf.

Index

Page numbers in this index followed by an italic *f* refer to figures; page numbers followed by an italic *t* refer to tables.